# ESSENTIALS
## OF
# ONCOLOGY CARE

MARY PAT LYNCH, CRNP, MSN, AOCN®

Oncology Nurse Practitioner and Administrator
Joan Karnell Cancer Center
at Pennsylvania Hospital
University of Pennsylvania Health System
Philadelphia, PA

D0639550

**MERCK**

**Compliments of Merck Oncology**

Professional Publishing Group, Ltd. • New York, NY

Professional Publishing Group, Ltd.
17 Battery Place, New York NY 10004
(646) 827-6448

ISBN 0-9713017-5-1

PRINTED IN THE UNITED STATES OF AMERICA

This book is dedicated to my colleagues and friends in oncology nursing and cancer care, in particular the wonderful staff at the Joan Karnell Cancer Center at Pennsylvania Hospital, the nation's first hospital. I am continually amazed, impressed and humbled by all you do for patients and families facing cancer. It is my hope that this handbook makes your job a little easier.

Love and thanks to John, Sean and Emma for the joy they bring to my life.

Special thanks to Marylou Osterman for her assistance and support on this project and many others, and to Cathy Fortenbaugh, RN, MSN, AOCN for her review, thoughtful suggestions and encouragement.

# Table of Contents

This pocket guide has been developed as an essential tool for oncology clinicians. It is intended to be a handy, quick reference for both the novice and experienced oncology clinician. The size and format allow it to be kept in one's pocket and available at the time it is needed. It does not replace the many excellent oncology textbooks and handbooks available today, but rather complements them, by offering essential clinical information at one's fingertips.

The content of this guide was developed and revised with the input of many colleagues who were eager to share their ideas of oncology care essentials — that information that they were always going back to look up or confirm. It also includes some of the concepts that they wished they had understood or had access to when they were beginning oncology clinicians. The content includes the essence of oncology nursing — chemotherapy drugs and regimens, side effects of those drugs and symptom management. It is not intended to be an exhaustive review of those topics but rather a quick reference to confirm or clarify the oncology knowledge database.

The 2005 edition of this book has been fully revised and new content has been added, including information on sexuality and fertility, anti-anxiety medications, and grief and bereavement. New information on biotherapy and new chemotherapy regimens has also been added. The staging section has been fully revised and updated. *Essentials of Oncology Care* includes expanded information on hypersensitivity reactions and anticoagulation therapy as well as the NCCN Clinical Practice Guidelines in Oncology v.1.2005 nausea and vomiting.

It is hoped that you will find this book to be a useful resource in your daily work with cancer patients and their families.

**1**

# Commonly Used Calculations

This section contains the most commonly used formulas and calculations in cancer care. These calculations are primarily used in the dosing of chemotherapy and other drugs.

## 1. Dosage Calculation

Chemotherapy dose = $(mg/m^2)$ x BSA

## 2. BSA – Body Surface Area Nomogram for Adults
(see Section 1, Figure 1)

## 3. Ideal Body Weight
(See Section 1, Table I)

Female: 45.5 kg + (2.3 kg x [height – 60 inches])

Male: 50 kg + (2.3 kg x [height – 60 inches])

## 4. Creatinine Clearance Estimation

$$\text{Creatinine clearance (male)} = \frac{(140 - \text{age}) \times (\text{lean body weight})}{(\text{serum creatinine}) \times 72}$$

Creatinine clearance (female) = 0.85 x creatinine clearance (male)

*Source: Cockcroft DW, Gault MH. Prediction of creatinine clearance from serum creatinine. Nephron. 1976;16:31-41.*

## 5. Carboplatin Dosing Calculation, Calvert Formula (area under the curve (AUC) method)

Dose (mg) = Target AUC x (creatinine clearance + 25)

Previously untreated patients: Target AUC = 6 to 8 mg/mL/min

Previously treated patients: Target AUC = 4 to 6 mg/mL/min

*Source: Calvert AH, et al. Carboplatin dosage: prospective evaluation of a simple formula based on renal function. J Clin Oncol. 1989;7:1748-1756.*

## 6. Absolute Neutrophil Count (ANC)

ANC = total WBC count x (% neutrophils + bands)

<1500 cells/mm$^3$ = increased risk of infection
<500 cells/mm$^3$ = serious risks of infection, especially if prolonged duration

## Estimation of Surface Area From Height and Weight

| Height | | Surface Area | Body Weight | |
|---|---|---|---|---|
| ft/in | cm | $m^2$ | lb | kg |

Note: An estimate of a patient's surface area can be obtained by marking the patient's height and weight and drawing a line between these two points; the point at which this line intersects the middle scale represents the patient's surface area.

Adapted from: Normal Laboratory Values. In: Dale DC, Federman DD, eds. Scientific American Medicine. Vol 3. New York, NY: Scientific American; 1996:19.

4

## Section 1: Table 1

**Ideal Body Weight Chart***

| Males | Height (cm) | Weight (kg) | Height (cm) | Weight (kg) | Height (cm) | Weight (kg) |
|---|---|---|---|---|---|---|
| | 145 | 51.9 | 159 | 59.9 | 173 | 68.7 |
| | 146 | 52.4 | 160 | 60.5 | 174 | 69.4 |
| | 147 | 52.9 | 161 | 61.1 | 175 | 70.1 |
| | 148 | 53.6 | 162 | 61.7 | 176 | 70.8 |
| | 149 | 54.0 | 163 | 62.3 | 177 | 71.6 |
| | 150 | 54.5 | 164 | 62.9 | 178 | 72.4 |
| | 151 | 55.0 | 165 | 63.5 | 179 | 73.3 |
| | 152 | 55.8 | 166 | 64.0 | 180 | 74.2 |
| | 153 | 56.1 | 167 | 64.6 | 181 | 75.0 |
| | 154 | 56.6 | 168 | 65.2 | 182 | 75.6 |
| | 155 | 57.2 | 169 | 65.9 | 183 | 76.5 |
| | 156 | 57.9 | 170 | 66.6 | 184 | 77.3 |
| | 157 | 57.9 | 171 | 67.3 | 185 | 78.1 |
| | 158 | 59.3 | 172 | 68.0 | 186 | 78.9 |

| Females | Height (cm) | Weight (kg) | Height (cm) | Weight (kg) | Height (cm) | Weight (kg) |
|---|---|---|---|---|---|---|
| | 140 | 44.9 | 150 | 50.4 | 160 | 56.2 |
| | 141 | 45.4 | 151 | 51.0 | 161 | 56.9 |
| | 142 | 45.9 | 152 | 51.5 | 162 | 57.6 |
| | 143 | 46.4 | 153 | 52.0 | 163 | 58.3 |
| | 144 | 47 | 154 | 52.5 | 164 | 58.9 |
| | 145 | 47.5 | 155 | 53.1 | 165 | 59.5 |
| | 146 | 48 | 156 | 53.7 | 166 | 60.1 |
| | 147 | 48.6 | 157 | 54.3 | 167 | 60.7 |
| | 148 | 49.2 | 158 | 54.9 | 168 | 61.4 |
| | 149 | 49.8 | 159 | 55.5 | 169 | 62.1 |

5

*Ideal body weight for height. This table corrects the 1960 Metropolitan Standards to nude weight without shoe heels.
Modified from Jellife DB. The Assessment of the Nutritional Status of the Community. *Geneva: WHO; 1986.*
*Source: Fischer DS, Knobf MT, Durivage HJ, Beaulieu NJ.* The Cancer Chemotherapy Handbook.
6th ed. *New York, NY: Mosby; 2003:517. Reprinted with permission.*

# Quick Guide to Staging for Common Cancers

Cancer is a group of diseases that are characterized by their abnormal cell structure, uncontrolled growth, ability to spread to distant parts of the body and ability to invade normal tissue. The grade of a tumor is based on the degree of differentiation of the cells. A grade 1 tumor is well differentiated; it appears similar to the specialized tissue from which it arose. The highest grade is given to a tumor that appears so undifferentiated that it is difficult to identify the tissue of origin.

> Grade 1 – Well differentiated
> Grade 2 – Moderately differentiated
> Grade 3 – Poorly differentiated
> Grade 4 – Undifferentiated

Different cancers are staged in different ways. Staging varies by site of cancer. The basic staging system used for most cancers is the TNM system.

> T = Tumor (local involvement)
> N = Node (nodal involvement)
> M = Metastasis (distant spread)

This section contains staging classification for the most common cancers, intended to be used as a quick reference for clinicians, not for pathologic staging. For complete staging information for all tumor types, the reader is referred to the American Joint Committee on Cancer (AJCC) *Cancer Staging Manual. 6th ed.* New York, NY: Springer-Verlag; 2002.

![bar]

**Bladder Cancer**

## TNM Classification

| | | |
|---|---|---|
| T (tumor) | TX | Primary tumor cannot be assessed |
| | T0 | No evidence of primary tumor |
| | Tis | Carcinoma in situ |
| | Ta | Noninvasive papillary carcinoma |
| | T1 | Tumor invades subepithelial connective tissue |
| | T2 | Tumor invades muscle<br>T2a superficial muscle<br>T2b deep muscle |
| | T3 | Tumor invades perivesical fat<br>T3a microscopic invasion<br>T3b macroscopic invasion |
| | T4 | Tumor invades contiguous viscera<br>T4a Prostate, uterus, vagina<br>T4b Pelvic wall or abdominal wall |

8

### Staging of Bladder Cancer

| | | | |
|---|---|---|---|
| Stage 0 | Ta or Tis | N0 | M0 |
| Stage I | T1 | N0 | M0 |
| Stage II | T2 | N0 | M0 |
| Stage III | T3 or T4 | N0 | M0 |
| Stage IV | T4b<br>any T | N0<br>N1-3 | M0<br>M0-1 |

**Breast Cancer**

### TNM Classification

| | | |
|---|---|---|
| T (tumor): | TX | Primary tumor cannot be assessed |
| | Tis | In situ carcinoma<br>Tis (DCIS) – Ductal CIS<br>Tis (LCIS) – Lobular CIS<br>Tis (Paget) – Paget's disease of the nipple with no tumor |
| | T0 | No evidence of tumor in breasts |
| | T1 | Tumor is 2 cm or less at its greatest dimension<br>T1mic – microinvasion $\leq$0.1 cm<br>T1a – >0.1 cm and $\leq$0.5 cm<br>T1b – >0.5 cm and $\leq$1.0 cm<br>T1c – >1.0 cm and $\leq$2.0 cm |
| | T2 | Tumor >2 cm and $\leq$5 cm |
| | T3 | Tumor >5 cm |
| | T4 | Any size tumor with extension to chest wall or skin<br>T4a – Extension to chest wall, not including pectoralis muscle<br>T4b – Skin ulceration, edema (including peau d'orange), or satellite nodules confined to same breast<br>T4c – Both T4a and T4b<br>T4d – Inflammatory carcinoma |
| N (nodes): | pN0 | No regional LN metastasis histologically |
| (pathologic) | pN1mi | Micrometastasis >0.2 to 2 mm |
| | pN1a | Metastasis to 1-3 nodes, any >2 mm |
| | pN2 | Metastasis 4-9 nodes or clinically apparent internal mammary lymph nodes without axillary LN metastasis |
| | pN3 | Metastasis to 10 or more axillary LN or to infraclavicular LN, or ipsilateral supraclavicular LN or clinically apparent mammary LN with axillary LN metastasis |
| M (metastasis) | M0 | No evidence of distant metastases |
| | M1 | Distant metastases |

*(continued on next page)*

## Breast Cancer

### Staging of Breast Cancer

| | | | |
|---|---|---|---|
| Stage 0 | Tis | N0 | M0 |
| Stage I | T1 | N0 | M0 |
| Stage IIA | T0 | N1 | M0 |
| | T1 | N1 | M0 |
| | T2 | N0 | M0 |
| Stage IIB | T2 | N1 | M0 |
| | T3 | N0 | M0 |
| Stage IIIA | T0 | N2 | M0 |
| | T1 | N2 | M0 |
| | T2 | N2 | M0 |
| | T3 | N1 | M0 |
| | T3 | N2 | M0 |
| Stage IIIB | T4 | any N | M0 |
| | Any T | N3 | M0 |
| Stage IV | any T | any N | M1 |

## Section 2: Table 3

**Cervical Cancer**

### Staging of Cervical Cancer

| | |
|---|---|
| Stage 0 | Carcinoma in situ (no stromal invasion) |
| Stage I | Strictly confined to the cervix (disregard extension to the corpus) |
| Stage IA | Preclinical carcinoma (diagnosed by microscopy) |
| Stage IA1 | Lesions with <3 mm depth of stromal invasion |
| Stage IA2 | Lesions detected microscopically that can be measured (>3-5 mm in depth of invasion from the originating epithelial base and ≤7 mm in horizontal spread) |
| Stage IB | Lesions of greater dimensions than IA2 whether seen clinically or not |
| Stage II | Cancer extends beyond the cervix but not to the pelvic sidewall |
| Stage IIA | Lesions involves the proximal vagina (upper two-thirds) |
| Stage IIB | Obvious parametrial involvement |
| Stage III | Tumor extends to the pelvic sidewall, or distal one-third of vagina, or hydronephrosis, or nonfunctioning kidney |
| Stage IV | Tumor extends beyond true pelvis, or biopsy-proven involvement of bladder or rectal mucosa |
| Stage IVa | Spread to adjacent organs |
| Stage IVb | Distant metastases |

**Colorectal Cancer**

**TNM Classification**

| | | |
|---|---|---|
| T (tumor) | TX | Primary tumor cannot be assessed |
| | T0 | No evidence of tumor in resected specimen |
| | Tis | Carcinoma in situ: intraepithelial or invasion of the lamina propria |
| | T1 | Invasion of the submucosa |
| | T2 | Invasion of the muscularis propria |
| | T3 | Invasion through muscularis propria into subserosa or into nonperitonealized pericolic or perirectal tissues |
| | T4 | Perforation of visceral peritoneum or direct invasion into adjacent organs or tissues |
| N (nodes) | NX | Nodes cannot be assessed (eg, local excision only) |
| | N0 | No regional node metastases |
| | N1 | 1 to 3 positive nodes |
| | N2 | 4 or more positive nodes |
| | N3 | Central nodes positive |
| M (metastases) | MX | Presence of distant metastases cannot be assessed |
| | M0 | No distant metastases |
| | M1 | Distant metastases present |

*(continued on next page)*

---

## Colorectal Cancer

### Duke Staging System for Colorectal Cancer

| | |
|---|---|
| Duke A = T1N0M0 | |
| | T2N0M0 |

| | |
|---|---|
| Duke B = T3N0M0 | |
| | T4N0M0 |

Duke C = Any T N1M0, any T N2M0

Duke D = Any T, any M M1

### TNM Staging for Colorectal Cancer

| Stage 0 | TisN0M0 |
|---|---|
| Stage I | T1, T2, N0, M0 |
| Stage II | T3, T4, N0, M0 |
| Stage III | Any T, N1, N2, M0 |
| Stage IV | Any T, any N, M1 |

## Section 2: Table 5

**Endometrial Cancer**

### FIGO Staging of Endometrial Cancer

| | |
|---|---|
| Stage 1 | Tumor confined to uterine fundus |
| Stage IA | Tumor limited to endometrium |
| Stage IB | Invasion to less than half of myometrium |
| Stage IC | Invasion to more than half of myometrium |

| | |
|---|---|
| Stage II | Tumor extends to the cervix |
| Stage IIA | Endocervical glandular involvement only |
| Stage IIB | Cervical stroma invasion |

| | |
|---|---|
| Stage III | Regional tumor spread |
| Stage IIIA | Tumor invades serosa or adnexa or positive peritoneal cytology |
| Stage IIIB | Vaginal metastases |
| Stage IIIC | Metastases to pelvic or para-aortic lymph nodes |

| | |
|---|---|
| Stage IV | Bulky pelvic disease or distant spread |
| Stage IVA | Tumor invasion of bladder and/or bowel mucosa |
| Stage IVB | Distant metastases including intra-abdominal and/or inguinal LN |

## Section 2: Table 6

**Esophageal Cancer**

### TNM Stages for Carcinoma of the Esophagus

| | |
|---|---|
| Tis | Carcinoma in situ |
| T1 | Invades lamina propria or submucosa |
| T2 | Invades muscularis propria |
| T3 | Invades adventitia |
| T4 | Invades adjacent structures |
| N0 | No nodal metastases |
| N1 | Regional node metastases |
| M0 | No distant metastases |
| M1 | Distant metastases |

*(continued on next page)*

## Esophageal Cancer

### Staging of Esophageal Cancer

| | |
|---|---|
| Stage 0 | Tis, N0, M0 |
| Stage I | T1, N0, M0 |
| Stage IIA | T2 or T3, N0, M0 |
| Stage IIB | T1 or T2, N1, M0 |
| Stage III | T3, N1, M0<br>T4, any N, M0 |
| Stage IV | Any T, any N, M1 |

![section separator bar]

## Gastric Cancer

**TNM Staging for Gastric Cancer**

**Primary Tumor**

| | |
|---|---|
| Tis | Carcinoma in situ |
| T1 | Invades lamina propria or submucosa |
| T2 | Invades muscularis propria or subserosa |
| T3 | Penetrates serosa (visceral peritoneum) |
| T4 | Invades adjacent structures |

**Regional lymph nodes**

| | |
|---|---|
| N0 | No nodal metastases |
| N1 | Metastases in 1-6 regional lymph nodes |
| N2 | Metastases in 7-15 regional lymph nodes |
| N3 | Metastases in more than 15 regional lymph nodes |

**Distant Metastases**

| | |
|---|---|
| M0 | None |
| M1 | Present |

*(continued on next page)*

## Gastric Cancer

### Staging of Gastric Cancer

| | |
|---|---|
| Stage 0 | TisN0M0 |
| Stage IA | T1N0M0 |
| Stage IB | T1N1M0 |
| | T2N0M0 |
| Stage II | T1N2M0 |
| | T2N1M0 |
| | T3N0M0 |
| Stage IIIA | T2N2M0 |
| | T3N1M0 |
| | T4N0M0 |
| Stage IIIB | T3N2M0 |
| Stage IV | T4N1M0 |
| | T1N3M0 |
| | T2N3M0 |
| | T3N3M0 |
| | T4N2M0 |
| | T4N3M0 |
| | Any T, any N, M1 |

17

## Head and Neck Cancers

### TNM Staging for Carcinomas of the Oral Cavity

| | |
|---|---|
| TX | No available information on primary tumor |
| T0 | No evidence of primary tumor |
| Tis | Carcinoma in situ |
| T1 | Greatest diameter of tumor $\leq$2 cm |
| T2 | Greatest diameter of tumor >2-4 cm |
| T3 | Greatest diameter of tumor >4 cm |
| T4 | Invasion to adjacent structures such as antrum, pterygoid muscles, base of tongue or skin of neck |
| NX | Nodes cannot be assessed |
| N0 | No clinically positive node |
| N1 | Single clinically positive ipsilateral node $\leq$3 cm in diameter |
| N2 | Single clinically positive ipsilateral node $\geq$3-6 cm; or multiple clinically positive nodes, none >6 cm; or bilateral or contralateral nodes, none >6 cm |
| N3 | Metastases in a lymph node >6 cm in greatest diameter |
| MX | Not assessed |
| M0 | No (known) distant metastases |
| M1 | Distant metastases present |

### Stage Grouping for Carcinomas of the Oral Cavity, Pharynx, Larynx, and Paranasal Sinuses

| | |
|---|---|
| Stage I | T1N0M0 |
| Stage II | T2N0M0 |
| Stage III | T3N0M0 |
| | T1 or T2 or T3, N1, M0 |
| Stage IV | T4, N0 or N1, M0 |
| | Any T, N2 or 3, M0 |
| | Any T, any N, M1 |

████████████████████████████████████████████

## Hepatocellular Cancer

**TNM Staging for Hepatocellular Carcinoma**

| | |
|---|---|
| Stage I | T1 (solitary tumor any size without vascular invasion), N0, M0 |
| Stage II | T2 (solitary tumor any size with vascular invasion; or multiple tumors, none greater than 5 cm), N0, M0 |
| Stage IIIA | T3 (multiple tumors >5 cm or tumor involving a major branch of the portal or hepatic veins), N0, M0 |
| Stage IIIB | T4 (direct invasion of adjacent organs other than gall bladder or with perforation of visceral peritoneum), N0, M0 |
| Stage IIIC | Any T, N1, M0 |
| Stage IVA | T4 (Multiple tumors involving more than one lobe or a major branch of the portal or hepatic veins), N0, M0 |
| Stage IVB | Any T, any N, M1 |

### Hodgkin's Disease and Non-Hodgkin's Lymphoma

#### Cotswold Modification of the Ann Arbor Staging System for Hodgkin's Disease

| | |
|---|---|
| Stage I | Involvement of a single lymph node region |
| Stage II | Involvement of two or more lymph node regions on the same side of the diaphragm |
| Stage III(1) | Involvement of lymph node regions or structures on both sides of the diaphragm, abdominal disease is limited to the upper abdomen, ie, spleen, splenic hilar, celiac, and/or porta hepatis nodes |
| Stage III(2) | Involvement of lymph node regions on both sides of the diaphragm, abdominal disease includes para-aortic, mesenteric, iliac, or inguinal nodes, with or without disease in the upper abdomen |
| Stage IV | Diffuse or disseminated involvement of one or more extralymphatic tissues or organs, with or without associated lymph node involvement |
| For all stages: | A = No symptoms<br>B = Fever (>38°C), drenching sweats, weight loss (>10% body weight over 6 months)<br>X = Bulky disease greater than one-third widening of the mediastinum<br>E = Involvement of a single extranodal site contiguous to a nodal site |

#### Non-Hodgkin's Lymphoma (NHL)

Can use Cotswold Modification of the Ann Arbor Staging System (above) or some clinicians use two stages of NHL:

> Limited disease – Stage I
> Advanced disease – Stages II, III, IV

#### Working Formulation Classification of Non-Hodgkin's Lymphoma

Low Grade

> A – Small lymphocytic; plasmacytoid
> B – Follicular, small cleaved cell
> C – Follicular, mixed (small cleaved and large cell)

*(continued on next page)*

## Hodgkin's Disease and Non-Hodgkin's Lymphoma

**Working Formulation Classification of Non-Hodgkin's Lymphoma:**

Intermediate Grade

| | |
|---|---|
| D | Follicular, large cell |
| E | Diffuse, small cleaved cell |
| F | Diffuse, mixed (small cleaved and large cell) |
| G | Diffuse, large cell |

High Grade

| | |
|---|---|
| H | Immunoblastic (large cell) |
| I | Lymphoblastic |
| J | Small, noncleaved (Burkitt, non-Burkitt) |

**International Prognostic Index for NHL**

| Variable | 0 point | 1 point |
|---|---|---|
| *All patients* | | |
| Age (yr) | ≤60 | >60 |
| Stage | I or II | III or IV |
| No. of extranodal sites | ≤1 | >1 |
| Performance status | 0 or 1 | ≥2 |
| LDH | normal | elevated |

Low risk 0 or 1; low intermediate risk 2; intermediate risk 3; high risk 4 or 5

| *Patients over age 60* | | |
|---|---|---|
| Stage | I or II | III or IV |
| Performance status | 0 or 1 | ≥2 |
| LDH | normal | elevated |

Low risk 0; low intermediate risk 1; high intermediate risk 2; high risk 3

## Leukemia

**FAB Classification of Acute Lymphoblastic Leukemia (ALL)**

| | |
|---|---|
| ALL-L1 | (Childhood form) |
| ALL-L2 | (Adult form) |
| ALL-L3 | (Burkitt type) |

**FAB Classification of Acute Myeloid Leukemia (AML)**

| Subtype | Morphologic Features |
|---|---|
| M0 | Myeloblastic without maturation |
| M1 | Myeloblastic with minimal maturation |
| M2 | Myeloblastic with maturation |
| M3 | Promyelocytic |
|    M3v | Promyelocytic microgranular variant |
| M4 | Myelomonocytic |
|    M4Eo | Myelomonoblasts with abnormal eosinophils |
| M5 | Monocytic leukemia |
|    M5a | Poorly differentiated |
|    M5b | Well differentiated |
| M6 | Erythroleukemia (usually progresses to M1, M2 or M4) |
| M7 | Megakaryoblastic leukemia |

**Chronic Myelogenous Leukemia (CML)**

No staging system is available for CML

*(continued on next page)*

22

**Leukemia**

### Rai Clinical Staging System for Chronic Lymphocytic Leukemia (CLL)

| | |
|---|---|
| Stage 0 | Lymphocytosis in blood (15,000/mcL or higher) and bone marrow ($\geq$40% lymphocytes) |
| Stage 1 | Stage 0 plus lymphadenopathy |
| Stage 2 | Stage 0 or 1 plus splenomegaly and/or hepatomegaly |
| Stage 3 | Stage 0, 1 or 2 plus anemia (hemoglobin <11 g/dL) |
| Stage 4 | Stage 0, 1 or 2 plus thrombocytopenia (platelets <100,000) |

**Section 2: Table 12**

**Lung Cancer**

### TNM Classification for Lung Cancer

| T (tumor) | TX | Primary tumor cannot be assessed or tumor proven by the presence of malignant cells in sputum or bronchial washings but not visualized by imaging or bronchoscopy |
|---|---|---|
| | T0 | No evidence of primary tumor |
| | Tis | In situ carcinoma |
| | T1 | Tumor is 3 cm or less at its greatest dimension, surrounded by lung or visceral pleura, without evidence of invasion proximal to a lobar bronchus at bronchoscopy (ie, not in the main bronchus) |
| | T2 | Tumor with any of the following features of size or extent: more than 3 cm in greatest diameter; involves main bronchus, 2 cm or more distal to the carina; invades the visceral pleura; or associated with atelectasis or obstructive pneumonitis which extends to the hilar region but does not involve the entire lung |
| | T3 | Tumor of any size that directly invades any of the following: chest wall (including superior sulcus tumors), diaphragm, mediastinal pleura, parietal pericardium, or tumor in the main bronchus less than 2 cm distal to the carina, but without involvement of the carina or associated atelectasis or obstructive pneumonitis of the entire lung |

*(continued on next page)*

**Lung Cancer**

| | T4 | Any size tumor that invades any of the following: mediastinum, heart, great vessels, trachea, esophagus, vertebral body, carina; or tumor with a malignant pleural effusion; or satellite tumor nodules within the ipsilateral primary tumor lobe of the lung |
|---|---|---|
| N (nodes) | NX | Regional lymph nodes cannot be assessed |
| | N0 | No regional lymph node metastasis |
| | N1 | Metastasis in ipsilateral peribronchial, hilar or intrapulmonary nodes, including direct extension |
| | N2 | Metastasis in ipsilateral mediastinal and/or subcarinal lymph nodes(s) |
| | N3 | Metastasis in contralateral mediastinal, contralateral hilar, ipsilateral, or contralateral scalene or supraclavicular lymph node(s) |
| M (metastasis) | MX | Presence of distant metastasis cannot be assessed |
| | M0 | No evidence of distant metastases |
| | M1 | Distant metastases |

**Staging of Lung Cancer**

| Stage Ia | T1 | N0 | M0 |
|---|---|---|---|
| Stage Ib | T2 | N0 | M0 |
| Stage IIa | T1 | N1 | M0 |
| Stage IIb | T2 | N1 | M0 |
| | T3 | N0 | M0 |
| Stage IIIa | T1 | N2 | M0 |
| | T2 | N2 | M0 |
| | T3 | N0 | M0 |
| | T3 | N1 | M0 |
| | T3 | N2 | M0 |
| Stage IIIb | Any T | N3 | M0 |
| | T4 | Any N | M0 |
| Stage IV | Any T | Any N | M1 |

24

**Melanoma**

**TNM Staging for Melanoma**

| | | | |
|---|---|---|---|
| T (tumor) | Tx | Primary tumor cannot be assessed | |
| | T0 | No evidence of primary tumor | |
| | Tis | Melanoma in situ | |
| | T1a | $\leq$1.0 mm thick without ulceration and level II or III | |
| | T1b | $\leq$1.0 mm thick with ulceration or level IV or V | |
| | T2a | 1.01 – 2.0 mm thick without ulceration | |
| | T2b | 1.01 – 2.0 mm thick with ulceration | |
| | T3a | 2.01-4.0 mm thick without ulceration | |
| | T3b | 2.01-4.0 mm thick with ulceration | |
| | T4a | >4.0 mm thick without ulceration | |
| | T4b | >4.0 mm thick with ulceration | |
| N (nodes) | NX | Regional lymph nodes cannot be assessed | |
| | N0 | No regional lymph node metastasis | |
| | N1 | Metastasis in one node | |
| | | N1a | Micrometastasis |
| | | N1b | Macrometastasis |
| | N2 | Metastasis in 2-3 regional lymph nodes or intralymphatic regional metastasis without nodal metastasis | |
| | | N2a | Micrometastasis |
| | | N2b | Macrometastasis |
| | | N2c | In-transit metastasis or satellites without metastatic nodes |
| | N3 | Metastasis in $\geq$4 nodes, or matted nodes, or in-transit metastasis/satellites(s) with metastatic nodes | |

**25**

*(continued on next page)*

## Melanoma

| M (metastases) | MX | Distant metastasis cannot be assessed |
|---|---|---|
| | M0 | No distant metastasis |
| | M1 | Distant metastasis is present |

| | | M1a | Metastasis to skin, SC tissue or distant LN; normal LDH |
|---|---|---|---|
| | | M1b | Metastasis to lung; normal LDH |
| | | M1c | Metastasis to all other visceral sites; or distant metastasis with an elevated LDH |

### Pathologic Stage Grouping

| Stage 0 | Tis N0 M0 |
|---|---|
| Stage IA | T1a N0 M0 |
| Stage IB | T1b2a N0 M0 |
| Stage IIA | T2b3a N0 M0 |
| Stage IIB | T3b4a N0 M0 |
| Stage IIC | T4b N0 M0 |
| Stage IIIA | T1a-4a N1a M0 (intermediate risk) |
| Stage IIIB | T1b-4b N1a,2a, M0; T1a-4a N1b 2b M0; T1a/b – 4a/b N2c M0 (high risk) |
| Stage IIIC | T1b-4b N1b, 2b M0; Any T N3 M0 (very high risk) |
| Stage IV | Any T Any N M1 |

### Clark Levels of Invasion for Malignant Melanoma

| Level 1 | Tumor confined to epidermis (in situ) |
|---|---|
| Level 2 | Tumor extends beyond basal lamina into papillary dermis |
| Level 3 | Tumor extends into papillary dermis and abuts onto but does not invade the reticular dermis |
| Level 4 | Tumor extends into the reticular dermis |
| Level 5 | Tumor extends into subcutaneous fat |

**Multiple Myeloma**

**Durie and Salmon Staging for Multiple Myeloma**

| Stage | Clinical Determinants |
|-------|----------------------|
| Stage I | **Low tumor mass** (<0.6 x $10^{12}$ plasma cells/m$^2$). Must have *all* of the following:<br><br>Hemoglobin >10 gm/dL<br><br>Serum calcium: normal or $\leq$12 mg/dL<br><br>Skeletal x-ray: normal or with a solitary plasmacytoma<br><br>Low M-component production rates:<br><br>    IgG value <5 gm/dL<br><br>    IgA value <3 gm/dL<br><br>    Urine light chain excretion <4g per 24 hrs. |
| Stage II | **Intermediate tumor mass** (0.6 – 1.2 x $10^{12}$ plasma cells/m$^2$)<br><br>Criteria that fits neither stage I or III |
| Stage III | **High tumor mass** (>1.2 x $10^{12}$ plasma cells/m$^2$)<br><br>*Any one or more* of the following:<br><br>Hemoglobin <8.5 gm/dL<br><br>Serum calcium >12 mg/dL<br><br>Extensive lytic bone lesions<br><br>High M-component production rates<br><br>    IgG >7 gm/dL<br><br>    IgA >5 gm/dL<br><br>    urine light chain excretion >12 gm/24 hrs |
| Substage A | Serum creatinine <2 mg/dL |
| Substage B | Serum creatinine $\geq$2 mg/dL |

**Ovarian Cancer**

**International Federation of Gynecology and Obstetrics (FIGO)
Staging System for Ovarian Cancer**

| | |
|---|---|
| Stage I | Cancer limited to ovaries |
| Stage Ia | Limited to one ovary, no ascites |
| Stage Ib | Both ovaries involved, no ascites |
| Stage Ic | Ia or Ib with ascites or positive peritoneal washings |
| Stage II | Cancer of one or both ovaries with extension limited to pelvic tissue |
| Stage IIa | Extension to uterus or tubes |
| Stage IIb | Extension to other pelvic tissues |
| Stage IIc | IIa or IIb with ascites or positive peritoneal washings |
| Stage III | Cancer involving one or both ovaries with peritoneal implants outside the pelvis and/or positive retroperitoneal or inguinal nodes. Tumor is limited to the true pelvis but with histologically proven extension to small bowel or omentum. |
| Stage IIIa | Tumor grossly limited to true pelvis with negative nodes but with histologically confirmed microscopic seeding of abdominal peritoneal surfaces. |
| Stage IIIb | Same as IIIa but abdominal peritoneal implants do not exceed 2 cm in diameter |
| Stage IIIc | Abdominal implants greater than 2 cm in diameter and/or positive retroperitoneal or inguinal lymph nodes |
| Stage IV | Distant metastases present (including cytology-positive pleural effusions and metastases to the liver parenchyma or peripheral superficial lymph nodes.) |

## Section 2: Table 16

### Pancreatic Cancer

#### TNM Staging for Pancreatic Cancer

| Stage I | TI (tumor <2 cm), T2 (tumor >2 cm, confined to pancreas), N0, M0 |
| --- | --- |
| Stage IIA | T3 (tumor extends to duodenum, bile duct, or peri-pancreatic tissue), N0, M0 |
| Stage IIB | T1-3, N1, M0 |
| Stage III | T4 (tumor extends to stomach, spleen, colon, or adjacent large vessels), N0-1, M0 |
| Stage IV | T1-4, N0-1, M1 (any distant metastases) |

## Section 2: Table 17

### Prostate Cancer

#### TNM Staging for Prostate Cancer

| TX | Primary tumor cannot be assessed |
| --- | --- |
| T0 | No evidence of primary tumor |
| T1 | Subclinical tumor not evident by palpation or imaging |
| | T1a  <5% cancerous tissue found incidentally on TURP |
| | T1b  >5% cancerous tissue found incidentally on TURP |
| | T1c  Tumor found by needle biopsy (eg, because of elevated PSA) |
| T2 | Tumor confined to the prostate |
| | T2a  Tumor involves ≤half of one lobe |
| | T2b  Tumor involves >half of one lobe |
| | T2c  Tumor involves both lobes |
| T3 | Tumor extends through prostate capsule |
| | T3a  Extracapsular extension (unilateral or bilateral) |
| | T3b  Seminal vesicle(s) involvement |
| T4 | Tumor is fixed or invades bladder neck, rectum, external sphincter, levator muscles, and/or pelvic wall |

*(continued on next page)*

**Prostate Cancer**

### TNM Staging for Prostate Cancer

| NX | Regional lymph nodes cannot be assessed |
|---|---|
| N0 | No regional lymph node metastasis |
| N1 | Metastasis in regional lymph node(s) |
| MX | Distant metastasis cannot be assessed |
| M0 | No distant metastasis |
| M1 | Distant metastasis is present |

| | M1a | Nonregional lymph node involvement (eg, supraclavicular) |
|---|---|---|
| | M1b | Bony metastasis |
| | M1c | Metastases to sites other than lymph nodes or bone (eg, liver) |

Histological Grade (G)

| G1 | Gleason 2-4 (well differentiated) |
|---|---|
| G2 | Gleason 5-6 (moderately differentiated) |
| G3 | Gleason 7-10 (poorly differentiated) |

---

## Renal Cell Carcinoma

### TNM Staging of Renal Cell Carcinoma

| | |
|---|---|
| TX | Primary tumor cannot be assessed |
| T0 | No evidence of primary tumor |
| T1a | Tumor $\leq 4$ cm and confined to the kidney |
| T1b | Tumor $>4$ cm, $\leq 7$ cm and confined to the kidney |
| T2 | Tumor $>7.0$ cm and confined to the kidney |
| T3a | Tumor invades adrenal gland or perinephric tissue but not beyond Gerota's fascia |
| T3b | Tumor extends into the renal vein (or its segmented branches) or vena cava below the diaphragm |
| T3c | Tumor extends into the vena cava above the diaphragm or invades the wall of the vena cava |
| T4 | Tumor invades beyond Gerota's fascia |
| NX | Regional lymph nodes cannot be assessed |
| N0 | No regional lymph node metastasis |
| N1 | Metastasis in a single regional lymph node |
| N2 | Metastases in more than one regional lymph node |
| MX | Distant metastasis cannot be assessed |
| M0 | No distant metastasis |
| M1 | Distant metastasis is present |

**31**

### Stage Groupings

| | |
|---|---|
| Stage 1 | T1 N0 M0 |
| Stage II | T2 N0 M0 |
| Stage III | T 1-2, N1, M0; T 3a,b,c, N0-1, M0 |
| Stage IV | T4 N0-1, M0; any T, N2, M0; any T any N M1 |

**Testicular Cancer**

### Staging of Testicular Cancer

| | |
|---|---|
| Stage A | Disease confined to the testes |
| Stage B | Metastases to the retroperitoneal lymph nodes |
| | Stage B1 Five or fewer encapsulated lymph nodes positive for tumor |
| | Stage B2 More than five lymph nodes positive for tumor |
| | Stage B3 Massive retroperitoneal lymph node disease |
| Stage C | Tumor involving supradiaphragmatic nodes, lungs, liver, bone, or brain |

## References

Casciato DA, ed. *Manual of Clinical Oncology.* 5th ed. Boston, Mass: Little, Brown and Company; 2004.

Govindan R, ed. *The Washington Manual of Oncology*. Philadelphia, Pa: Lippincott, Williams and Wilkins; 2002.

Skeel RT, ed. *Handbook of Cancer Chemotherapy.* 6th ed. Philadelphia, Pa: Lippincott, Williams and Wilkins; 2003.

American Joint Committee on Cancer (AJCC). *Cancer Staging Manual.* 6th ed. New York, NY: Springer-Verlag; 2002.

# Chemotherapy Regimens for Common Cancers

Chemotherapy drugs were initially used as single agents in the 1950s. By the 1960s and 1970s, drugs were combined to attack the tumor at different points in the cell cycle. Increases in complete responses as well as longer duration of response were seen and combination therapy has become the mainstay of chemotherapeutic treatment for cancer. Factors to consider when combining drugs include cell cycle specificity, toxicity, synergy and modes of action.

There are hundreds of combination chemotherapy regimens. This section will list the most common regimens for the most common tumor types seen in adults. It is intended as a quick reference guide for oncology professionals who are familiar with the therapy. There are many excellent textbooks available for more detailed information and for those who are novices in the field. The National Cancer Institute (NCI) provides the Physician's Data Query (PDQ), an online computer service which lists many combination regimens and new protocols, as well as information about diagnosis and treatment of various cancers. This service provides the most up to date listings of current treatment and new protocols.

When this book is used as a guide, it is imperative to consult the original or cited literature to verify dosage, check timing or sequencing and to ascertain the need for additional measures such as hydration or antiemetics. Supportive measures with most chemotherapy regimens will include hydration and antiemetics. Colony-stimulating factors may be indicated with some therapies. Oncology professionals should be familiar with these supportive measures. They are listed with some of the regimens and drugs but this list is not exhaustive or specific, rather a reminder to consider the supportive needs of the regimen.

When combination chemotherapy is used in conjunction with radiation therapy, dosage reduction is usually indicated. Toxicities from the drugs may also result in dosage reduction.

Only board certified or board eligible oncologists or oncology fellows should order chemotherapy, after a period of supervision and continuing oversight. It should not be given as a verbal order except to reduce a dose. Patients should be treated and monitored by oncology nurses trained and certified to give chemotherapy, preferably on a dedicated oncology unit or in an outpatient setting. It should be dispensed by oncology trained and certified pharmacists. The chemotherapy orders should be independently verified by all those involved.

This section lists only proven regimens with FDA approved drugs. Ongoing protocols with cooperative clinical research groups may offer newer drugs and combinations. These should be considered when determining treatment for most patients. Ongoing clinical trials can be accessed through the NCI website (www.cancer.gov).

### Biological Therapies

Biological therapy is a type of treatment that works with the immune system. It can help fight cancer or help control side effects from other cancer treatments like chemotherapy. Biological therapy and chemotherapy are both treatments that fight cancer. While they may seem alike, they work in different ways. Biological therapy helps the immune system fight cancer. Chemotherapy attacks the cancer cells directly. Biological therapy can be given in conjunction with chemotherapy and radiation therapy or as a single therapy. It is thought that biological therapies:

- Stop or slow the growth of cancer cells.

- Make it easier for the immune system to destroy cancer cells.

- Keep cancer from spreading to other parts of the body.

The immune system includes the spleen, lymph nodes, tonsils, bone marrow, and white blood cells which all help protect the patient from getting infections and diseases. White blood cells include:

- Monocytes

- Lymphocytes
  - B cells
  - T cells
  - Natural killer cells

Just like other forms of cancer treatment, biological therapy sometimes causes side effects. Side effects can include rashes or swelling at the injection site, flu-like symptoms such as fever, chills, nausea, vomiting, loss of appetite, fatigue, bone pain and muscle aches, and hypotension.

Cancer vaccines are also a form of biological therapy. While other vaccines are given before a person gets sick, cancer vaccines are given after the cancer diagnosis in an attempt to fight the cancer and prevent it from recurring. Current cancer vaccine research is being done in melanoma, lymphoma, and kidney, breast, ovarian, prostate, colon, and rectal cancers.

**Common Biological Therapy Treatments for Cancer**

- BCG or Bacillus Calmette-Guérin treats bladder tumors or bladder cancer.

- IL-2 or Interleukin-2 treats certain types of cancer.

- Interferon alpha treats certain types of cancer.

- Rituxan® or Rituximab treats non-Hodgkin's lymphoma.

- Herceptin® or Trastuzumab treats breast cancer.

- Bevicizamab (Avastin™) or Cetuximab (Erbitux™) for colorectal cancer.

**Common Biological Therapy Treatments for Controlling Side Effects**

- Neupogen®, Neulasta® or G-CSF increases white blood cell counts and helps prevent infection in people who are getting chemotherapy.

- Procrit®, or Erythropoietin and Darbepoetin (Aranesp®) help make red blood cells in people who have anemia.

- IL-11, Interleukin-11, Oprelvekin® or Neumega® helps make platelets (a type of blood cell).

*Source: National Cancer Institute; www.cancer.gov; updated 1/14/2004.*

**Targeted Therapies**

Targeted cancer therapies use drugs that block the growth and spread of cancer. They interfere with specific molecules involved in carcinogenesis and tumor growth. By focusing on molecular and cellular changes that are specific to cancer, targeted cancer therapies may be more effective than current treatments and less harmful to normal cells.

Most targeted therapies are in preclinical testing but some are in clinical trials or have been approved by the FDA. Targeted cancer therapies are being studied for use alone, in combination with each other, and in combination with other cancer treatments, such as chemotherapy.

Targeted therapies interfere with cancer cell growth and division in different ways and at various points during the development, growth, and spread of cancer. Many of these therapies focus on proteins that are involved in the signal process. By blocking the signals that tell cancer cells to grow and divide uncontrollably, targeted cancer therapies can help to stop the growth and division of cancer cells.

Some examples of targeted cancer therapies include:

- "Small molecule" drugs that block specific enzymes and growth factor receptors involved in cancer cell growth. Gleevac® (imatinib mesylate) and Iressa® (gefitinib) are examples of small molecule drugs.

- "Apoptosis-inducing" drugs cause cancer cells to undergo cell death by interfering with proteins involved in the process. Velcade® (bortezomib) is an example of an apoptosis-inducing drug.

- Monoclonal antibodies, cancer vaccines, angiogenesis inhibitors and gene therapy are considered by some to be targeted therapies because they interfere with the growth of cancer cells.

*Source: National Cancer Institute; www.cancer.gov; reviewed 4/27/2004.*

## Chemotherapy Regimens

Chemotherapeutic agents are commonly divided into several classes. Within the classes are several types of agents. In Table 1, these agents are grouped according to their mechanism of action, biochemical structure or physiologic action. Knowledge of these classifications can be helpful in planning therapy, in understanding why two classifications can or cannot be used together, and in predicting cross-resistance between two drugs.

### Section 3: Table 1

**Useful Chemotherapeutic Agents**

| Class and Type | Agents |
| --- | --- |
| Alkylating agents | |
| Alkyl sulfonate | Busulfan |
| Ethylenimine derivative | Thiotepa (triethylenethiophosphoramide) |
| Metal salt | Carboplatin, cisplatin, oxaliplatin |
| Nitrogen mustard | Chlorambucil, cyclophosphamide, estramustine, ifosfamide, mechlorethamine, melphalan |
| Nitrosourea | Carmustine, lormustine, streptozocin |
| triazene | Dacarbazine, temozolamide |
| Antimetabolites | |
| Antifolates | Methotrexate, pemetrexed, raltitrexed, trimetrexate |
| Purine analogs | Mercaptopurine, thioguanine, pentostatin, cladribine, fludarabine |
| Pyrimidine analogs | Azacitidine, capecitabine, cytarabine, floxuridine, fluorouracil, gemcitabine |
| Natural products | |
| Antibiotics | Bleomycin, dactinomycin, daunorubicin, doxorubicin, epirubicin, idarubicin, mitomycin, mitoxantrone, valrubicin |
| Enzyme | Asparaginase |
| Microtubule polymer stabilizer | Docetaxel, paclitaxel |

*(continued on next page)*

## Useful Chemotherapeutic Agents

| Class and Type | Agents |
|---|---|
| Mitotic inhibiter | Vinblastine, vincristine, vindesine, vinorelbine |
| Topoisomerase I inhibitors | Irinotecan, topotecan |
| Topoisomerase II inhibitors | Etoposide, teniposide |
| **Hormones and hormone antagonists** | |
| Androgen | Fluoxymesterone and others |
| Androgen antagonist | Bicalutamide, flutamide, nilutamide |
| Aromatase inhibitor | Aminoglufethimide, anastrozole, letrozole, exemestane |
| Corticosteroid | Dexamethasone, prednisone |
| Estrogen | Diethylstilbestrol |
| Estrogen antagonist (selective estrogen receptor modulator) | Fulvestrant, raloxifene, tamoxifen, toremifene |
| Luteinizing hormone–releasing hormone agonist | Goserelin, leuprolide, triptorelin |
| Progestin | Megestrol acetate, medroxyprogesterone acetate |
| Thyroid hormones | Levothyroxine, liothyronine |
| **Molecularly targeted agents** | |
| Gene expression modulators | Retinoids, rexinoids |
| Monoclonal antibody | Alemtozumab, cetuximab, gemtuzumab, ibritumomab tiuxetan, trastuzumab (Herceptin), rituximab, $^{131}$I-tositumomab |
| Tyrosine kinase inhibitor (includes receptor tyrosine kinase inhibitors) | Imatinib mesylate, semaxanib (SU5416), ZD1839 (getitinib, Iressa) |
| **Biologic response modifiers** | |
| Interferons | Interferon-$\alpha_{2a}$, interferon-$\alpha_{2b}$ |
| Interleukins | Aldesleukin (interleukin-2), oprelvekin, denileukin diftitox |
| Myeloid- and erythroid-stimulating factors | Epoetin, filgrastim, sargramostim |
| Nonspecific immuno-modulation | Thalidomide |

*(continued on next page)*

**Useful Chemotherapeutic Agents**

| Class and Type | Agents |
|---|---|
| **Miscellaneous agents** | |
| Adrenocortical suppressant | Mitotane |
| Bisphosphonates | Pamidronate, zoledronic acid |
| Cytoprotector (reactive species antagonists) | Amifostine, dexrazoxane, mesna |
| Growth factor-binding inhibitor | Suramin |
| Methylhydrazine derivative | Procarbazine |
| Photosensitizing agents | Porfimer |
| Platelet-reducing agents | Anagrelide |
| Salt | Arsenic trioxide |
| Somatostatin analog | Octreotide |
| Substituted melamine | Altretamine (hexamethylmelamine) |
| Substituted urea | Hydroxyurea |

*Skeel R.* Handbook of Cancer Chemotherapy. *6th ed. Philadelphia, Pa: Lippincott Williams & Wilkins; 2003. Reprinted with permission.*

---

## Common Chemotherapy Regimens by Diagnosis

---

### 5+2

**Use:**  Acute myelocytic leukemia (AML; reinduction). *Cycle:* 7 days. Regimen given once after an induction regimen has been used.

**Regimen:**  Cytarabine 100 to 200 mg/m$^2$/day continuous IV infusion, days 1 through 5
*with*
Daunorubicin 45 mg/m$^2$ IV, days 1 and 2
*or*
Mitoxantrone 12 mg/m$^2$ IV, days 1 and 2

---

### 7+3

**Use:**  Acute myelocytic leukemia (AML; induction). *Cycle:* 7 days. Give 1 cycle only.

**Regimen:**  Cytarabine 100 to 200 mg/m$^2$/day continuous IV infusion, days 1 through 7
*with*
Daunorubicin 30 or 45 mg/m$^2$/day IV, days 1 through 3
*or*
Idarubicin 12 mg/m$^2$/day IV, days 1 through 3
*or*
Mitoxantrone 12 mg/m$^2$/day IV, days 1 through 3

41

---

### 7+3+7

**Use:**  Acute myelogenous leukemia (AML; induction-adults). *Cycle:* 21 days. Give 1 cycle. If patient has persistent leukemia at day 21, give 1 to 2 additional cycles.

**Regimen:**  Cytarabine 100 mg/m$^2$/day continuous IV infusion, days 1 through 7
Daunorubicin 50 mg/m$^2$/day IV, days 1 through 3
Etoposide 75 mg/m$^2$/day IV, days 1 through 7

---

### "8 in 1"

**Use:**  Brain tumors (pediatrics). *Cycle:* 14 days

**Regimen:**  Methylprednisolone 300 mg/m$^2$/dose PO every 6 hours for 3 doses, day 1, starting at hour 0
Vincristine 1.5 mg/m$^2$ (2 mg maximum dose) IV, day 1, hour 0
Lomustine 100 mg/m$^2$ PO, day 1, hour 0
Procarbazine 75 mg/m$^2$ PO, day 1, hour 1
Hydroxyurea 3,000 mg/m$^2$ PO, day 1, hour 2

---

*(continued on next page)*

**Common Chemotherapy Regimens by Diagnosis**

---

**"8 in 1"** *(continued)*

Cisplatin 90 mg/m$^2$ IV, day 1, starting at hour 3 (6-hour infusion)
Cytarabine 300 mg/m$^2$ IV, day 1, hour 9
Dacarbazine 150 mg/m$^2$ IV, day 1, hour 12

---

**ABV**

Use:        Kaposi sarcoma. *Cycle:* 28 days

Regimen:    Doxorubicin 40 mg/m$^2$ IV, day 1
            Bleomycin 15 units IV, days 1 and 15
            Vinblastine 6 mg/m$^2$ IV, day 1

---

Use:        Kaposi sarcoma. *Cycle:* 28 days

Regimen:    Doxorubicin 10 mg/m$^2$ IV, days 1 and 15
            Bleomycin 15 units IV, days 1 and 15
            Vincristine 1 mg IV, days 1 and 15

---

**ABVD**

Use:        Lymphoma (Hodgkin). *Cycle:* 28 days

Regimen:    Doxorubicin 25 mg/m$^2$ IV, days 1 and 15
            Bleomycin 10 units/m$^2$ IV, days 1 and 15
            Vinblastine 6 mg/m$^2$ IV, days 1 and 15
            *with*
            Dacarbazine 375 mg/m$^2$ IV, days 1 and 15
            *or*
            Dacarbazine 150 mg/m$^2$ IV, days 1 through 5

---

**AC (see also CY/A)**

Use:        Breast cancer. *Cycle:* 21 days

Regimen:    Doxorubicin 60 mg/m$^2$ IV, day 1
            Cyclophosphamide 600 mg/m$^2$ IV, day 1

---

Use:        Sarcoma (bone). *Cycle:* 21 to 28 days

Regimen:    Doxorubicin 30 mg/m$^2$/day continuous IV infusion, days 1 through 3
            Cisplatin 100 mg/m$^2$ IV, day 4

---

Use:        Neuroblastoma (pediatrics). *Cycle:* 21 to 28 days

Regimen:    Cyclophosphamide 150 mg/m$^2$/day PO, days 1 through 7
            Doxorubicin 35 mg/m$^2$ IV, day 8

*(continued on next page)*

## Section 3: Table 2

## Common Chemotherapy Regimens by Diagnosis

### AC/Paclitaxel, Sequential

Use: Breast cancer. *Cycle:* 21 days

Regimen: Give 4 cycles of AC regimen for breast cancer
*followed by*
Paclitaxel 175 mg/m$^2$ IV, day 1 for 4 cycles

### ACE (CAE)

Use: Lung cancer (small cell). *Cycle:* 21 to 28 days

Regimen: Cyclophosphamide 1,000 mg/m$^2$ IV, day 1
Doxorubicin 45 mg/m$^2$ IV, day 1
Etoposide 50 mg/m$^2$/day IV, days 1 through 5

### ACe

Use: Breast cancer. *Cycle:* 21 to 28 days

Regimen: Cyclophosphamide 200 mg/m$^2$/day PO, days 3 through 6
Doxorubicin 40 mg/m$^2$ IV, day 1

### AD

Use: Sarcoma (soft tissue or bone). *Cycle:* 21 days

Regimen: Doxorubicin 45 to 60 mg/m$^2$ IV, day 1
Dacarbazine 200 to 250 mg/m$^2$/day IV, days 1 through 5
*or*
Doxorubicin 15 mg/m$^2$/day continuous IV infusion, days 1 through 4
Dacarbazine 250 mg/m$^2$/day continuous IV infusion, days 1 through 4

### Advanced Stage Burkitt or B-Cell ALL Pediatric Protocol

Use: Lymphoma (Burkitt or B-cell ALL-pediatrics). *Cycle:* 18 to 25 days, based on hematologic recovery. Give Treatment A, then follow with Treatment B after hematologic recovery; repeat alternating treatments a total of 4 times over 5 to 6 months.

Regimen: Treatment A
Methotrexate 10 mg/m$^2$ intrathecal, hours 0 and 72 for first cycle;
then hour 0 only of subsequent cycles
Cytarabine 50 mg/m$^2$ intrathecal, hours 0 and 72 for first cycle;
then hour 0 only of subsequent cycles
Cyclophosphamide 300 mg/m$^2$/dose IV, every 12 hours for 6 doses, given at hours 0, 12, 24, 36, 48, and 60
Vincristine 1.5 mg/m$^2$ IV, hour 72 (first cycle only: an additional dose at day 11)

*(continued on next page)*

**Common Chemotherapy Regimens by Diagnosis**

---

**Advanced Stage Burkitt or B-Cell ALL Pediatric Protocol** *(continued)*

Doxorubicin 50 mg/m$^2$ IV, hour 72

### Treatment B
Methotrexate 12 mg/m$^2$ intrathecal, hour 0

Methotrexate 200 mg/m$^2$ IV, hour 0 (on day 1)

*then*

Methotrexate 800 mg/m$^2$/day continuous IV infusion over 24 hours, begin hour 0 (on day 1)

Cytarabine 50 mg/m$^2$ intrathecal, hour 24 (on day 2, give at end of methotrexate infusion)

Cytarabine 200 mg/m$^2$/day continuous IV infusion, days 2 and 3 for first cycle. Increase to 400 mg/m$^2$/day continuous IV infusion, days 2 and 3 for second cycle; 800 mg/m$^2$/day continuous IV infusion, days 2 and 3 for third cycle; and 1,600 mg/m$^2$/day continuous IV infusion, days 2 and 3 for final cycle.

Leucovorin 30 mg/m$^2$/dose IV, every 6 hours for 2 doses at hours 36 and 42

*then*

Leucovorin 3 mg/m$^2$/dose IV, every 12 hours for 3 doses at hours 54, 66, and 78

---

**AP**

| | |
|---|---|
| Use: | Ovarian, endometrial cancer. *Cycle:* 21 to 28 days |
| Regimen: | Doxorubicin 50 to 60 mg/m$^2$ IV, day 1 |
| | Cisplatin 50 to 60 mg/m$^2$ IV, day 1 |

---

**ARAC-DNR**

| | |
|---|---|
| Use: | Acute myelocytic leukemia (AML). |
| Regimen: | Cytarabine 100 mg/m$^2$/day continuous IV infusion, days 1 through 7 |
| | Daunorubicin 30 or 45 mg/m$^2$/day IV, days 1 through 3 |
| | If leukemia is persistent, additional doses are given: cytarabine on days 1 through 5, daunorubicin on days 1 and 2 |

---

**AT**

| | |
|---|---|
| Use: | Breast cancer. *Cycle:* 21 days for up to 8 cycles |
| Regimen: | Doxorubicin 50 mg/m$^2$ IV, day 1 |
| | Paclitaxel 220 mg/m$^2$ IV over 3 hours, day 2 (given 24 hours after doxorubicin) |

*(continued on next page)*

▬▬▬▬▬▬▬▬▬▬▬▬▬▬▬▬▬▬▬▬▬▬▬▬▬▬▬▬

## Common Chemotherapy Regimens by Diagnosis

---

**ATRA + CT-see DA + ATRA**

---

### B-CAVe

**Use:** Lymphoma (Hodgkin). *Cycle:* 28 days

**Regimen:** Bleomycin 5 units/m$^2$ IV, days 1, 28, and 35
Lomustine 100 mg/m$^2$ PO, day 1
Doxorubicin 60 mg/m$^2$ IV, day 1
Vinblastine 5 mg/m$^2$ IV, day 1

---

### BCVPP

**Use:** Lymphoma (Hodgkin). *Cycle:* 28 days

**Regimen:** Carmustine 100 mg/m$^2$ IV, day 1
Cyclophosphamide 600 mg/m$^2$ IV, day 1
Vinblastine 5 mg/m$^2$ IV, day 1
Procarbazine 50 mg/m$^2$ PO, day 1
Procarbazine 100 mg/m$^2$/day PO, days 2 through 10
Prednisone 60 mg/m$^2$/day PO, days 1 through 10

45

---

### BEACOPP

**Use:** Lymphoma (Hodgkin). *Cycle:* 21 days

**Regimen:** Bleomycin 10 units/m$^2$ IV, day 8
Etoposide 100 mg/m$^2$ IV, days 1 through 3
Doxorubicin 25 mg/m$^2$ IV, day 1
Cyclophosphamide 650 mg/m$^2$ IV, day 1
Vincristine 1.4 mg/m$^2$ (2 mg maximum dose) IV, day 1
Procarbazine 100 mg/m$^2$/day PO, days 1 through 7
Prednisone 40 mg/m$^2$/day PO, days 1 through 14
Filgrastim 300 to 480 mcg/day subcutaneously, starting on day 8,
give for 3 days or more or until leukocytes exceed 2,000
cells/mm$^3$ for 3 days

---

### BEP

**Use:** Testicular cancer, germ cell tumors. *Cycle:* 21 days

**Regimen:** Bleomycin 30 units IV, days 2, 9, and 16
Etoposide 100 mg/m$^2$/day IV, days 1 through 5
Cisplatin 20 mg/m$^2$/day IV, days 1 through 5

▬▬▬▬▬▬▬▬▬▬▬▬▬▬▬▬▬▬▬▬▬▬▬▬▬▬▬▬

*(continued on next page)*

## Common Chemotherapy Regimens by Diagnosis

---

### Bicalutamide + LHRH-A

Use:        Prostate cancer. *Cycle:* ongoing

Regimen:    Bicalutamide 50 mg PO daily
            *with*
            Goserelin acetate 3.6 mg/dose implant subcutaneously, every 28 days
            *or*
            Leuprolide depot 7.5 mg/dose IM, every 28 days

---

### Bio-Chemotherapy (see Interleukin 2-Interferon alfa 2)

---

### BIP

Use:        Cervical cancer. *Cycle:* 21 days

Regimen:    Bleomycin 30 units/day continuous IV infusion over 24 hours, day 1
            Cisplatin 50 mg/m$^2$ IV, day 2
            Ifosfamide 5,000 mg/m$^2$/day continuous IV infusion over 24 hours, day 2
            Mesna 6,000 mg/m$^2$/cycle continuous IV infusion over 36 hours, day
                2 (start with ifosfamide)

---

### BOMP

Use:        Cervical cancer. *Cycle:* 6 weeks

Regimen:    Bleomycin 10 units IM, days 1, 8, 15, 22, 29, and 36
            Vincristine 1 mg/m$^2$ (2 mg maximum dose) IV, days 1, 8, 22, and 29
            Cisplatin 50 mg/m$^2$ IV, days 1 and 22
            Mitomycin 10 mg/m$^2$ IV, day 1

---

### C-MOPP-see COPP

---

### CA

Use:        Acute myelocytic leukemia (AML; induction-pediatrics). *Cycle:* 7
            days. Give 2 cycles. If patient has persistent blasts at day 15, give a
            third cycle.

Regimen:    Cytarabine 3,000 mg/m$^2$/dose IV every 12 hours for 4 doses,
            days 1 and 2
            Asparaginase 6,000 units/m$^2$ IM, at hour 42

*(continued on next page)*

**Common Chemotherapy Regimens by Diagnosis**

---

**CA-VP16**

| | |
|---|---|
| **Use:** | Lung cancer (small cell). *Cycle:* 21 days |
| **Regimen:** | Cyclophosphamide 1,000 mg/m$^2$ IV, day 1 |
| | Doxorubicin 45 mg/m$^2$ IV, day 1 |
| | Etoposide 80 mg/m$^2$/day, days 1 through 3 |

---

**CABO**

| | |
|---|---|
| **Use:** | Head and neck cancer. *Cycle:* 21 days |
| **Regimen:** | Cisplatin 50 mg/m$^2$ IV, day 4 |
| | Methotrexate 40 mg/m$^2$ IV, days 1 and 15 |
| | Bleomycin 10 units/dose IV, days 1, 8, and 15 |
| | Vincristine 2 mg/dose IV, days 1, 8, and 15 |

---

**CAE (see ACE)**

47

---

**CAF**

| | |
|---|---|
| **Use:** | Breast cancer. *Cycle:* 28 days |
| **Regimen:** | Cyclophosphamide 100 mg/m$^2$/day PO, days 1 through 14 |
| | Doxorubicin 30 mg/m$^2$ IV, days 1 and 8 |
| | Fluorouracil 500 mg/m$^2$ IV, days 1 and 8 |

| | |
|---|---|
| **Use:** | Breast cancer. *Cycle:* 21 days |
| **Regimen:** | Cyclophosphamide 500 mg/m$^2$ IV, day 1 |
| | Doxorubicin 50 mg/m$^2$ IV, day 1 |
| | Fluorouracil 500 mg/m$^2$ IV, day 1 |

---

**CAL-G**

| | |
|---|---|
| **Use:** | Acute lymphocytic leukemia (ALL; induction-adult). *Cycle:* 4 weeks. Give 1 cycle only. |
| **Regimen:** | Cyclophosphamide 1,200 mg/m$^2$ IV, day 1 |
| | Daunorubicin 45 mg/m$^2$/day IV, days 1 through 3 |
| | Vincristine 2 mg/day IV, days 1, 8, 15, and 22 |
| | Prednisone 60 mg/m$^2$/day PO or IV, days 1 through 21 |
| | *with* |
| | Asparaginase 6,000 units/m$^2$/day subcutaneously, days 5, 8, 11, 15, 18, and 22 |

---

*(continued on next page)*

**Common Chemotherapy Regimens by Diagnosis**

---

**CAMP**

Use: Lung cancer (non-small cell). *Cycle:* 28 days

Regimen: Cyclophosphamide 300 mg/m$^2$ IV, days 1 and 8
Doxorubicin 20 mg/m$^2$ IV, days 1 and 8
Methotrexate 15 mg/m$^2$ IV, days 1 and 8
Procarbazine 100 mg/m$^2$/day PO, days 1 through 10

---

**CAP**

Use: Lung cancer (non-small cell). *Cycle:* 28 days

Regimen: Cyclophosphamide 400 mg/m$^2$ IV, day 1
Doxorubicin 40 mg/m$^2$ IV, day 1
Cisplatin 60 mg/m$^2$ IV, day 1

---

**Capecitabine-Docetaxel**

Use: Breast cancer. *Cycle:* 21 days

Regimen: Capecitabine 1,250 mg/m$^2$/dose PO twice daily, days 1 through 14
Docetaxel 75 mg/m$^2$ IV, day 1

---

**Carboplatin-Fluorouracil (see CF)**

---

**Carbo-Tax (see also CaT)**

Use: Ovarian cancer. *Cycle:* 21 days

Regimen: Paclitaxel 175 mg/m$^2$ IV over 3 hours, day 1
Carboplatin IV dose by Calvert equation to AUC 7.5 mg/mL/min,
day 1 (after paclitaxel)
*or*
Paclitaxel 185 mg/m$^2$ IV over 3 hours, day 1
Carboplatin IV dose by Calvert equation to AUC 6 mg/mL/min,
day 1 (after paclitaxel)

---

Use: Adenocarcinoma (unknown primary). *Cycle:* 21 days for up to 8 cycles

Regimen: Paclitaxel 200 mg/m$^2$ IV over 3 hours, day 1 (after carboplatin)
Carboplatin IV dose by Calvert equation to AUC 6 mg/mL/min, day 1
Filgrastim 300 mcg/day subcutaneously, days 5 to 12

---

**CaT (see also Carbo-Tax)**

Use: Adenocarcinoma (unknown primary), lung cancer (non-small cell),
ovarian cancer. *Cycle:* 21 days

48

*(continued on next page)*

## Common Chemotherapy Regimens by Diagnosis

**CaT (see also Carbo-Tax)** *(continued)*

Regimen: Carboplatin IV dose by Calvert equation to AUC 7.5 mg/mL/min, day 1 or 2 (give after paclitaxel infusion)

*with*

Paclitaxel 175 mg/m$^2$ IV over 3 hours, day 1
*or*
Paclitaxel 135 mg/m$^2$/day continuous IV infusion over 24 hours, on day 1

Use: Lung cancer (non-small cell). *Cycle:* 21 days

Regimen: Carboplatin IV dose by Calvert equation to AUC 6 mg/mL/min, day 1 (give after paclitaxel)

Paclitaxel 225 mg/m$^2$ IV over 3 hours, day 1

**CAV (VAC)**

Use: Lung cancer (small cell). *Cycle:* 21 days

Regimen: Cyclophosphamide 1,000 mg/m$^2$ IV, day 1
Doxorubicin 40 to 50 mg/m$^2$ IV, day 1
Vincristine 1 to 1.4 mg/m$^2$ (2 mg maximum dose) IV, day 1

**CAV/EP**

Use: Lung cancer (small cell). *Cycle:* 42 days for 3 cycles

Regimen: Cyclophosphamide 1,000 mg/m$^2$ IV, day 1
Doxorubicin 50 mg/m$^2$ IV, day 1
Vincristine 1.2 mg/m$^2$ IV, day 1
Etoposide 100 mg/m$^2$/day IV, days 22, 23, and 24
Cisplatin 25 mg/m$^2$/day IV, days 22, 23, and 24

**CAVE**

Use: Lung cancer (small cell). *Cycle:* 21 days

Regimen: Cyclophosphamide 1,000 mg/m$^2$ IV, day 1
Doxorubicin 50 mg/m$^2$ IV, day 1
Vincristine 2 mg IV, day 1
Etoposide 100 mg/m$^2$/day IV, days 2 through 4

**CC**

Use: Ovarian cancer. *Cycle:* 28 days

Regimen: Cyclophosphamide 600 mg/m$^2$ IV, day 1
Carboplatin 300 to 350 mg/m$^2$ IV, day 1

49

*(continued on next page)*

## Common Chemotherapy Regimens by Diagnosis

### CDB

Use: Melanoma. *Cycle:* 21 days

Regimen: Cisplatin 25 mg/m$^2$/day IV, days 1 through 3
Dacarbazine 220 mg/m$^2$/day IV, days 1 through 3
Carmustine 150 mg/m$^2$ IV, day 1 of odd-numbered cycles only
(eg, cycle 1, 3, 5)

### CDB + Tamoxifen (Dartmouth regimen)

Use: Melanoma. *Cycle:* 21 days

Regimen: Tamoxifen 10 mg PO twice daily, continuously, started 1 week prior
to cytotoxic chemotherapy
Cisplatin 25 mg/m$^2$/day IV, days 1 through 3
Dacarbazine 220 mg/m$^2$/day IV, days 1 through 3
Carmustine 150 mg/m$^2$ IV, day 1 of odd-numbered cycles only
(eg, cycle 1, 3, 5), given before cisplatin and dacarbazine

### CDDP/VP-16

Use: Brain tumors (pediatrics). *Cycle:* 21 days

Regimen: Cisplatin 90 mg/m$^2$ IV, day 1
Etoposide 150 mg/m$^2$/day IV, days 3 and 4

### CDE

Use: Lymphoma (HIV-related, non-Hodgkin-adult). *Cycle:* 28 days

Regimen: Cyclophosphamide 200 mg/m$^2$/day continuous IV infusion, days 1
through 4
Doxorubicin 12.5 mg/m$^2$/day continuous IV infusion, days 1 through 4
Etoposide 60 mg/m$^2$/day continuous IV infusion, days 1 through 4
Filgrastim 5 mcg/kg/day subcutaneously starting on day 6, at least
24 hours after the end of the continuous infusions, and ending
when the absolute neutrophil count (ANC) is 10,000 cells/mm$^3$
or higher

### CEF (see also FEC)

Use: Breast cancer. *Cycle:* 28 days

Regimen: Cyclophosphamide 75 mg/m$^2$/day PO, days 1 through 14
Epirubicin 60 mg/m$^2$ IV, days 1 and 8
Fluorouracil 500 mg/m$^2$ IV, days 1 and 8
Cotrimoxazole 2 tablets PO twice daily, days 1 through 28

*(continued on next page)*

**Common Chemotherapy Regimens by Diagnosis**

---

**CEPP(B)**

Use: Lymphoma (non-Hodgkin). *Cycle:* 28 days

Regimen: Cyclophosphamide 600 to 650 mg/m$^2$ IV, days 1 and 8
Etoposide 70 to 85 mg/m$^2$/day IV, days 1 through 3
Prednisone 60 mg/m$^2$/day PO, days 1 through 10
Procarbazine 60 mg/m$^2$/day PO, days 1 through 10
*may or may not give with*
Bleomycin 15 units/m$^2$ IV, days 1 and 15

---

**CEV**

Use: Lung cancer (small cell). *Cycle:* 21 days

Regimen: Cyclophosphamide 1,000 mg/m$^2$ IV, day 1
Etoposide 50 mg/m$^2$ IV, day 1
Etoposide 100 mg/m$^2$/day PO, days 2 through 5
Vincristine 1.4 mg/m$^2$ (2 mg maximum dose) IV, day 1

51

---

**CF**

Use: Adenocarcinoma, head and neck cancer. *Cycle:* 21 to 28 days

Regimen: Cisplatin 100 mg/m$^2$ IV, day 1
Fluorouracil 1,000 mg/m$^2$/day continuous IV infusion, days 1 through 4 or days 1 through 5

---

Use: Head and neck cancer. *Cycle:* 21 to 28 days

Regimen: Carboplatin 400 mg/m$^2$ IV, day 1
Fluorouracil 1,000 mg/m$^2$/day continuous IV infusion, days 1 through 4 or days 1 through 5

---

**CFM (see CNF)**

---

**CHAMOCA (Modified Bagshawe)**

Use: Gestational trophoblastic neoplasm. *Cycle:* 18 days or longer, as toxicity permits

Regimen: Hydroxyurea 500 mg/dose PO every 6 hours for 4 doses, day 1 (start at 6 am)
Dactinomycin 0.2 mg/day IV, days 1 through 3 (give at 7 pm)
Dactinomycin 0.5 mg/day IV, days 4 and 5 (give at 7 pm)
Cyclophosphamide 500 mg/m$^2$ IV, days 3 and 8 (give at 7 pm)
Vincristine 1 mg/m$^2$ IV (2 mg maximum dose), day 2 (give at 7 am)
Methotrexate 100 mg/m$^2$ IV push, day 2 (give at 7 pm)

---

*(continued on next page)*

**Common Chemotherapy Regimens by Diagnosis**

---

**CHAMOCA (Modified Bagshawe)** *(continued)*

Methotrexate 200 mg/m² IV over 12 hours, day 2 (give after IV
    push dose)
Leucovorin 14 mg/dose IM every 6 hours for 6 doses, days 3
     through 5 (begin at 7 pm on day 3)
Doxorubicin 30 mg/m² IV, day 8 (give at 7 pm)

---

**CHAP**

Use:             Ovarian cancer. *Cycle:* 28 days

Regimen:     Cyclophosphamide 150 mg/m²/day PO, days 2 through 8
                 *or*
                 Cyclophosphamide 400 mg/m² IV, day 1
                 *with*
                 Altretamine 150 mg/m²/day PO, days 2 through 8
                 Doxorubicin 30 mg/m² IV, day 1
                 Cisplatin 50 to 60 mg/m² IV, day 1

---

**ChIVPP**

Use:             Lymphoma (Hodgkin). *Cycle:* 28 days

Regimen:     Chlorambucil 6 mg/m²/day (10 mg/day maximum dose) PO, days 1
                  through 14
                 Vinblastine 6 mg/m² (10 mg/day maximum dose) IV, days 1 and 8
                 Procarbazine 100 mg/m²/day (150 mg/day maximum dose) PO,
                  days 1 through 14
                 Prednisone 40 to 50 mg/day PO, days 1 through 14*
                 *Note: Prednisolone is recommended in the British literature. In the
                    US, prednisone is the preferred corticosteroid. The doses of
                    these 2 corticosteroids are equivalent (ie, prednisone 40 mg
                    PO = prednisolone 40 mg PO).

---

**ChIVPP/EVA**

Use:             Lymphoma (Hodgkin). *Cycle:* 28 days

Regimen:     Chlorambucil 10 mg/day PO, days 1 through 7
                 Vinblastine 10 mg IV, day 1
                 Procarbazine 150 mg/day PO, days 1 through 7
                 Prednisone 50 mg/day PO, days 1 through 7*
                 *with*
                 Etoposide 200 mg/m² IV, day 8
                 Vincristine 2 mg IV, day 8

---

*(continued on next page)*

═══════════════════════════════════════════════════

## Common Chemotherapy Regimens by Diagnosis

---

**ChIVPP/EVA** *(continued)*

Doxorubicin 50 mg/m² IV, day 8

*Note: Prednisolone is recommended in the British literature. In the US, prednisone is the preferred corticosteroid. The doses of these 2 corticosteroids are equivalent (ie, prednisone 40 mg PO = prednisolone 40 mg PO).

---

### CHOP

| | |
|---|---|
| Use: | Lymphoma (non-Hodgkin), HIV-related lymphoma. *Cycle:* 21 to 28 days |
| Regimen: | Cyclophosphamide 750 mg/m² IV, day 1 |
| | Doxorubicin 50 mg/m² IV, day 1 |
| | Vincristine 1.4 mg/m² (2 mg maximum dose) IV, day 1 |
| | Prednisone 100 mg/day PO, days 1 through 5 |

---

Use: Lymphoma (non-Hodgkin-pediatrics, induction, and consolidation)

Regimen: **Induction.** Give 1 cycle only (6 weeks).
Cyclophosphamide 750 mg/m² IV, days 1 and 22
Doxorubicin 40 mg/m² IV, days 1 and 22
Vincristine 1.5 mg/m² (2 mg maximum dose) IV weekly, weeks 1 through 6
Prednisone 40 mg/m²/day PO, days 1 through 28
*may be used in conjunction with*
Radiation therapy

**Consolidation therapy.** *Cycle:* 21 days
Cyclophosphamide 750 mg/m² IV, day 1
Doxorubicin 40 mg/m² IV, day 1
Vincristine 1.5 mg/m² (2 mg maximum dose) IV, day 1
Prednisone 40 mg/m²/day PO, days 1 through 5
Note: CHOP refers to induction and consolidation phase. Protocol also includes maintenance and central nervous system prophylaxis.

**53**

---

### CHOP-BLEO

| | |
|---|---|
| Use: | Lymphoma (non-Hodgkin). *Cycle:* 21 to 28 days |
| Regimen: | **Add to CHOP:** Bleomycin 15 units/day IV, days 1 through 5 |

---

### CHOP + Rituximab (R-CHOP)

| | |
|---|---|
| Use: | Lymphoma (B-cell). *Cycle:* 21 days for up to 8 cycles |
| Regimen: | **Add to CHOP:** Rituximab 375 mg/m² IV, day 1 |

---

*(continued on next page)*

**Common Chemotherapy Regimens by Diagnosis**

---

**CISCA**

Use:          Bladder cancer. *Cycle:* 21 to 28 days

Regimen:     Cyclophosphamide 650 mg/m$^2$ IV, day 1
Doxorubicin 50 mg/m$^2$ IV, day 1
Cisplatin 100 mg/m$^2$ IV, day 2

---

**CISCA II/VB IV**

Use:          Germ cell tumors. *Cycle:* Individualized based on duration of
myelosuppression

Regimen:     Cyclophosphamide 500 mg/m$^2$/day IV, days 1 and 2
Doxorubicin 40 to 45 mg/m$^2$/day IV, days 1 and 2
Cisplatin 100 to 120 mg/m$^2$ IV, day 3
*alternating with*
Vinblastine 3 mg/m$^2$/day continuous IV infusion, days 1 through 5
Bleomycin 30 units/day continuous IV infusion, days 1 through 5

---

**Cisplatin-Docetaxel**

Use:          Bladder cancer. *Cycle:* Every 7 days for 8 weeks

Regimen:     Cisplatin 30 mg/m$^2$ IV, day 1
Docetaxel 40 mg/m$^2$ IV, day 4
*used in conjunction with*
Radiation therapy

---

Use:          Bladder cancer. *Cycle:* 21 days

Regimen:     Cisplatin 75 mg/m$^2$ IV, day 1
Docetaxel 75 mg/m$^2$ IV, day 1

---

**Cisplatin-Fluorouracil**

Use:          Cervical cancer. *Cycle:* 21 days

Regimen:     Cisplatin 75 mg/m$^2$ IV, day 1
*followed by*
Fluorouracil 1,000 mg/m$^2$/day continuous IV infusion, days 1 through
4 (for 96 hours total)
*used in conjunction with*
Radiation therapy

---

Use:          Cervical cancer. *Cycle:* 28 days

Regimen:     Cisplatin 50 mg/m$^2$ IV, day 1 starting 4 hours before external beam
radiotherapy
Fluorouracil 1,000 mg/m$^2$/day continuous IV infusion, days 2 through 5

*(continued on next page)*

## Common Chemotherapy Regimens by Diagnosis

---

**Cisplatin-Vinorelbine (see also Vinorelbine-Cisplatin)**

Use: Cervical cancer. *Cycle:* 21 days

Regimen: Cisplatin 80 mg/m$^2$ IV, day 1
Vinorelbine 25 mg/m$^2$ IV, days 1 and 8

---

**CLD-BOMP**

Use: Cervical cancer. *Cycle:* 21 days

Regimen: Bleomycin 5 units/day continuous IV infusion, days 1 through 7
Cisplatin 10 mg/m$^2$/day IV, days 1 through 7
Vincristine 0.7 mg/m$^2$ IV, day 7
Mitomycin 7 mg/m$^2$ IV, day 7

---

**CMF**

Use: Breast cancer. *Cycle:* 28 days

Regimen 1: *Patients aged 65 years and younger:*
Methotrexate 40 mg/m$^2$ IV, days 1 and 8
Fluorouracil 600 mg/m$^2$ IV, days 1 and 8
*with*
Cyclophosphamide 100 mg/m$^2$/day PO, days 1 through 14
*or*
Cyclophosphamide 750 mg/m$^2$ IV, day 1

Regimen 2: *Patients older than 65 years of age:*
Methotrexate 30 mg/m$^2$ IV, days 1 and 8
Fluorouracil 400 mg/m$^2$ IV, days 1 and 8
Cyclophosphamide 100 mg/m$^2$/day PO, days 1 through 14

---

**CMF-IV**

Use: Breast cancer. *Cycle:* 21 days

Regimen: Cyclophosphamide 600 mg/m$^2$ IV, day 1
Methotrexate 40 mg/m$^2$ IV, day 1
Fluorouracil 600 mg/m$^2$ IV, day 1

---

**CMFP**

Use: Breast cancer. *Cycle:* 28 days

Regimen: Cyclophosphamide 100 mg/m$^2$/day PO, days 1 through 14
Methotrexate 30 to 40 mg/m$^2$ IV, days 1 and 8
Fluorouracil 400 to 600 mg/m$^2$ IV, days 1 and 8
Prednisone 40 mg/m$^2$/day PO, days 1 through 14

---

*(continued on next page)*

**Common Chemotherapy Regimens by Diagnosis**

---

**CMFVP**

Use: Breast cancer. *Cycle:* 28 days

Regimen: Cyclophosphamide 400 mg/m$^2$ IV, day 1
Methotrexate 30 mg/m$^2$ IV, days 1 and 8
Fluorouracil 400 mg/m$^2$ IV, days 1 and 8
Vincristine 1 mg IV, days 1 and 8
Prednisone 80 mg/day PO, days 1 through 7

---

**CMV**

Use: Bladder cancer. *Cycle:* 21 days

Regimen: Cisplatin 100 mg/m$^2$ IV, day 2 (at least 12 hours after methotrexate)
Methotrexate 30 mg/m$^2$ IV, days 1 and 8
Vinblastine 4 mg/m$^2$ IV, days 1 and 8

---

**56**

**CNF**

Use: Breast cancer. *Cycle:* 21 days

Regimen: Cyclophosphamide 500 mg/m$^2$ IV, day 1
Mitoxantrone 10 mg/m$^2$ IV, day 1
Fluorouracil 500 mg/m$^2$ IV, day 1

---

**CNOP**

Use: Lymphoma (non-Hodgkin). *Cycle:* 21 to 28 days

Regimen: Cyclophosphamide 750 mg/m$^2$ IV, day 1
Mitoxantrone 12 mg/m$^2$ IV, day 1
Vincristine 1.4 mg/m$^2$ (2 mg maximum dose) IV, day 1
Prednisone 50 mg/m$^2$/day PO, days 1 through 5

---

**COB**

Use: Head and neck cancer. *Cycle:* 21 days

Regimen: Cisplatin 100 mg/m$^2$ IV, day 1
Vincristine 1mg IV, days 2 and 5
Bleomycin 30 units/day continuous IV infusion, days 2 through 5

---

**CODE**

Use: Lung cancer (small cell). *Cycle:* 9-week regimen

Regimen: Cisplatin 25 mg/m$^2$ IV, every week for 9 weeks
Vincristine 1 mg/m$^2$ (2 mg maximum dose) IV weekly, weeks 1, 2, 4, 6, and 8
Doxorubicin 40 mg/m$^2$ IV weekly, weeks 1, 3, 5, 7, and 9
Etoposide 80 mg/m$^2$ IV, day 1 of weeks 1, 3, 5, 7, and 9

*(continued on next page)*

**Common Chemotherapy Regimens by Diagnosis**

---

**CODE** *(continued)*

Etoposide 80 mg/m$^2$/day PO, days 2 and 3 of weeks 1, 3, 5, 7, and 9
*used in conjunction with*
Prednisone 50 mg PO daily for 5 weeks, then alternate days until
  chemotherapy completion, then taper over 2 weeks

---

**CODOX-M/IVAC***

Use: Lymphoma (advanced B-cell). *Cycle:* Give 4 cycles as myelosuppre-
sion permits. Give next cycle when granulocyte count is above
1,000 cells/mm$^3$ and platelet count is above 50,000 cells/mm$^3$.

Regimen: **Treatment A**-CODOX-M (cycles 1 and 3)
Cyclophosphamide 800 mg/m$^2$ IV, day 1
Cyclophosphamide 200 mg/m$^2$/day IV, days 2 through 5
Vincristine 1.5 mg/m$^2$ (2 mg maximum dose) IV, days 1 and 8
Doxorubicin 40 mg/m$^2$ IV, day 1
Methotrexate 1,200 mg/m$^2$ IV over 1 hour, day 10
Methotrexate 240 mg/m$^2$/hour continuous IV infusion over 23 hours,
  day 10 (begin after 1,200 mg/m$^2$ dose)
Leucovorin 192 mg/m$^2$ IV, day 11, given 36 hours after the start of
  the methotrexate infusion
Leucovorin 12 mg/m$^2$/dose IV every 6 hours, day 11, beginning 42
  hours after the start of the methotrexate infusion and continued
  until the methotrexate concentration is below 0.05 microMol/L
Cytarabine 70 mg intrathecal, days 1 and 3
Methotrexate 12 mg intrathecal, day 15
Filgrastim 5 mcg/kg/day subcutaneously, starting on day 13 and
  continuing until granulocyte count is above 1,000 cells/mm$^3$

**Treatment B**-IVAC (cycles 2 and 4)
Ifosfamide 1,500 mg/m$^2$/day IV, days 1 through 5
Mesna 1,500 mg/m$^2$/day continuous IV infusion, days 1 through 5
Etoposide 60 mg/m$^2$/day IV, days 1 through 5
Cytarabine 2,000 mg/m$^2$/dose IV every 12 hours for 4 doses, days
  1 and 2
Methotrexate 12 mg intrathecal, day 5
Filgrastim 5 mcg/kg/day subcutaneously, starting on day 7 and
  continuing until granulocyte count is above 1,000 cells/mm$^3$
*Note: These two regimens are normally used in combination with
  each other and are rarely given alone. Patients with malignant
  pleocytosis receive additional intrathecal drugs:
Cycle 1 (CODOX-M) cytarabine 70 mg intrathecal day 5 and
  methotrexate 12 mg intrathecal day 15
Cycle 2 (IVAC) cytarabine 70 mg intrathecal on days 7 and 9

*(continued on next page)*

━━━━━━━━━━━━━━━━━━━━━━━━━━━━━━━━━━━━━━━━━━━━━━━━

## Common Chemotherapy Regimens by Diagnosis

---

**COMLA**

Use: Lymphoma (non-Hodgkin). *Cycle:* 78 to 85 days

Regimen: Cyclophosphamide 1,500 mg/m$^2$ IV, day 1
Vincristine 1.4 mg/m$^2$ (2 mg maximum dose) IV, days 1, 8, and 15
Methotrexate 120 mg/m$^2$ IV, days 22, 29, 36, 43, 50, 57, 64, and 71
Leucovorin 25 mg/m$^2$/dose PO every 6 hours for 4 doses, beginning
    24 hours after each methotrexate dose
Cytarabine 300 mg/m$^2$ IV, days 22, 29, 36, 43, 50, 57, 64, and 71

---

**COMP**

Use: Lymphoma (non-Hodgkin-pediatrics).

Regimen: **Induction.** *Cycle:* Give 1 cycle only
Cyclophosphamide 1,200 mg/m$^2$ IV, day 1
Vincristine 2 mg/m$^2$ (2 mg maximum dose) IV, days 3, 10, 17, and 24
Methotrexate 300 mg/m$^2$ IV, day 12 or 17
Prednisone 60 mg/m$^2$/day (60 mg/day maximum dose) PO in 4
    divided doses, days 3 through 30, then taper for 7 to 10 days
*used in conjunction with*
Intrathecal chemotherapy

**Maintenance therapy.** *Cycle:* 28 days for 15 cycles
Cyclophosphamide 1,000 mg/m$^2$ IV, day 1
Vincristine 1.5 mg/m$^2$ (2 mg maximum dose) IV, days 1 and 15
Methotrexate 300 mg/m$^2$ IV, day 15
Prednisone 60 mg/m$^2$/day (60 mg/day maximum dose) PO in 4
    divided doses, days 1 through 5, cycles 2 through 15
*used in conjunction with*
Intrathecal chemotherapy

---

**Cooper Regimen**

Use: Breast cancer. *Cycle:* 36 weeks

Regimen: Cyclophosphamide 2 mg/kg/day PO, weeks 1 through 36
Methotrexate 0.7 mg/kg IV weekly, weeks 1 through 8
Methotrexate 0.7 mg/kg IV every other week, weeks 10, 12, 14, 16,
    18, 20, 22, 24, 26, 28, 30, 32, 34, and 36
Fluorouracil 12 mg/kg IV weekly, weeks 1 through 8
Fluorouracil 12 mg/kg IV every other week, weeks 10, 12, 14, 16,
    18, 20, 22, 24, 26, 28, 30, 32, 34, and 36
Vincristine 0.035 mg/kg IV (2 mg maximum dose) weekly, weeks 1
    through 5

*(continued on next page)*

**Common Chemotherapy Regimens by Diagnosis**

---

**Cooper Regimen** *(continued)*

Vincristine 0.035 mg/kg IV monthly, weeks 8, 12, 16, 20, 24, 28, 32, and 36

Prednisone 0.75 mg/kg/day PO, days 1 through 10, then taper off over next 40 days

---

**COP**

| | |
|---|---|
| **Use:** | Lymphoma (non-Hodgkin). *Cycle:* 14 to 28 days |
| **Regimen:** | Cyclophosphamide 800 to 1,000 mg/m$^2$ IV, day 1 |
| | Vincristine 2 mg IV, day 1 |
| | Prednisone 60 mg/m$^2$/day (or 100 mg/day) PO, days 1 through 5, then taper off over next 3 days |

---

**COPE**

| | |
|---|---|
| **Use:** | Lung cancer (small cell). *Cycle:* 21 days |
| **Regimen:** | Cyclophosphamide 750 mg/m$^2$ IV, day 1 |
| | Vincristine 2 mg/cycle IV, day 14 |
| | Cisplatin 50 mg/m$^2$ IV, day 2 |
| | Etoposide 100 mg/m$^2$/day IV, days 1 through 3 |

---

**COPE (Baby Brain I)**

| | |
|---|---|
| **Use:** | Brain tumors (pediatrics). *Cycle:* 28 days |
| **Regimen:** | Alternate cycles AABAAB. |

**Cycle A:** Vincristine 0.065 mg/kg (1.5 mg maximum dose) IV, days 1 and 8

Cyclophosphamide 65 mg/kg IV, day 1

**Cycle B:** Cisplatin 4 mg/kg IV, day 1

Etoposide 6.5 mg/kg/day IV, days 3 and 4

---

**COPP (C-MOPP)**

| | |
|---|---|
| **Use:** | Lymphoma (non-Hodgkin or Hodgkin). *Cycle:* 28 days |
| **Regimen:** | Cyclophosphamide 450 to 650 mg/m$^2$ IV, days 1 and 8 |

Vincristine 1.4 to 2 mg/m$^2$ (2 mg maximum dose) IV, days 1 and 8

Procarbazine 100 mg/m$^2$/day PO, days 1 through 14

Prednisone 40 mg/m$^2$/day PO, cycles 1 and 4,* days 1 through 14

*Note: Some clinicians give prednisone with every cycle of COPP. The original clinical trials gave prednisone only with the first and fourth cycles.

*(continued on next page)*

▨▨▨▨▨▨▨▨▨▨▨▨▨▨▨▨▨▨▨▨▨▨▨▨▨▨▨▨▨▨▨▨▨▨▨▨▨▨▨▨

**Common Chemotherapy Regimens by Diagnosis**

---

**CP**

| | |
|---|---|
| **Use:** | Chronic lymphocytic leukemia (CLL). *Cycle:* 14 days |
| **Regimen:** | Chlorambucil 30 mg/m$^2$/day PO, day 1 |
| | Prednisone 80 mg/day PO, days 1 through 5 |

---

| | |
|---|---|
| **Use:** | Ovarian cancer. *Cycle:* 21 to 28 days |
| **Regimen:** | Cyclophosphamide 600 to 1,000 mg/m$^2$ IV, day 1 |
| | Cisplatin 60 to 80 mg/m$^2$ IV, day 1 |

---

**CT**

| | |
|---|---|
| **Use:** | Ovarian cancer. *Cycle:* 21 days |
| **Regimen:** | Cisplatin 75 mg/m$^2$ IV, day 1 or 2 (given immediately after paclitaxel infusion) |
| | *with* |
| | Paclitaxel 175 mg/m$^2$ IV infusion over 3 hours, day 1 |
| | *or* |
| | Paclitaxel 135 mg/m$^2$/day continuous IV infusion over 24 hours, on day 1 |

---

| | |
|---|---|
| **Use:** | Lung cancer (non-small cell). *Cycle:* 21 days |
| **Regimen:** | Cisplatin 75 mg/m$^2$ IV, day 2 (given after paclitaxel) |
| | Paclitaxel 135 mg/m$^2$/day continuous IV infusion over 24 hours, day 1 |

---

**CVD**

| | |
|---|---|
| **Use:** | Malignant melanoma. *Cycle:* 21 days |
| **Regimen:** | Cisplatin 20 mg/m$^2$/day IV, days 2 through 5 |
| | Vinblastine 1.6 mg/m$^2$/day IV, days 1 through 5 |
| | Dacarbazine 800 mg/m$^2$ IV, day 1 |

---

**CVD + IL-N2I**

| | |
|---|---|
| **Use:** | Malignant melanoma. *Cycle:* 21 days |
| **Regimen:** | Cisplatin 20 mg/m$^2$/day IV, days 1 through 4 |
| | Vinblastine 1.6 mg/m$^2$/day IV, days 1 through 4 |
| | Dacarbazine 800 mg/m$^2$ IV, day 1 |
| | Aldesleukin 9 million units/m$^2$/day continuous IV infusion, days 1 through 4 |
| | Interferon alfa 5 million units/m$^2$/day subcutaneously, days 1 through 5, 7, 9, 11, and 13 |

60

*(continued on next page)*

---

## Common Chemotherapy Regimens by Diagnosis

---

### CVI (VIC)

Use:      Lung cancer (non-small cell). *Cycle:* 28 days

Regimen:    Carboplatin 300 to 350 mg/m$^2$ IV, day 1
Etoposide 60 to 100 mg/m$^2$ IV, days 1, 3, and 5
Ifosfamide 1,500 mg/m$^2$ IV, days 1, 3, and 5
Mesna 400 mg/m$^2$ IV before ifosfamide given, days 1, 3, and 5
Mesna 1,600 mg/m$^2$/day continuous IV infusion, days 1, 3, and 5
    (give after mesna bolus)

---

### CVP

Use:      Lymphoma (non-Hodgkin), chronic lymphocytic leukemia (CLL).
*Cycle:* 21 days

Regimen:    Cyclophosphamide 300 to 400 mg/m$^2$/day PO, days 1 through 5
Vincristine 1.2 to 1.4 mg/m$^2$ (2 mg maximum dose) IV, day 1
Prednisone 40 to 100 mg/m$^2$/day PO, days 1 through 5

**61**

---

### CVPP

Use:      Lymphoma (Hodgkin). *Cycle:* 28 days

Regimen:    Lomustine 75 mg/m$^2$ PO, day 1
Vinblastine 4 mg/m$^2$ IV, days 1 and 8
Procarbazine 100 mg/m$^2$/day PO, days 1 through 14
Prednisone 40 mg/m$^2$/day PO, cycles 1 and 4, days 1 through 14

---

### CY/A (see AC)

---

### Cyclophosphamide-Fludarabine

Use:      Chronic lymphocytic leukemia (CLL). *Cycle:* 28 days

Regimen:    Cyclophosphamide 250 mg/m$^2$/day IV, days 1 through 3
Fludarabine 25 to 30 mg/m$^2$/day IV, days 1 through 3

---

### CYVADIC

Use:      Sarcoma (bony or soft tissue). *Cycle:* 21 days

Regimen:    Cyclophosphamide 500 mg/m$^2$ IV, day 1
Vincristine 1 mg/m$^2$ (2 mg maximum dose) IV, days 1 and 5
Doxorubicin 50 mg/m$^2$ IV, day 1
Dacarbazine 250 mg/m$^2$/day IV, days 1 through 5

*(continued on next page)*

▰▰▰▰▰▰▰▰▰▰▰▰▰▰▰▰▰▰▰▰▰▰▰▰▰▰▰▰▰▰▰▰▰▰▰▰

**Common Chemotherapy Regimens by Diagnosis**

---

### DA

| | |
|---|---|
| Use: | Acute myelocytic leukemia (AML; induction-pediatrics) |
| Regimen: | Daunorubicin 45 to 60 $mg/m^2$/day IV, days 1 through 3 |
| | Cytarabine 100 $mg/m^2$/day continuous IV infusion, days 1 through 7 |

---

### DA + ATRA (ATRA + CT)

Use: Acute promyelocytic leukemia (APL; induction and consolidation)

Regimen: Tretinoin 45 $mg/m^2$/day PO, days 1 through 90, or until complete remission, whichever occurs earlier

**Induction.** *Cycle:* Give 1 induction cycle followed by 2 consolidation cycles after hematologic recovery.
Daunorubicin 60 $mg/m^2$/day IV, days 3 through 5
Cytarabine 200 $mg/m^2$/day continuous IV infusion, days 3 through 9

**First consolidation.** *Cycle:* Give 1 cycle.
Daunorubicin 60 $mg/m^2$/day IV, days 1 through 3
Cytarabine 200 $mg/m^2$/day continuous IV infusion, days 1 through 7

**Second consolidation.** *Cycle:* Give 1 cycle. Do not give to elderly patients.
Daunorubicin 45 $mg/m^2$/day IV, days 1 through 3
Cytarabine 1,000 $mg/m^2$/dose IV every 12 hours for 8 doses, days 1 through 4

---

### Dartmouth Regimen (see CDB + Tamoxifen)

---

### DAT

Use: Acute myelocytic leukemia (AML; induction-pediatrics). *Cycle:* 14 to 21 days

Regimen: Cytarabine 100 $mg/m^2$/dose IV every 12 hours for 14 doses, days 1 through 7
Thioguanine 100 $mg/m^2$/dose PO, every 12 hours for 14 doses, days 1 through 7
Daunorubicin 60 $mg/m^2$/day continuous IV infusion, days 5 through 7

---

Use: Acute myelocyctic leukemia (AML; induction-pediatrics)

Regimen: **Remission induction.** *Cycle:* Give 1 cycle only
Daunorubicin 45 $mg/m^2$/day IV, days 1 through 3
Cytarabine 100 $mg/m^2$/day continuous IV infusion, days 1 through 7
Thioguanine 100 $mg/m^2$/day PO, days 1 through 7

---

*(continued on next page)*

████████████████████████████████████████████████████████████

**Common Chemotherapy Regimens by Diagnosis**

---

**DAT** *(continued)*

**Second induction.** *Cycle:* Give a single cycle 14 days after initial
remission induction course; delay until hematologic recovery in
patients with remission or with hypoplastic marrow.
Daunorubicin 45 mg/m$^2$/day IV, days 1 and 2
Cytarabine 100 mg/m$^2$/day continuous IV infusion, days 1 through 5
Thioguanine 100 mg/m$^2$/day PO, days 1 through 5
*used in conjunction with*
Intrathecal chemotherapy

---

**DAV**

Use:         Acute myelocytic leukemia (AML; induction-pediatrics). *Cycle:* Give a
             single cycle

Regimen:     Cytarabine 100 mg/m$^2$/day continuous IV infusion, days 1 through 2
             Cytarabine 100 mg/m$^2$/dose IV every 12 hours for 12 doses, days 3      **63**
                 through 8
             Daunorubicin 60 mg/m$^2$/day IV, days 3 through 5
             Etoposide 150 mg/m$^2$/day IV, days 6 through 8

---

**DCT**

Use:         Acute myelocytic leukemia (AML; induction-adults). *Cycle:* 7 days.
             Give once. May be given a second time based on individual
             response. Time between cycles not specified.

Regimen:     Daunorubicin 40 mg/m$^2$/day IV, days 1 through 3
             Cytarabine 100 mg/m$^2$/dose IV every 12 hours for 14 doses,
                 days 1 through 7
             Thioguanine 100 mg/m$^2$/dose PO every 12 hours for 14 doses,
                 days 1 through 7

---

**DHAOx**

Use:         Lymphoma (non-Hodgkin). *Cycle:* 21 days

Regimen:     Oxaliplatin 130 mg/m$^2$ IV, day 1
             Dexamethasone 40 mg/day PO or IV, days 1 through 4
             Cytarabine 2,000 mg/m$^2$/dose IV every 12 hours for 2 doses
                 (total dose 4,000 mg/m$^2$), day 2
             Filgrastim 5 mcg/kg/day subcutaneously, starting on day 3 and
                 continued until granulocyte count is above 500 cells/mm$^3$

████████████████████████████████████████████████████████████

*(continued on next page)*

---

## Common Chemotherapy Regimens by Diagnosis

---

**DHAP**

Use:      Lymphoma (non-Hodgkin). *Cycle:* 21 to 28 days

Regimen:      Cisplatin 100 mg/m²/day continuous IV infusion, day 1

       Dexamethasone 40 mg/day PO or IV, days 1 through 4

       Cytarabine 2,000 mg/m²/dose IV every 12 hours for 2 doses
         (total dose, 4,000 mg/m²), day 2

---

**DI**

Use:      Sarcoma (soft-tissue). *Cycle:* 21 days

Regimen:      Doxorubicin 50 mg/m² IV, day 1

       Ifosfamide 5,000 mg/m²/day continuous IV infusion, day 1
         (after doxorubicin given)

       Mesna 600 mg/m² IV bolus before ifosfamide infusion, day 1

       Mesna 2,500 mg/m²/day continuous IV infusion over 36 hours, day 1
         (give after mesna bolus)

---

**Docetaxel-Cisplatin**

Use:      Lung cancer (non-small cell). *Cycle:* 21 days

Regimen:      Docetaxel 75 mg/m² IV, day 1

       Cisplatin 75 mg/m² IV, day 1 (after docetaxel)

---

**Docetaxel-Estramustine**

Use:      Prostate cancer. *Cycle:* 21 days (6 cycles maximum)

Regimen:      Estramustine 280 mg/dose PO every 6 hours for 5 doses, day 1

       Docetaxel 70 mg/m² IV, day 1 (given 12 hours after first estramustine
         dose)

---

**Dox ⟶ CMF, Sequential**

Use:      Breast cancer. *Cycle:* 21 days

Regimen:      Doxorubicin 75 mg/m² IV, day 1 for 4 cycles
       *followed by*
       CMF-IV for 8 cycles

---

**DTIC/Tamoxifen**

Use:      Malignant melanoma. *Cycle:* 21 days

Regimen:      Dacarbazine 250 mg/m²/day IV, days 1 through 5

       Tamoxifen 20 mg/m²/day PO, days 1 through 5

---

*(continued on next page)*

**64**

████████████████████████████████████████████████████████

## Common Chemotherapy Regimens by Diagnosis

---

### DVP

| | |
|---|---|
| **Use:** | Acute lymphocytic leukemia (ALL; induction-pediatrics). *Cycle:* 35 days. Give a single cycle. |
| **Regimen:** | Daunorubicin 25 mg/m$^2$ IV, days 1, 8, and 15 |
| | Vincristine 1.5 mg/m$^2$ (2 mg maximum dose) IV, days 1, 8, 15, and 22 |
| | Prednisone 60 mg/m$^2$ day PO, days 1 through 28 then taper over next 14 days |
| | *used in conjunction with* |
| | Intrathecal chemotherapy |

---

### EAP

| | |
|---|---|
| **Use:** | Gastric, small bowel cancer. *Cycle:* 21 to 28 days |
| **Regimen:** | Etoposide 100 to 120 mg/m$^2$/day IV, days 4 through 6 |
| | Doxorubicin 20 mg/m$^2$ IV, days 1 and 7 |
| | Cisplatin 40 mg/m$^2$ IV, days 2 and 8 |

**65**

---

### EC

| | |
|---|---|
| **Use:** | Lung cancer. *Cycle:* 21 to 28 days |
| **Regimen:** | Etoposide 100 to 120 mg/m$^2$/day IV, days 1 through 3 |
| | Carboplatin 300 to 350 mg/m$^2$ IV, day 1 |
| | *or* |
| | Carboplatin IV dose by Calvert equation to AUC 6 mg/mL/min, day 1 |

---

### ECF

| | |
|---|---|
| **Use:** | Gastric cancer. *Cycle:* 21 days for up to 8 cycles |
| **Regimen:** | Epirubicin 50 mg/m$^2$ IV, day 1 |
| | Cisplatin 60 mg/m$^2$ IV, day 1 |
| | Fluorouracil 200 mg/m$^2$/day continuous IV infusion, days 1 through 180 |

---

### EFP

| | |
|---|---|
| **Use:** | Gastric, small bowel cancer. *Cycle:* 21 to 28 days |
| **Regimen:** | Etoposide 80 to 100 mg/m$^2$ IV, days 1, 3, and 5 |
| | Fluorouracil 800 to 900 mg/m$^2$/day continuous IV infusion, days 1 through 5 |
| | Cisplatin 20 mg/m$^2$/day IV, days 1 through 5 |

*(continued on next page)*

---

**Common Chemotherapy Regimens by Diagnosis**

---

**ELF**

Use: Gastric cancer. *Cycle:* 21 to 28 days

Regimen: Etoposide 120 mg/m$^2$/day IV, days 1 through 3
Leucovorin 300 mg/m$^2$/day IV, days 1 through 3
Fluorouracil 500 mg/m$^2$/day IV, days 1 through 3 (after leucovorin)

---

**EMA 86**

Use: Acute myelocytic leukemia (AML; induction-adults). *Cycle:* Give a
single cycle.

Regimen: Mitoxantrone 12 mg/m$^2$/day IV, days 1 through 3
Etoposide 200 mg/m$^2$/day continuous IV infusion, days 8 through 10
Cytarabine 500 mg/m$^2$/day continuous IV infusion, days 1 through 3
and days 8 through 10

---

**66**   **EM-V (see Estramustine/Vinblastine)**

---

**EP**

Use: Testicular cancer. *Cycle:* 21 days

Regimen: Etoposide 100 mg/m$^2$/day IV, days 1 through 5
Cisplatin 20 mg/m$^2$/day IV, days 1 through 5

---

Use: Lung cancer, adenocarcinoma. *Cycle:* 21 to 28 days

Regimen: Etoposide 80 to 120 mg/m$^2$/day IV, days 1 through 3
Cisplatin 80 to 100 mg/m$^2$ IV, day 1

---

**ESHAP**

Use: Lymphoma (non-Hodgkin). *Cycle:* 21 to 28 days

Regimen: Methylprednisolone 250 to 500 mg/day IV, days 1 through 4 or 1
through 5
Etoposide 40 to 60 mg/m$^2$/day IV, days 1 through 4
Cytarabine 2,000 mg/m$^2$ IV, day 5 (after etoposide and cisplatin finished)
Cisplatin 25 mg/m$^2$/day continuous IV infusion, days 1 through 4

---

**Estramustine/Vinblastine (EM-V)**

Use: Prostate cancer. *Cycle:* 8 weeks

Regimen: Vinblastine 4 mg/m$^2$ IV weekly, weeks 1 through 6
*with*
Estramustine 10 mg/kg/day PO given in 3 divided doses, days 1
through 42

---

*(continued on next page)*

**Common Chemotherapy Regimens by Diagnosis**

---

**Estramustine/Vinblastine (EM-V)** *(continued)*

*or*

Estramustine 600 mg/m$^2$/day PO given in 2 to 3 divided doses, days
  1 through 42

---

**EVA**

Use: Lymphoma (Hodgkin). *Cycle:* 28 days

Regimen: Etoposide 100 mg/m$^2$/day IV, days 1 through 3
Vinblastine 6 mg/m$^2$ IV, day 1
Doxorubicin 50 mg/m$^2$ IV, day 1

---

**F-CL (FU/LV)**

Use: Colorectal cancer. *Cycle:* 4 to 8 weeks

Regimen: Leucovorin 500 mg/m$^2$ IV, weekly for 6 weeks, then 2-week rest
  period
Fluorouracil 600 mg/m$^2$ IV, weekly for 6 weeks (after starting leucovorin),
*then*
2-week rest period
*or*
Leucovorin 20 mg/m$^2$/day IV, days 1 through 5
Fluorouracil 370 to 425 mg/m$^2$/day IV, days 1 through 5 (after starting
  leucovorin)
*or*
Leucovorin 200 mg/m$^2$/day IV, days 1 through 5
Fluorouracil 370 mg/m$^2$/day IV, days 1 through 5 (after starting
  leucovorin)

67

---

**FAC**

Use: Breast cancer. *Cycle:* 21 to 28 days

Regimen: Fluorouracil 500 mg/m$^2$ IV, days 1 and 8
Doxorubicin 50 mg/m$^2$ IV, day 1
Cyclophosphamide 500 mg/m$^2$ IV, day 1

---

**FAM**

Use: Adenocarcinoma, gastric cancer. *Cycle:* 8 weeks

Regimen: Fluorouracil 600 mg/m$^2$ IV, days 1, 8, 29, and 36
Doxorubicin 30 mg/m$^2$ IV, days 1 and 29
Mitomycin 10 mg/m$^2$ IV, day 1

---

*(continued on next page)*

## Common Chemotherapy Regimens by Diagnosis

### FAMTX

Use: Gastric cancer. *Cycle:* 28 days

Regimen: Methotrexate 1,500 mg/m$^2$ IV, day 1
Fluorouracil 1,500 mg/m$^2$ IV, day 1 (give after methotrexate)
Leucovorin 15 mg/m$^2$/dose PO every 6 hours for 8 doses (start 24 hours after methotrexate); increase dose to 30 mg/m$^2$/dose PO every 6 hours for 16 doses if 24-hour methotrexate level is 2.5 mol/L or higher.
Doxorubicin 30 mg/m$^2$ IV, day 15

### FAP

Use: Gastric cancer. *Cycle:* 5 weeks

Regimen: Fluorouracil 300 mg/m$^2$/day IV, days 1 through 5
Doxorubicin 40 mg/m$^2$ IV, day 1
Cisplatin 60 mg/m$^2$ IV, day 1

### FEC (see also CEF)

Use: Breast cancer. *Cycle:* 21 days

Regimen: Fluorouracil 500 mg/m$^2$ IV, day 1
Cyclophosphamide 500 mg/m$^2$ IV, day 1
Epirubicin 100 mg/m$^2$ IV, day 1

### FED

Use: Lung cancer (non-small cell). *Cycle:* 21 days

Regimen: Cisplatin 100 mg/m$^2$ IV, day 1
Fluorouracil 960 mg/m$^2$/day continuous IV infusion, days 2 through 4
Etoposide 80 mg/m$^2$/day IV, days 2 through 4

### FL

Use: Prostate cancer. *Cycle:* Ongoing

Regimen: Flutamide 250 mg/dose PO every 8 hours
*with*
Leuprolide acetate 1 mg subcutaneously daily
*or*
Leuprolide depot 7.5 mg IM/dose, every 28 days
*or*
Leuprolide depot 22.5 mg IM/dose, every 3 months

*(continued on next page)*

**Common Chemotherapy Regimens by Diagnosis**

---

### FLAG-Ida

**Use:** Acute myelocytic leukemia (AML; remission induction). *Cycle:* Give a single cycle.
May be given a second time based on individual response. Time between cycles not specified.

**Regimen:** Filgrastim 300 mcg/day subcutaneously, day 1 until neutropenia resolves
Fludarabine 30 mg/m$^2$/day IV over 30 minutes, days 2 through 6
Cytarabine 2,000 mg/m$^2$/day IV, days 2 through 6 (begin 4 hours after starting fludarabine)
Idarubicin 8 mg/m$^2$/day IV, days 2 through 4

---

### Fle

**Use:** Colorectal cancer. *Cycle:* 1 year

**Regimen:** Fluorouracil 450 mg/m$^2$/day IV, days 1 through 5
Fluorouracil 450 mg/m$^2$/week IV, weeks 5 through 52
Levamisole 50 mg/dose PO every 8 hours, days 1 through 3 of every other week for 1 year

---

### Fludarabine-Cyclophosphamide

**Use:** Chronic lymphocytic leukemia (CLL). *Cycle:* 4 to 6 weeks based on recovery of myelosuppression

**Regimen:** Fludarabine 30 mg/m$^2$/day IV, days 1 through 3
Cyclophosphamide 300 mg/m$^2$/day IV, days 1 through 3

---

### FNC—SEE CNF

---

### FOLFOX-4

**Use:** Colorectal cancer. *Cycle:* 14 days

**Regimen:** Oxaliplatin 85 mg/m$^2$ IV, day 1 (begin with leucovorin)
Leucovorin 200 mg/m$^2$/day IV, days 1 and 2
*then*
Fluorouracil 400 mg/m$^2$/day IV bolus, days 1 and 2
*then*
Fluorouracil 600 mg/m$^2$/dose continuous infusion over 22 hours, days 1 and 2

---

### FU/LV-see F-CL

---

69

*(continued on next page)*

**Common Chemotherapy Regimens by Diagnosis**

### FU/LV/CPT-11

Use:        Metastatic colorectal cancer.* *Cycle:* 42 days

Regimen:    Fluorouracil 500 mg/m$^2$ IV, days 1, 8, 15, and 22
Leucovorin 20 mg/m$^2$ IV, days 1, 8, 15, and 22
Irinotecan 125 mg/m$^2$ IV, days 1, 8, 15, and 22
*Note: A recent study analysis found an increased risk of early
deaths (within 60 days of initiating treatment) with use of this
regimen. Specific risk factors that may have contributed to
death were not identified. Intensive patient monitoring and
dosage modification are recommended to reduce the risk of
severe adverse effects.

---

Use:        Metastatic colorectal cancer. *Cycle:* 14 days

Regimen:    Fluorouracil 400 mg/m$^2$ IV bolus, day 1
*then*
Fluorouracil 600 mg/m$^2$/dose continuous IV infusion over 22 hours,
day 1
Leucovorin 200 mg/m$^2$/day IV, days 1 and 2
Irinotecan 180 mg/m$^2$ IV, day 1
*or*
Fluorouracil 2,300 mg/m$^2$/day continuous IV infusion, days 1 and 8
Leucovorin 500 mg/m$^2$ IV, days 1 and 8
Irinotecan 80 mg/m$^2$ IV, days 1 and 8

---

### FUP

Use:        Gastric cancer. *Cycle:* 28 days

Regimen:    Fluorouracil 1,000 mg/m$^2$/day continuous IV infusion, days 1 through 5
Cisplatin 100 mg/m$^2$ IV, day 2

---

### FZ

Use:        Prostate cancer. *Cycle:* Ongoing

Regimen:    Flutamide 250 mg/dose PO every 8 hours
*with*
Goserelin acetate 3.6 mg/dose implant subcutaneously every 28 days
*or*
Goserelin acetate 10.8 mg/dose implant subcutaneously every 12 weeks

---

### G + V (see also Gemcitabine-Vinorelbine)

Use:        Lung cancer (non-small cell). *Cycle:* 21 days for up to 6 cycles

Regimen:    Gemcitabine 1,200 mg/m$^2$ IV, days 1 and 8
Vinorelbine 30 mg/m$^2$ IV, days 1 and 8

*(continued on next page)*

## Common Chemotherapy Regimens by Diagnosis

---

**Gemcitabine-Carboplatin**

Use: Lung cancer (non-small cell). *Cycle:* 28 days

Regimen: Gemcitabine 1,000 or 1,100 mg/m$^2$ IV, days 1 and 8
Carboplatin IV dose by Calvert equation to AUC 5 mg/mL/min, day 8

---

**Gemcitabine-Cis**

Use: Lung cancer (non-small cell). *Cycle:* 28 days

Regimen: Gemcitabine 1,000 to 1,200 mg/m$^2$ IV, days 1, 8, and 15
Cisplatin 100 mg/m$^2$ IV, day 15*
*Note: Some references state that a single dose of cisplatin may be
given on day 1, 2, or 15 of each cycle. However, the best
results are seen when cisplatin is given on day 15.

---

**Gemcitabine-Cisplatin**

Use: Metastatic bladder cancer. *Cycle:* 28 days for up to 6 cycles

Regimen: Gemcitabine 1,000 mg/m$^2$ IV, days 1, 8, and 15
Cisplatin 70 mg/m$^2$ IV, day 2

**71**

---

**Gemcitabine-Irinotecan**

Use: Pancreatic cancer. *Cycle:* 21 days

Regimen: Gemcitabine 1,000 mg/m$^2$ IV, days 1 and 8
Irinotecan 100 mg/m$^2$ IV, days 1 and 8 (after gemcitabine)

---

**Gemcitabine-Vinorelbine (see also G + V)**

Use: Lung cancer (non-small cell). *Cycle:* 28 days for up to 6 cycles

Regimen: Gemcitabine 800 or 1,000 mg/m$^2$ IV, days 1, 8, and 15
Vinorelbine 20 mg/m$^2$ IV, days 1, 8, and 15

---

**HDMTX**

Use: Sarcoma (bone). *Cycle:* 1 to 4 weeks

Regimen: Methotrexate 8,000 to 12,000 mg/m$^2$ (20,000 mg maximum dose)
IV, day 1
Leucovorin 15 mg/m$^2$/dose PO or IV every 6 hours for 10 doses,
beginning 20 to 30 hours after beginning of methotrexate infusion

*(continued on next page)*

## Section 3: Table 2

## Common Chemotherapy Regimens by Diagnosis

### HEC

**Use:** Breast cancer. *Cycle:* 21 days for up to 8 cycles

**Regimen:** Epirubicin 100 mg/m$^2$ IV, day 1
Cyclophosphamide 830 mg/m$^2$ IV, day 1

### Hexa-CAF

**Use:** Ovarian cancer. *Cycle:* 28 days

**Regimen:** Altretamine 150 mg/m$^2$/day PO, days 1 through 14
Cyclophosphamide 100 to 150 mg/m$^2$/day PO, days 1 through 14
Methotrexate 40 mg/m$^2$ IV, days 1 and 8
Fluorouracil 600 mg/m$^2$ IV, days 1 and 8

### Hi-C DAZE

**Use:** Acute myelogenous leukemia (AML; induction-pediatrics). *Cycle:* Give a single cycle

**Regimen:** Daunorubicin 30 mg/m$^2$/day IV, days 1 through 3
Cytarabine 3,000 mg/m$^2$/dose IV every 12 hours, days 1 through 4 (total of 8 doses)
Etoposide 200 mg/m$^2$/day IV, days 1 through 3 and days 6 through 8
5-azacytidine* 150 mg/m$^2$/day IV, days 3 through 5 and days 8 through 10
*Note: 5-azacytidine is an investigational Group C drug. Although it is not currently marketed in the United States, the product may be obtained from the NCI.

### Hyper-CVAD/HD MTX Ara-C*

**Use:** Lymphoma (mantle cell). *Cycle:* 21 days, delay subsequent cycles until hematologic recovery. Give up to 4 cycles.

**Regimen:** **Treatment A**-Hyper-CVAD (cycles 1 and 3)
Cyclophosphamide 300 mg/m$^2$/dose IV every 12 hours for 6 doses, days 1 through 3
Doxorubicin 25 mg/m$^2$/day continuous IV infusion, days 4 and 5
Vincristine 2mg IV, day 4 (given 12 hours after last cyclophosphamide dose) and day 11
Dexamethasone 40 mg/day IV or PO, days 1 through 4 and days 11 through 14
Filgrastim 5 mcg/kg/day subcutaneously, starting on day 6 and continued until granulocyte count exceeds 4,500 cells/mm$^3$

**Treatment B**-HD MTX Ara-C (cycles 2 and 4)
Methotrexate 200 mg/m$^2$ IV bolus, day 1
*then*

*(continued on next page)*

**Common Chemotherapy Regimens by Diagnosis**

---

**Hyper-CVAD/HD MTX Ara-C\*** *(continued)*

Methotrexate 800 mg/m$^2$/day continuous IV infusion, day 1

Cytarabine 3,000 mg/m$^2$/dose IV every 12 hours for 4 doses, days 2 and 3

Leucovorin 50 mg PO, day 3, given 24 hours after methotrexate infusion finished

Leucovorin 15 mg/dose PO every 6 hours for 8 doses, days 3 through 5, starting 30 hours after methotrexate infusion finished

Filgrastim 5 mcg/kg/day subcutaneously, starting on day 6 and continued until granulocyte count exceeds 4,500 cells/mm$^3$

*used in conjunction with*

Autologous stem cell transplantation

\*Note: These two regimens are normally used in combination with each other and are rarely given alone.

---

**Use:** Acute lymphocytic leukemia (ALL; induction-adults). *Cycle:* 21 days, delay subsequent cycles until hematologic recovery. Give 8 cycles.

**Regimen:** **Treatment A**-Hyper-CVAD (cycles 1, 3, 5, and 7)

Cyclophosphamide 300 mg/m$^2$/dose IV every 12 hours for 6 doses, day 1 through 3

Mesna 600 mg/m$^2$/day continuous IV infusion, days 1 through 3 (begin with cyclophosphamide)

Doxorubicin 50 mg/m$^2$ IV, day 4

Vincristine 2 mg IV, days 4 and 11

Dexamethasone 40 mg/day IV or PO, days 1 through 4 and days 11 through 14

Filgrastim 10 mcg/kg/day subcutaneously, starting day 5 and continued until granulocyte count exceeds 3,000 cells/mm$^3$

**Treatment B**-HD MTX Ara-C (cycles 2, 4, 6, and 8)

Methotrexate 200 mg/m$^2$ IV bolus, day 1

*then*

Methotrexate 800 mg/m$^2$/day continuous IV infusion, day 1

Cytarabine 3,000 mg/m$^2$/dose IV every 12 hours for 4 doses, days 2 and 3

Leucovorin 15 mg PO or IV every 6 hours for 8 doses, beginning on day 3, starting 24 hours after methotrexate infusion finished and continued until methotrexate concentration is less than 0.1 microMol/L; increase dose to 50 mg/dose PO or IV every 6 hours if the methotrexate concentration is greater than 20 microMol/L at the end of the infusion or greater than 1 microMol/L 24 hours after the end of the infusion, or greater than 0.1 microMol/L 48 hours after the end of the infusion.

**73**

*(continued on next page)*

**Common Chemotherapy Regimens by Diagnosis**

---

**Hyper-CVAD/HD MTX Ara-C\*** *(continued)*

Methylprednisolone 50 mg/dose IV twice daily, days 1 through 3

Filgrastim 10 mcg/kg/day subcutaneously, starting day 4 and
    continued until granulocyte count exceeds 3,000 cells/mm$^3$

CNS *prophylaxis:* Given for cycle 1 and 2 for low-risk patients, cycle
    1 through 4 for unknown risk, and all 8 cycles for high-risk patients.

Methotrexate 12 mg intrathecal, day 2

Cytarabine 100 mg intrathecal, day 8

*used in conjunction with antimicrobial prophylaxis*

Flucanazole 200 mg/day PO, continuously

*plus*

Ciprofloxacin 500 mg PO twice daily, continuously

*or*

Levofloxacin 500 mg/day PO, continuously

*plus*

Acyclovir 200 mg PO twice daily, continuously

*or*

Valacyclovir 500 mg/day PO, continuously

\*Note: These two regimens are normally used in combination with
    each other and are rarely given alone.

---

**ICE (see MICE)**

---

**ICE + Autologous Stem Cell Transplantation**

Use:      Lymphoma (non-Hodgkin-adults). *Cycle:* 14 days for 3 cycles

Regimen:      Etoposide 100 mg/m$^2$/day IV, days 1 through 3

Ifosfamide 5,000 mg/m$^2$/day continuous IV infusion, day 2\*

Mesna 5,000 mg/m$^2$/day continuous IV infusion, day 2\*

Carboplatin IV dose by Calvert equation to AUC 5 mg/mL/min
    (800 mg maximum dose), day 2

Filgrastim 5 mcg/kg/day subcutaneously, days 5 through 12;
    increased in third cycle to 10 mcg/kg/day subcutaneously, from
    day 5 until leukapheresis

*used in conjunction with*

Autologous stem cell transplantation

\*Note: Ifosfamide and mesna may be mixed and administered in the
    same infusion bag.

---

**ICE Protocol (see Idarubicin, Cytarabine, Etoposide)**

---

*(continued on next page)*

═══════════════════════════════════════════════

## Common Chemotherapy Regimens by Diagnosis

---

### ICE-T

Use:            Breast cancer, sarcoma, lung cancer (non-small cell). *Cycle:* 28 days

Regimen:     Ifosfamide 1,250 mg/m$^2$/day IV, days 1 through 3
Carboplatin 300 mg/m$^2$ IV, day 1
Etoposide 80 mg/m$^2$/day IV, days 1 through 3
Paclitaxel 175 mg/m$^2$ IV over 3 hours, day 4
*with*
Mesna 20% of ifosfamide dose IV before, then mesna 40% of ifosfamide
     dose PO given 4 and 8 hours after ifosfamide, days 1 through 3
*or*
Mesna 1,250 mg/m$^2$ IV, days 1 through 3

---

### IDA-based BF12 (see Idarubicin, Cytarabine, Etoposide)

---

### Idarubicin, Cytarabine, Etoposide (ICE Protocol)

Use:            Acute myelogenous leukemia (AML; induction-adults). *Cycle:* Give a
single cycle

Regimen:     Idarubicin 6 mg/m$^2$/day IV, days 1 through 5
Cytarabine 600 mg/m$^2$/day IV, days 1 through 5
Etoposide 150 mg/m$^2$/day IV, days 1 through 3

---

### Idarubicin, Cytarabine, Etoposide (IDA-based BF12)

Use:            Acute myelogenous leukemia (AML; induction-adults). *Cycle:* Usually
1 cycle used.
A second cycle may be considered for patients with partial response.
Time between cycles not specified.

Regimen:     Idarubicin 5 mg/m$^2$/day IV, days 1 through 5
Cytarabine 2,000 mg/m$^2$/dose IV every 12 hours, days 1 through 5
     (total of 10 doses)
Etoposide 100 mg/m$^2$/day IV, days 1 through 5

---

### IDMTX

Use:            Acute lymphocytic leukemia (ALL; intensification—pediatrics).
*Cycle:* 14 days, for 12 cycles

Regimen:     Methotrexate 1,000 mg/m$^2$/day continuous IV infusion, day 1
     (24-hour infusion)
Mercaptopurine 1,000 mg/m$^2$ IV over 6 hours following
     methotrexate, day 2

*(continued on next page)*

**Common Chemotherapy Regimens by Diagnosis**

**IDMTX** *(continued)*

Leucovorin 5 mg/m$^2$/dose IV over 6 hours for at least 5 doses, days 3 and 4, starting 48 hours after the start of the methotrexate infusion and continued until metho-trexate concentration is less than 0.1 microMol/L

Methotrexate 20 mg/m$^2$ IM, day 8

Mercaptopurine 50 mg/m$^2$/day PO, days 8 through 14

---

**IDMTX/6-MP**

Use:        Acute lymphocytic leukemia (ALL; consolidation—pediatrics). *Cycle:* 2 weeks, up to 12 cycles

Regimen:    **Week 1:** Methotrexate 200 mg/m$^2$ IV bolus, day 1

Mercaptopurine 200 mg/m$^2$ IV bolus, day 1

*then*

Methotrexate 800 mg/m$^2$/day continuous IV infusion, day 1

Mercaptopurine 800 mg/m$^2$ IV over 8 hours, day 1

Leucovorin 5 mg/m$^2$/dose PO or IV every 6 hours for 5 to 13 doses, beginning 24 hours after methotrexate infusion finished

**Week 2:** Methotrexate 20 mg/m$^2$ IM, day 8

Mercaptopurine 50 mg/m$^2$/day PO, days 8 through 14

---

**IE**

Use:        Sarcoma (soft-tissue). *Cycle:* 21 days

Regimen:    Ifosfamide 1,800 mg/m$^2$/day IV, days 1 through 5

Etoposide 100 mg/m$^2$/day IV, days 1 through 5

*with*

Mesna 1,800 mg/m$^2$/day IV, days 1 through 5

*or*

Mesna 20% of ifosfamide dose prior to, then 4 and 8 hours after ifosfamide, days 1 through 5

---

**IfoVP**

Use:        Sarcoma (osteosarcoma-pediatrics). *Cycle:* 21 days

Regimen:    Ifosfamide 1,800 mg/m$^2$/day IV, days 1 through 5

Etoposide 100 mg/m$^2$/day IV, days 1 through 5

Mesna 1,800 mg/m$^2$/day IV, days 1 through 5

*(continued on next page)*

▬▬▬▬▬▬▬▬▬▬▬▬▬▬▬▬▬▬▬▬▬▬▬▬▬▬▬▬▬▬▬▬

## Common Chemotherapy Regimens by Diagnosis

---

### Interferon-Cytarabine-Hydroxyurea

**Use:** Chronic myelogenous leukemia (CML). *Cycle:* 28 days

**Regimen:** Interferon alfa-2b 5 million units/day subcutaneously, continuously; adjust dose to white blood cell count

Hydroxyurea 50 mg/kg/day PO, continuously; adjust dose to white blood cell count

Cytarabine 20 mg/m$^2$/day subcutaneously, days 15 through 24 (therapy modified based on white blood cell count and therapeutic response)

---

### Interleukin 2-Interferon alfa 2

**Use:** Renal cell carcinoma. *Cycle:* 56 days

**Regimen:** Aldesleukin 20 million units/m$^2$/dose subcutaneously, 3 times weekly, weeks 1 and 4

Aldesleukin 5 million units/m$^2$/dose subcutaneously, 3 times weekly, weeks 2, 3, 5, and 6

Interferon alfa 6 million units/m$^2$/dose subcutaneously, once weekly, weeks 1 and 4

Interferon alfa 6 million units/m$^2$/dose subcutaneously, 3 times weekly, weeks 2, 3, 5, and 6

---

**Use:** Renal cell carcinoma

**Regimen:** **Remission induction.** *Cycle:* 11 days for 2 cycles

Aldesleukin 18 million units/m$^2$/day continuous IV infusion, days 1 through 5

Interferon alfa-2a 6 million units/dose subcutaneously, days 1, 3, and 5

**Maintenance.** *Cycle:* 26 days for 4 cycles

Aldesleukin 18 million units/m$^2$/day continuous IV infusion, days 1 through 5

Interferon alfa-2a 6 million units/dose subcutaneously, days 1, 3, and 5

---

### IPA

**Use:** Hepatoblastoma (pediatrics). *Cycle:* 21 days

**Regimen:** Ifosfamide 500 mg/m$^2$ IV bolus, day 1

Ifosfamide 1,000 mg/m$^2$/day continuous IV infusion, days 1 through 3

Cisplatin 20 mg/m$^2$/day IV, days 4 through 8

Doxorubicin 30 mg/m$^2$/day continuous IV infusion, days 9 and 10

**77**

▬▬▬▬▬▬▬▬▬▬▬▬▬▬▬▬▬▬▬▬▬▬▬▬▬▬▬▬▬▬▬▬

*(continued on next page)*

**Common Chemotherapy Regimens by Diagnosis**

---

**Linker Protocol**

Use:          Acute lymphocytic leukemia (ALL; induction and consolidation)

Regimen:     **Remission induction.** Give 1 cycle only

Daunorubicin 50 mg/m$^2$/day IV, days 1 through 3

Vincristine 2mg IV, days 1, 8, 15, and 22

Prednisone 60 mg/m$^2$/day PO, days 1 through 28

Asparaginase 6,000 units/m$^2$/day IM, days 17 through 28

*if residual leukemia in marrow on day 14:*

Daunorubicin 50 mg/m$^2$ IV, day 15

*if residual leukemia in marrow on day 28:*

Daunorubicin 50 mg/m$^2$/day IV, days 29 and 30

Vincristine 2mg IV, days 29 and 36

Prednisone 60 mg/m$^2$/day PO, days 29 through 42

Asparaginase 6,000 units/m$^2$/day IM, days 29 through 35

**Consolidation therapy.** *Cycle:* 28 days

**Treatment A** (cycles 1, 3, 5, and 7)

    Daunorubicin 50 mg/m$^2$/day IV, days 1 and 2

    Vincristine 2mg IV, days 1 and 8

    Prednisone 60 mg/m$^2$/day PO, days 1 through 14

    Asparaginase 12,000 units/m$^2$ IM, days 2, 4, 7, 9, 11, and 14

**Treatment B** (cycles 2, 4, 6, and 8)

    Teniposide 165 mg/m$^2$ IV, days 1, 4, 8, and 11

    Cytarabine 300 mg/m$^2$ IV, days 1, 4, 8, and 11

**Treatment C** (cycle 9)

    Methotrexate 690 mg/m$^2$ IV over 42 hours

    Leucovorin 15 mg/m$^2$/dose IV every 6 hours for 12 doses

       (start at end of methotrexate infusion)

---

**M-2**

Use:          Multiple myeloma. *Cycle:* 5 weeks

Regimen:     Vincristine 0.03 mg/kg (2 mg maximum dose) IV, day 1

Carmustine 0.5 mg/kg IV, day 1

Cyclophosphamide 10 mg/kg IV, day 1

Prednisone 1 mg/kg/day PO, days 1 through 7, tapered over next

    14 days

*with*

Melphalan 0.25 mg/kg/day PO, days 1 through 4

*or*

Melphalan 0.1 mg/kg/day PO, days 1 through 7 or days 1 through 10

---

*(continued on next page)*

---

## Common Chemotherapy Regimens by Diagnosis

---

### m-BACOD (see also M-BACOD)*

Use: Lymphoma (non-Hodgkin). *Cycle:* 21 days

Regimen: Bleomycin 4 units/m$^2$ IV, day 1
Doxorubicin 45 mg/m$^2$ IV, day 1
Cyclophosphamide 600 mg/m$^2$ IV, day 1
Vincristine 1 mg/m$^2$ (2 mg maximum dose) IV, day 1
Dexamethasone 6 mg/m$^2$/day PO, days 1 through 5
Methotrexate 200 mg/m$^2$ IV, days 8 and 15
Leucovorin 10 mg/m$^2$/dose PO every 6 hours for 8 doses, begin
24 hours after each methotrexate dose
Sargramostim 5 mcg/kg/day subcutaneously, days 4 through 13
*used in conjunction with*
Intrathecal chemotherapy
*Notes: m-BACOD and M-BACOD differ in the dose and timing of
the methotrexate. Leucovorin dose not specified in original
articles; the dose given here is derived from the Wooldridge
reference, a tertiary book.

---

### m-BACOD (Reduced Dose)*

Use: Lymphoma (non-Hodgkin) associated with HIV infection. *Cycle:* 21 days

Regimen: Bleomycin 4 units/m$^2$ IV, day 1
Doxorubicin 25 mg/m$^2$ IV, day 1
Cyclophosphamide 300 mg/m$^2$ IV, day 1
Vincristine 1.4 mg/m$^2$ (2 mg maximum dose) IV, day 1
Dexamethasone 3 mg/m$^2$/day PO, days 1 through 5
Methotrexate 200 mg/m$^2$ IV, day 15
Sargramostim 5 mcg/kg/day subcutaneously, days 4 through 13
(added during subsequent cycles), for granulocyte count less than
500 cells/mm$^3$ at any time during the cycle or less than 1,000
cells/mm$^3$ on day 22 of any chemotherapy cycle
*used in conjunction with*
Intrathecal chemotherapy
*Note: m-BACOD (reduced dose) has decreased doses of
cyclophosphamide and dexamethasone, and decreased
number of methotrexate doses compared with M-BACOD.

---

### M-BACOD (see also m-BACOD)*

Use: Lymphoma (non-Hodgkin). *Cycle:* 21 days

Regimen: Bleomycin 4 units/m$^2$ IV, day 1
Doxorubicin 45 mg/m$^2$ IV, day 1
Cyclophosphamide 600 mg/m$^2$ IV, day 1

---

*(continued on next page)*

**Common Chemotherapy Regimens by Diagnosis**

---

**M-BACOD (see also m-BACOD)\*** *(continued)*

Vincristine 1 mg/m$^2$ (2 mg maximum dose) IV, day 1
Dexamethasone 6 mg/m$^2$/day PO, days 1 through 5
Methotrexate 3,000 mg/m$^2$ IV, day 15
Leucovorin 10 mg/m$^2$/dose PO every 6 hours for 8 doses, begin
    24 hours after methotrexate dose
Sargramostim 5 mcg/kg/day subcutaneously, days 4 through 13
\*Notes: m-BACOD and M-BACOD differ in the dose and timing of
    the methotrexate. Leucovorin dose not specified in original
    articles; the dose given here is derived from the Wooldridge
    reference, a tertiary book.

---

**M-VAC**

| | |
|---|---|
| Use: | Bladder cancer. *Cycle:* 28 days |
| Regimen: | Methotrexate 30 mg/m$^2$ IV, days 1, 15, and 22 |
| | Vinblastine 3 mg/m$^2$ IV, days 2, 15, and 22 |
| | Doxorubicin 30 mg/m$^2$ IV, day 2 |
| | Cisplatin 70 mg/m$^2$ IV, day 2 |

---

**MAC III**

| | |
|---|---|
| Use: | Gestational trophoblastic neoplasm (high-risk). *Cycle:* 21 days |
| Regimen: | Methotrexate 1 mg/kg IM, days 1, 3, 5, and 7 |
| | Leucovorin 0.1 mg/kg IM, days 2, 4, 6, and 8 (give 24 hours after each methotrexate dose) |
| | Dactinomycin 0.012 mg/kg/day IV, days 1 through 5 |
| | Cyclophosphamide 3 mg/kg/day IV, days 1 through 5 |

---

**MACC**

| | |
|---|---|
| Use: | Lung cancer (non-small cell). *Cycle:* 21 days |
| Regimen: | Methotrexate 30 to 40 mg/m$^2$ IV, day 1 |
| | Doxorubicin 30 to 40 mg/m$^2$ IV, day 1 (total cumulative dose 550 mg/m$^2$) |
| | Cyclophosphamide 400 mg/m$^2$ IV, day 1 |
| | Lomustine 30 mg/m$^2$/day PO, day 1 |

---

**MACOP-B**

| | |
|---|---|
| Use: | Lymphoma, (non-Hodgkin). *Cycle:* Give only a single cycle |
| Regimen: | Methotrexate 400 mg/m$^2$ IV weekly, weeks 2, 6, and 10 |
| | Leucovorin 15 mg/dose PO every 6 hours for 6 doses, begin 24 hours after each methotrexate dose |

*(continued on next page)*

**Common Chemotherapy Regimens by Diagnosis**

---

**MACOP-B** *(continued)*

Doxorubicin 50 mg/m$^2$ IV weekly, weeks 1, 3, 5, 7, 9, and 11
Cyclophosphamide 350 mg/m$^2$ IV weekly, weeks 1, 3, 5, 7, 9, and 11
Vincristine 1.4 mg/m$^2$ (2 mg maximum dose) IV weekly, weeks 2, 4,
   6, 8, 10, and 12
Bleomycin 10 units/m$^2$ IV weekly, weeks 4, 8, and 12
Prednisone 75 mg/day PO for 12 weeks, tapered over last 2 weeks
*used in conjunction with*
Intrathecal chemotherapy
*used in conjunction with*
antimicrobial prophylaxis
Ketoconazole 200 mg/day PO, continuously
Cotrimoxazole double-strength (160/800) 2 tablets PO twice daily,
   continuously

---

**MAID**

81

| Use: | Sarcoma (soft-tissue, bony). *Cycle:* 21 days |
|---|---|
| Regimen: | Mesna 2,000 mg/m$^2$/day continuous IV infusion, days 1 through 4* |
| | Doxorubicin 15 mg/m$^2$/day continuous IV infusion, days 1 through 4 |
| | Ifosfamide 2,000 mg/m$^2$/day continuous IV infusion, days 1 through 3* |
| | Dacarbazine 250 mg/m$^2$/day continuous IV infusion, days 1 through 4 |
| | *Note: Ifosfamide and mesna may be mixed and administered in the same infusion bag. |

---

**MBC**

| Use: | Head and neck cancer. *Cycle:* 21 days |
|---|---|
| Regimen: | Methotrexate 40 mg/m$^2$ IV, days 1 and 14 |
| | Bleomycin 10 units/m$^2$ IM or IV, days 1, 7, and 14 |
| | Cisplatin 50 mg/m$^2$ IV, day 4 |

---

**MC**

| Use: | Acute myelocytic leukemia (AML; induction-adults). *Cycle:* Give a single cycle |
|---|---|
| Regimen: | Mitoxantrone 12 mg/m$^2$/day IV, days 1 through 3 |
| | Cytarabine 100 to 200 mg/m$^2$/day continuous IV infusion or IV, days 1 through 7 |

*(continued on next page)*

![gray bar]

**Common Chemotherapy Regimens by Diagnosis**

---

**MCF**

Use: Gastric cancer. *Cycle:* 42 days for up to 4 cycles

Regimen: Mitomycin 7 mg/m$^2$ (14 mg maximum dose) IV, day 1
Cisplatin 60 mg/m$^2$ IV, days 1 and 22
Fluorouracil 300 mg/m$^2$/day continuous IV infusion, days 1 through 180

---

**MF**

Use: Breast cancer. *Cycle:* 28 days

Regimen: Methotrexate 100 mg/m$^2$ IV, days 1 and 8
Fluorouracil 600 mg/m$^2$ IV, days 1 and 8, given 1 hour after methotrexate
Leucovorin 10 mg/m$^2$/dose IV or PO every 6 hours for 6 doses,
starting 24 hours after methotrexate

---

**82**

**MICE (ICE)**

Use: Sarcoma (adults), osteosarcoma (pediatrics), lung cancer.
*Cycle:* 21 to 28 days

Regimen: Ifosfamide 1,250 to 1,500 mg/m$^2$/day IV, days 1 through 3
Carboplatin 300 to 635 mg/m$^2$ IV, once on day 1 or 3
Etoposide 80 to 100 mg/m$^2$/day IV, days 1 through 3
*with*
Mesna 1,250 mg/m$^2$/day IV, days 1 through 3
*or*
Mesna 20% of ifosfamide dose IV before, 4 hours after, and 8 hours
after each ifosfamide infusion, days 1 through 3

---

**MINE**

Use: Lymphoma (non-Hodgkin). *Cycle:* 21 days

Regimen: Mesna 1,330 mg/m$^2$/day IV, days 1 through 3, given with ifosfamide
Mesna 500 mg/dose PO, 4 hours after ifosfamide, days 1 through 3
Ifosfamide 1,330 mg/m$^2$/day IV, days 1 through 3
Mitoxantrone 8 mg/m$^2$ IV, day 1
Etoposide 65 mg/m$^2$/day IV, days 1 through 3

---

**MINE-ESHAP**

Use: Lymphoma (non-Hodgkin). *Cycle:* 21 days

Regimen: Give MINE for 6 cycles, then give ESHAP for 3 to 6 cycles

---

*(continued on next page)*

**Common Chemotherapy Regimens by Diagnosis**

### mini-BEAM

**Use:** Lymphoma (Hodgkin). *Cycle:* 4 to 6 weeks

**Regimen:** Carmustine 60 mg/m$^2$ IV, day 1
Etoposide 75 mg/m$^2$/day IV, days 2 through 5
Cytarabine 100 mg/m$^2$/dose IV every 12 hours for 8 doses, days
2 through 5
Melphalan 30 mg/m$^2$ IV, day 6

### MOBP

**Use:** Cervical cancer. *Cycle:* 6 weeks

**Regimen:** Bleomycin 30 units/day continuous IV infusion, days 1 through 4
Vincristine 0.5 mg/m$^2$ IV, days 1 and 4
Cisplatin 50 mg/m$^2$ IV, days 1 and 22
Mitomycin 10 mg/m$^2$ IV, day 2

### MOP

**Use:** Brain tumors (pediatrics). *Cycle:* 28 days

**Regimen:** Mechlorethamine 6 mg/m$^2$ IV, days 1 and 8
Vincristine 1.5 mg/m$^2$ (2 mg maximum dose) IV, days 1 and 8
Procarbazine 100 mg/m$^2$/day PO, days 1 through 14

### MOPP

**Use:** Lymphoma (Hodgkin-adults). *Cycle:* 28 days

**Regimen:** Mechlorethamine 6 mg/m$^2$ IV, days 1 and 8
Vincristine 1.4 mg/m$^2$ (2 mg maximum dose) IV, days 1 and 8
Procarbazine 100 mg/m$^2$/day PO, days 1 through 14
Prednisone 40 mg/m$^2$/day PO, cycles 1 and 4,* days 1 through 14
*Note: Some clinicians give prednisone with every cycle of MOPP.
The original clinical trials gave prednisone only with the first
and fourth cycles.

**Use:** Lymphoma (Hodgkin – pediatrics). *Cycle:* 28 days

**Regimen:** Mechlorethamine 6 mg/m$^2$ IV, days 1 and 8
Vincristine 1.4 mg/m$^2$ (2 mg maximum dose) IV, days 1 and 8
Procarbazine 50 mg PO, day 1
Procarbazine 100 mg/m$^2$/day PO, days 2 through 14
Prednisone 40 mg/m$^2$/day PO, cycles 1 and 4,* days 1 through 14
*Note: Some clinicians give prednisone with every cycle of MOPP.
The original clinical trials gave prednisone only with the first
and fourth cycles.

*(continued on next page)*

**Common Chemotherapy Regimens by Diagnosis**

---

**MOPP** *(continued)*

Use: Brain cancer (medulloblastoma). *Cycle:* 28 days

Regimen: Mechlorethamine 3 mg/m² IV, days 1 and 8
Vincristine 1.4 mg/m² (2 mg maximum dose) IV, days 1 and 8
Prednisone 40 mg/m²/day PO, days 1 through 10
Procarbazine 50 mg PO, day 1
Procarbazine 100 mg PO, day 2
Procarbazine 100 mg/m²/day PO, days 3 through 10

---

**MOPP/ABV**

Use: Lymphoma (Hodgkin). *Cycle:* 28 days

Regimen: Mechlorethamine 6 mg/m² IV, day 1
Vincristine 1.4 mg/m² (2 mg maximum dose) IV, day 1
Procarbazine 100 mg/m²/day PO, days 1 through 7
Prednisone 40 mg/m²/day PO, days 1 through 14
Doxorubicin 35 mg/m² IV, day 8
Bleomycin 10 units/m² IV, day 8
Vinblastine 6 mg/m² IV, day 8

---

**MOPP/ABVD**

Use: Lymphoma (Hodgkin). *Cycle:* 28 days

Regimen: Alternate MOPP and ABVD regimens every month

---

**MP**

Use: Multiple myeloma. *Cycle:* 21 to 28 days

Regimen: Melphalan 8 mg/m²/day PO, days 1 through 4
Prednisone 60 mg/m²/day PO, days 1 through 4

---

Use: Prostate cancer. *Cycle:* 21 days

Regimen: Mitoxantrone 12 mg/m² IV, day 1
Prednisone 5 mg/dose PO twice daily

---

**MTX/6-MP**

Use: Acute lymphocytic leukemia (ALL; continuation-pediatrics). *Cycle:* Ongoing, weeks 25 through 130

Regimen: Methotrexate 20 mg/m² IM weekly
Mercaptopurine 50 mg/m²/day PO
*used in conjunction with*
Intrathecal therapy once every 12 weeks

---

*(continued on next page)*

84

▓▓▓▓▓▓▓▓▓▓▓▓▓▓▓▓▓▓▓▓▓▓▓▓▓▓▓▓▓▓▓▓▓▓▓▓▓▓▓▓▓▓▓▓▓▓▓▓▓

**Common Chemotherapy Regimens by Diagnosis**

---

**MTX/6-MP/VP**

Use:      Acute lymphocytic leukemia (ALL; continuation-pediatrics).
*Cycle:* Ongoing, 2 to 3 years

Regimen:      Methotrexate 20 mg/m$^2$/dose PO weekly
Mercaptopurine 75 mg/m$^2$/day PO
Vincristine 1.5 mg/m$^2$ IV, once monthly
Prednisone 40 mg/m$^2$/day PO for 5 days each month

---

**MTX-CDDPAdr**

Use:      Osteosarcoma (pediatrics). *Cycle:* 28 days

Regimen:      Methotrexate 12,000 mg/m$^2$ IV, days 1 and 8
Leucovorin 20 mg/m$^2$/dose IV every 3 hours for 8 doses then give
PO every 6 hours for 8 doses (begin 16 hours after end of
methotrexate infusion)
Cisplatin 75 mg/m$^2$ IV, day 15 of cycles 1 through 7
Cisplatin 120 mg/m$^2$ IV, day 15 of cycles 8 through 10
Doxorubicin 25 mg/m$^2$/day IV, days 15 through 17 of cycles 1 through 7

---

**MV**

Use:      Breast cancer. *Cycle:* 6 to 8 weeks

Regimen:      Mitomycin 20 mg/m$^2$ IV, day 1
Vinblastine 0.15 mg/kg IV, days 1 and 21

---

Use:      Acute myelocytic leukemia (AML; induction). *Cycle:* Give 1 cycle.
Second cycle may be considered if complete response not achieved
(ie, persistent blasts present on day 21).

Regimen:      Mitoxantrone 10 mg/m$^2$/day IV, days 1 through 5
Etoposide 100 mg/m$^2$/day IV, days 1 through 5

---

**MVP**

Use:      Lung cancer (non-small cell). *Cycle:* 6 weeks

Regimen:      Mitomycin 8 mg/m$^2$ IV, day 1
Vinblastine 6 mg/m$^2$ IV, days 1 and 22
Cisplatin 50 mg/m$^2$ IV, days 1 and 22

---

**MVPP**

Use:      Lymphoma (Hodgkin). *Cycle:* 6 weeks

Regimen:      Mechlorethamine 6 mg/m$^2$ (10 mg maximum dose) IV, days 1 and 8
Vinblastine 4 to 6 mg/m$^2$ (10 mg maximum dose) IV, days 1 and 8

85

▓▓▓▓▓▓▓▓▓▓▓▓▓▓▓▓▓▓▓▓▓▓▓▓▓▓▓▓▓▓▓▓▓▓▓▓▓▓▓▓▓▓▓▓▓▓▓▓▓

*(continued on next page)*

**Common Chemotherapy Regimens by Diagnosis**

---

**MVPP** *(continued)*

Procarbazine 100 mg/m$^2$/day (150 mg maximum dose) PO, days
1 through 14
Prednisone 40 mg/m$^2$/day (50 mg maximum dose) PO, cycles 1
and 4,* days 1 through 14
*Note: Some clinicians give prednisone with every cycle of MVPP. The
original clinical trials gave prednisone only with the first and
fourth cycles. Prednisolone is recommended in the British literature. In the US, prednisone is the preferred corticosteroid.
The doses of these 2 corticosteroids are equivalent (ie, prednisone 40 mg PO = prednisolone 40 mg PO).

---

**NA–see Vinorelbine-Doxorubicin**

---

**NFL**

Use:          Breast cancer. *Cycle:* 21 days

Regimen:      Mitoxantrone 12 mg/m$^2$ IV, day 1
Fluorouracil 350 mg/m$^2$/day IV, days 1 through 3 after leucovorin
Leucovorin 300 mg/day IV, days 1 through 3
*or*
Mitoxantrone 10 mg/m$^2$ IV, day 1
Fluorouracil 1,000 mg/m$^2$/day continuous IV infusion, days 1 through 3
Leucovorin 100 mg/m$^2$/day IV, days 1 through 3, give before
fluorouracil on day 1

---

**NOVP**

Use:          Lymphoma (Hodgkin). *Cycle:* 21 days

Regimen:      Mitoxantrone 10 mg/m$^2$ IV, day 1
Vinblastine 6 mg/m$^2$ IV, day 1
Prednisone 100 mg/day PO, days 1 through 5
Vincristine 1.4 mg/m$^2$ (2 mg maximum dose) IV, day 8

---

**OPA**

Use:          Lymphoma (Hodgkin-pediatrics). *Cycle:* 15 days. Up to 2 cycles
used. Time between cycles not specified.

Regimen:      Vincristine 1.5 mg/m$^2$ (2 mg maximum dose) IV, days 1, 8, and 15
Prednisone 60 mg/m$^2$/day PO in 3 divided doses, days 1 through 15
Doxorubicin 40 mg/m$^2$ IV, days 1 and 15

---

*(continued on next page)*

## Common Chemotherapy Regimens by Diagnosis

### OPPA

| | |
|---|---|
| Use: | Lymphoma (Hodgkin-pediatrics). *Cycle:* 15 days. Up to 2 cycles used. Time between cycles not specified. |
| Regimen: | **Add to OPA:** Procarbazine 100 mg/m$^2$/day PO in 2 to 3 divided doses, days 1 through 15 |

### PA-CI

| | |
|---|---|
| Use: | Hepatoblastoma (pediatrics). *Cycle:* 21 days |
| Regimen: | Cisplatin 90 mg/m$^2$ IV, day 1<br>Doxorubicin 20 mg/m$^2$/day continuous IV infusion, days 2 through 5 |

### PAC

| | |
|---|---|
| Use: | Ovarian, endometrial cancer. *Cycle:* 28 days |
| Regimen: | Cisplatin 50 mg/m$^2$ IV, day 1<br>Doxorubicin 50 mg/m$^2$ IV, day 1<br>Cyclophosphamide 500 mg/m$^2$ IV, day 1 |

87

### PAC-I (Indiana Protocol)

| | |
|---|---|
| Use: | Ovarian cancer. *Cycle:* 21 days |
| Regimen: | Cisplatin 50 mg/m$^2$ IV, day 1 (total cumulative dose 300 mg/m$^2$)<br>Doxorubicin 50 mg/m$^2$ IV, day 1<br>Cyclophosphamide 750 mg/m$^2$ IV, day 1 |

### Paclitaxel-Carboplatin-Etoposide

| | |
|---|---|
| Use: | Adenocarcinoma (unknown primary), lung cancer (small cell). *Cycle:* 21 days |
| Regimen: | Paclitaxel 200 mg/m$^2$ IV over 1 hour, day 1<br>Carboplatin IV dose by Calvert equation to AUC 6 mg/mL/min, day 1 (give after paclitaxel)<br>Etoposide 50 mg/day PO alternated with 100 mg/day PO, days 1 through 10 |

### Paclitaxel-Herceptin

| | |
|---|---|
| Use: | Breast cancer. *Cycle:* 7 days |
| Regimen: | Paclitaxel 70 to 90 mg/m$^2$ IV over 1 hour, day 1 (give after trastuzumab)<br>Trastuzumab 4 mg/kg IV, day 1 for first cycle only (loading dose); then trastuzumab 2 mg/kg IV, day 1 for subsequent cycles |

*(continued on next page)*

## Section 3: Table 2

---

## Common Chemotherapy Regimens by Diagnosis

---

### Paclitaxel-Vinorelbine

| | |
|---|---|
| Use: | Breast cancer. *Cycle:* 28 days |
| Regimen: | Paclitaxel 135 mg/m$^2$ IV over 3 hours, day 1 (after vinorelbine infusion) |
| | Vinorelbine 30 mg/m$^2$ IV, days 1 and 8 |

---

### PC

| | |
|---|---|
| Use: | Lung cancer (non-small cell). *Cycle:* 21 days |
| Regimen: | Paclitaxel 135 mg/m$^2$/day continuous IV infusion over 24 hours, day 1 |
| | Carboplatin IV dose by Calvert equation to AUC 7.5 mg/mL/min, day 2 (after paclitaxel) |

---

| | |
|---|---|
| Use: | Lung cancer (non-small cell). *Cycle:* 21 days |
| Regimen: | Paclitaxel 175 mg/m$^2$ IV over 3 hours, day 1 |
| | Cisplatin 80 mg/m$^2$ IV, day 1 (after paclitaxel) |

---

| | |
|---|---|
| Use: | Bladder cancer. *Cycle:* 21 days |
| Regimen: | Paclitaxel 200 or 225 mg/m$^2$ IV over 3 hours, day 1 |
| | Carboplatin IV dose by Calvert equation to AUC 5 to 6 mg/mL/min, day 1 (after paclitaxel) |

---

### PCV

| | |
|---|---|
| Use: | Brain tumor. *Cycle:* 6 to 8 weeks |
| Regimen: | Lomustine 110 mg/m$^2$/day PO, day 1 |
| | Procarbazine 60 mg/m$^2$/day PO, days 8 through 21 |
| | Vincristine 1.4 mg/m$^2$ (2 mg maximum dose) IV, days 8 and 29 |

---

### PE

| | |
|---|---|
| Use: | Prostate cancer. *Cycle:* 21 days |
| Regimen: | Paclitaxel 30 mg/m$^2$/day continuous IV infusion over 24 hours, days 1 through 4 |
| | Estramustine 600 mg/m$^2$/day PO given in 2 to 3 divided doses (start 24 hours before first paclitaxel infusion) |

---

### PFL

| | |
|---|---|
| Use: | Head and neck, gastric cancer. *Cycle:* 28 days |
| Regimen: | Cisplatin 25 mg/m$^2$/day continuous IV infusion, days 1 through 5 |
| | Fluorouracil 800 mg/m$^2$/day continuous IV infusion, days 2 through 6 |
| | Leucovorin 500 mg/m$^2$/day continuous IV infusion, days 1 through 6 |

---

*(continued on next page)*

▬▬▬▬▬▬▬▬▬▬▬▬▬▬▬▬▬▬▬▬▬▬▬▬▬▬▬▬▬

**Common Chemotherapy Regimens by Diagnosis**

---

**PFL** *(continued)*

Use:         Head and neck, gastric cancer. *Cycle:* 21 days

Regimen:    Cisplatin 100 mg/m$^2$ IV, day 1

Fluorouracil 600 to 800 mg/m$^2$/day continuous IV infusion, days 1 through 5

Leucovorin 50 mg/m$^2$/dose PO every 4 to 6 hours, days 1 through 6

---

**POC**

Use:         Brain tumors (pediatrics). *Cycle:* 6 weeks

Regimen:    Prednisone 40 mg/m$^2$/day PO, days 1 through 14

Vincristine 1.5 mg/m$^2$ IV (2 mg maximum dose), days 1, 8, and 15

Lomustine 100 mg/m$^2$/day PO, day 1

---

**ProMACE**

Use:         Lymphoma (non-Hodgkin). *Cycle:* 28 days

Regimen:    Prednisone 60 mg/m$^2$/day PO, days 1 through 14

Methotrexate 750 mg/m$^2$ IV, day 14

Leucovorin 50 mg/m$^2$/dose IV every 6 hours for 5 doses, day 15 (start 24 hours after methotrexate)

Doxorubicin 25 mg/m$^2$ IV, days 1 and 8

Cyclophosphamide 650 mg/m$^2$ IV, days 1 and 8

Etoposide 120 mg/m$^2$ IV, days 1 and 8

---

**ProMACE/cytaBOM**

Use:         Lymphoma (non-Hodgkin). *Cycle:* 21 days

Regimen:    Prednisone 60 mg/m$^2$/day PO, days 1 through 14

Doxorubicin 25 mg/m$^2$ IV, day 1

Cyclophosphamide 650 mg/m$^2$ IV, day 1

Etoposide 120 mg/m$^2$ IV, day 1

Cytarabine 300 mg/m$^2$ IV, day 8

Bleomycin 5 units/m$^2$ IV, day 8

Vincristine 1.4 mg/m$^2$ (2 mg maximum dose) IV, day 8

Methotrexate 120 mg/m$^2$ IV, day 8

Leucovorin 25 mg/m$^2$/dose PO every 6 hours for 4 doses (start 24 hours after methotrexate dose)

Cotrimoxazole double-strength (160/800) 2 tablets PO twice daily, days 1 through 21

▬▬▬▬▬▬▬▬▬▬▬▬▬▬▬▬▬▬▬▬▬▬▬▬▬▬▬▬▬

*(continued on next page)*

---

## Common Chemotherapy Regimens by Diagnosis

---

**ProMACE/MOPP**

| | |
|---|---|
| **Use:** | Lymphoma (non-Hodgkin). *Cycle:* 28 days |
| **Regimen:** | Prednisone 60 mg/m$^2$/day PO, days 1 through 14 |
| | Doxorubicin 25 mg/m$^2$ IV, day 1 |
| | Cyclophosphamide 650 mg/m$^2$ IV, day 1 |
| | Etoposide 120 mg/m$^2$ IV, day 1 |
| | Mechlorethamine 6 mg/m$^2$ IV, day 8 |
| | Vincristine 1.4 mg/m$^2$ (2 mg maximum dose) IV, day 8 |
| | Procarbazine 100 mg/m$^2$/day PO, days 8 through 14 |
| | Methotrexate 500 mg/m$^2$ IV, day 15 |
| | Leucovorin 50 mg/m$^2$/dose PO every 6 hours for 4 doses |
| | (start 24 hours after methotrexate dose) |

---

**Pt/VM**

| | |
|---|---|
| **Use:** | Neuroblastoma (pediatrics). *Cycle:* 21 to 28 days |
| **Regimen:** | Cisplatin 90 mg/m$^2$ IV, day 1 |
| | Teniposide 100 mg/m$^2$ IV, day 3 |

---

**PVA**

| | |
|---|---|
| **Use:** | Acute lymphocytic leukemia (ALL; induction-pediatrics). *Cycle:* 28 days. Give a single cycle. |
| **Regimen:** | Prednisone 40 mg/m$^2$/day (60 mg maximum dose) PO, given in 3 divided doses, days 1 through 28 |
| | Vincristine 1.5 mg/m$^2$ (2 mg maximum dose) IV, days 1, 8, 15, and 22 |
| | *with* |
| | Asparaginase 6,000 units/m$^2$/dose IM, 3 times weekly for 2 weeks (ie, days 2, 5, 7, 9, 12, and 14) |
| | *or* |
| | Asparaginase 6,000 units/m$^2$/dose IM, days 2, 5, 8, 12, 15, and 19 |
| | *or* |
| | Asparaginase 5,000 units/m$^2$/dose IM, days 2, 5, 8, 12, 15, and 18 |
| | *used in conjunction with* |
| | Intrathecal therapy |

---

**PVB**

| | |
|---|---|
| **Use:** | Testicular cancer, adenocarcinoma. *Cycle:* 21 days |
| **Regimen:** | Cisplatin 20 mg/m$^2$/day IV, days 1 through 5 |
| | Vinblastine 0.15 mg/kg/day IV, days 1 and 2 |
| | Bleomycin 30 units IV, days 2, 9, and 16 |

---

*(continued on next page)*

## Section 3: Table 2

**Common Chemotherapy Regimens by Diagnosis**

---

**PVDA**

Use: Acute lymphocytic leukemia (ALL; induction-pediatrics). *Cycle:* 28 days. Give a single cycle.

Regimen: Prednisone 40 mg/m$^2$/day PO, days 1 through 28
Vincristine 1.5 mg/m$^2$ (2 mg maximum dose) IV, days 1, 8, 15, and 22
Daunorubicin 25 mg/m$^2$ IV, days 1, 8, 15, and 22
Asparaginase 10,000 units/m$^2$ IM, 3 times weekly for 12 doses, beginning on day 1
*used in conjunction with*
Intrathecal therapy
Cotrimoxazole 5 mg/kg/day (as trimethoprim) PO in 2 divided doses, days 1 through 28

---

Use: Acute lymphocytic leukemia (ALL; induction-pediatrics). *Cycle:* 28 days. Give a single cycle.

Regimen: Prednisone 40 mg/m$^2$/day PO, days 1 through 28
Vincristine 1.5 mg/m$^2$ (2 mg maximum dose) IV, days 2, 8, 15, and 22
Daunorubicin 25 mg/m$^2$ IV days 2, 8, 15, and 22
Asparaginase 5,000 units/m$^2$/dose IM, days 2, 5, 8, 12, 15, 19
*used in conjunction with*
Intrathecal therapy

---

**R-CHOP (see CHOP + Rituximab)**

---

**Sequential AC/Paclitaxel (see AC/Paclitaxel, Sequential)**

---

**Sequential Dox i CMF (see Dox i CMF, Sequential)**

---

**SMF**

Use: Pancreatic cancer. *Cycle:* 8 weeks

Regimen: Streptozocin 1,000 mg/m$^2$ IV, days 1, 8, 29, and 36
Mitomycin 10 mg/m$^2$ IV, day 1
Fluorouracil 600 mg/m$^2$ IV, days 1, 8, 29, and 36

---

**Stanford V**

Use: Lymphoma (Hodgkin). *Cycle:* 28 days

Regimen: Mechlorethamine 6 mg/m$^2$ IV, day 1
Doxorubicin 25 mg/m$^2$ IV, days 1 and 15
Vinblastine 6 mg/m$^2$ IV, days 1 and 15
Vincristine 1.4 mg/m$^2$ (2 mg maximum dose) IV, days 8 and 22
Bleomycin 5 units/m$^2$ IV, days 8 and 22

---

*(continued on next page)*

**Common Chemotherapy Regimens by Diagnosis**

**Stanford V** *(continued)*

Etoposide 60 mg/m$^2$/day IV, days 15 and 16

Prednisone 40 mg/m$^2$/dose PO, every other day continually for 10
    weeks, then taper off by 10 mg every other day for next 14 days

*used in conjunction with*

antimicrobial prophylaxis

Cotrimoxazole double-strength (160/800) 2 tablets PO twice daily,
    continuously

Ketoconazole 200 mg/day PO, continuously

Acyclovir 200 mg PO 3 times daily, continuously

---

**TAC**

| | |
|---|---|
| Use: | Breast cancer. *Cycle:* 21 days (up to 8 cycles) |
| Regimen: | Doxorubicin 50 mg/m$^2$ IV, day 1 |
| | Cyclophosphamide 500 mg/m$^2$ IV, day 1 (after doxorubicin) |
| | Docetaxel 75 mg/m$^2$ IV, day 1 (after cyclophosphamide) |
| | Ciprofloxacin 500 mg PO twice daily, days 5 through 15 |

---

**TAD**

| | |
|---|---|
| Use: | Acute myelocytic leukemia (AML; induction-adults). *Cycle:* 21 days. Give 2 cycles. |
| Regimen: | Daunorubicin 60 mg/m$^2$/day IV, days 3 through 5 |
| | Cytarabine 100 mg/m$^2$/day continuous IV infusion, days 1 and 2 |
| | Cytarabine 100 mg/m$^2$/dose IV every 12 hours for 12 doses, days 3 through 8 |
| | Thioguanine 100 mg/m$^2$/dose PO every 12 hours for 14 doses, days 3 through 9 |

---

**Tamoxifen-Epirubicin**

| | |
|---|---|
| Use: | Breast cancer. *Cycle:* 28 days for 6 cycles |
| Regimen: | Tamoxifen 20 mg PO daily, continuously for 4 years |
| | Epirubicin 50 mg/m$^2$ IV, on days 1 and 8 |

---

**TC**

| | |
|---|---|
| Use: | Gastric cancer. *Cycle:* 21 days (up to 8 cycles) |
| Regimen: | Docetaxel 85 mg/m$^2$ IV, day 1 |
| | Cisplatin 75 mg/m$^2$ IV, day 1 (after docetaxel) |

*(continued on next page)*

**Common Chemotherapy Regimens by Diagnosis**

---

**TCF**

Use:            Esophageal cancer. *Cycle:* 28 days

Regimen:      Paclitaxel 175 mg/m$^2$ IV over 3 hours, day 1
                 Cisplatin 20 mg/m$^2$/day IV, days 1 through 5 (give after paclitaxel)
                 Fluorouracil 750 mg/m$^2$/day, continuous IV infusion days 1 through 5

---

**TEC**

Use:            Prostate cancer. *Cycle:* 28 days

Regimen:      Estramustine 10 mg/kg/day (840 mg maximum daily dose) PO given
                 in 3 divided doses, start 2 days before chemotherapy and continue
                 for 2 days after chemotherapy, 5 days total (days 21 to +3 of each
                 cycle)
                 Paclitaxel 100 mg/m$^2$ IV over 1 hour, days 1, 8, 15, and 22
                 Carboplatin IV dose by Calvert equation to AUC 6 mg/mL/min
                 (1,000 mg maximum dose), day 1

**93**

---

**TIP**

Use:            Head and neck, esophageal cancer. *Cycle:* 21 to 28 days

Regimen:      Paclitaxel 175 mg/m$^2$ IV over 3 hours, day 1
                 Ifosfamide 1,000 mg/m$^2$/day IV, days 1 through 3
                 Mesna 400 mg/m$^2$/day IV pre-ifosfamide, days 1 through 3
                 Mesna 200 mg/m$^2$/dose IV given 4 hours after ifosfamide, days 1
                 through 3
                 Cisplatin 60 mg/m$^2$ IV, given after paclitaxel infusion, day 1

---

Use:            Testicular cancer. *Cycle:* 21 days (4 cycles)

Regimen:      Paclitaxel 175 to 250 mg/m$^2$/day continuous IV infusion over 24
                 hours, day 1
                 Ifosfamide 1,200 mg/m$^2$/day IV, days 2 through 6
                 Cisplatin 20 mg/m$^2$/day IV, days 2 through 6
                 Mesna 400 mg/m$^2$/dose IV prior to, then 4 and 8 hours after
                 ifosfamide, days 2 through 6

---

**TIT**

Use:            Acute lymphocytic leukemia (ALL; CNS prophylaxis-pediatrics).

Regimen:      Doses are based on patient's age. Give during weeks 1, 2, 3, 7, 13,
                 19, and 25 of intensification and every 12 weeks during maintenance.*
                 *Age 1 to 2 years:*
                 Methotrexate 8 mg intrathecal

*(continued on next page)*

**Common Chemotherapy Regimens by Diagnosis**

---

**TIT** *(continued)*

Cytarabine 16 mg intrathecal
Hydrocortisone 8 mg intrathecal
*Age 2 to 3 years:*
Methotrexate 10 mg intrathecal
Cytarabine 20 mg intrathecal
Hydrocortisone 10 mg intrathecal
*Age 3 to 9 years:*
Methotrexate 12 mg intrathecal
Cytarabine 24 mg intrathecal
Hydrocortisone 12 mg intrathecal
*Age 9 years and older:*
Methotrexate 15 mg intrathecal
Cytarabine 30 mg intrathecal
Hydrocortisone 15 mg intrathecal
*Note: All three drugs may be mixed and administered in a single syringe, if diluted with preservative-free 0.9% sodium chloride. Regimen used in combination with an induction/maintenance regimen.

---

**Use:** Acute lymphocytic leukemia (ALL; CNS prophylaxis-pediatrics).

**Regimen:** Doses are based on patient's age. Give on day 1 of induction, during weeks 1, 2, 3, 6, 11, 16, 21, and 26 of intensification, during week 31, and every 12 weeks during maintenance.*
*Age 1 year:*
Methotrexate 10 mg intrathecal
Cytarabine 20 mg intrathecal
Hydrocortisone 10 mg intrathecal
*Age 2 years:*
Methotrexate 12.5 mg intrathecal
Cytarabine 25 mg intrathecal
Hydrocortisone 12.5 mg intrathecal
*Age greater than 3 years:*
Methotrexate 15 mg intrathecal
Cytarabine 30 mg intrathecal
Hydrocortisone 15 mg intrathecal
*Note: All three drugs may be mixed and administered in a single syringe, if diluted with preservative-free 0.9% sodium chloride. Regimen used in combination with an induction/maintenance regimen.

---

*(continued on next page)*

**Common Chemotherapy Regimens by Diagnosis**

---

**TIT** *(continued)*

Use: Acute lymphocytic leukemia (ALL; CNS prophylaxis-adults).

Regimen: Give on days 1 and 5 of week 1, day 1 of week 4, days 1 and 5 of
week 7, day 1 of week 10, days 1 and 5 of week 13, and day 1
of week 16.

Methotrexate 15 mg intrathecal

Cytarabine 40 mg intrathecal

Dexamethasone 4 mg intrathecal*

*Note: No preservative-free product is available; dexamethasone 4
mg/mL injection contains benzyl alcohol 10 mg/mL, a preser-
vative that is unsuitable for intrathecal injection. Because other
intrathecal regimens are available that do not include benzyl
alcohol-containing products, this regimen should be reserved
for use when no other options are available and the benefit to
the patient clearly outweighs the risk of benzyl alcohol toxicity.
Regimen used in combination with an induction/maintenance
regimen.

**95**

---

**Topo/CTX**

Use: Sarcomas (bone and soft-tissue-pediatrics). *Cycle:* 21 days

Regimen: Cyclophosphamide 250 mg/m$^2$/day IV, days 1 through 5

Topotecan 0.75 mg/m$^2$/day IV, days 1 through 5 after
cyclophosphamide

Mesna 150 mg/m$^2$/dose IV before and 3 hours after each
cyclophosphamide dose, days 1 through 5

---

**Trastuzumab-Paclitaxel**

Use: Breast cancer. *Cycle:* 21 days for at least 6 cycles

Regimen: Paclitaxel 175 mg/m$^2$/dose IV over 3 hours, day 1

Trastuzumab 4 mg/kg IV, day 1 first cycle only (loading dose)

Trastuzumab 2 mg/kg IV weekly, days 1, 8, and 15, except for day
1 of first cycle

---

**VAB-6**

Use: Testicular cancer. *Cycle:* 21 to 28 days

Regimen: Cyclophosphamide 600 mg/m$^2$ IV, day 1

Dactinomycin 1 mg/m$^2$ IV, day 1

Vinblastine 4 mg/m$^2$ IV, day 1

Cisplatin 120 mg/m$^2$ IV, day 4

---

*(continued on next page)*

**Common Chemotherapy Regimens by Diagnosis**

**VAB-6** *(continued)*

Bleomycin 30 units IV push, day 1 (omit from cycle 3)
*then*
Bleomycin 20 units/m$^2$/day continuous IV infusion, days 1 through 3
   (omit from cycle 3)

**VAC Pediatric**

Use:       Sarcoma (pediatrics). *Cycle:* 21 days

Regimen:    Vincristine 2 mg/m$^2$ IV (2 mg maximum dose), day 1
Dactinomycin 1 mg/m$^2$ IV, day 1
Cyclophosphamide 600 mg/m$^2$ IV, day 1

**VAC Pulse**

Use:       Sarcomas.

Regimen:    Vincristine 2 mg/m$^2$ (2 mg maximum dose) IV weekly, for 12 weeks
Dactinomycin 0.015 mg/kg/day (0.5 mg/day maximum dose)
   continuous IV infusion, days 1 through 5, every 3 months for 5
   courses
Cyclophosphamide 10 mg/kg/day IV or PO, days 1 through 7, every
   6 weeks

**VAC Standard**

Use:       Sarcomas.

Regimen:    Vincristine 2 mg/m$^2$ (2 mg maximum dose) IV weekly, for 12 weeks
Dactinomycin 0.015 mg/kg/day (0.5 mg/day maximum dose)
   continuous IV infusion, days 1 through 5, every 3 months for 5
   courses
Cyclophosphamide 2.5 mg/kg/day PO, daily for 2 years

**VACAdr**

Use:       Sarcoma (bone and soft-tissue-pediatrics).

Regimen:    Vincristine 1.5 mg/m$^2$ (2 mg maximum dose) IV, days 1, 8, 15, 22,
   29, and 36
Cyclophosphamide 500 mg/m$^2$ IV, days 1, 8, 15, 22, 29, and 36
Doxorubicin 60 mg/m$^2$ IV, day 36
*followed by 6-week rest period, then*
Dactinomycin 0.015 mg/kg/day IV, days 1 through 5
Vincristine 1.5 mg/m$^2$ (2 mg maximum dose) IV, days 14, 21, 28, 35,
   and 42

*(continued on next page)*

**Common Chemotherapy Regimens by Diagnosis**

---

**VACAdr** (continued)

Cyclophosphamide 500 mg/m² IV, days 14, 21, 28, 35, and 42
Doxorubicin 60 mg/m² IV, day 42 (give on day of final vincristine and
   cyclophosphamide doses)

---

**VAD**

Use:    Multiple myeloma. *Cycle:* 3 to 4 weeks

Regimen:    Vincristine 0.4 mg/day (dose is not in mg/m²) continuous IV infusion,
   days 1 through 4*
   Doxorubicin 9 mg/m²/day continuous IV infusion, days 1 through 4*
   Dexamethasone 40 mg/day PO, days 1 through 4, days 9 through
   12, and days 17 through 20†
   *Note: Vincristine and doxorubicin may be mixed and administered in
   the same infusion bag, if diluted with 0.9% sodium chloride.
   †Note: After completing the first 2 cycles of VAD, some clinicians
   give dexamethasone only on days 1 through 4 of each cycle
   to reduce the risk of infection. Antibiotic prophylaxis with cotrimoxazole also has been used for this purpose.

97

---

Use:    Acute lymphocytic leukemia. *Cycle:* 24 to 28 days

Regimen:    Vincristine 0.4 mg/day (dose is not in mg/m²) continuous IV infusion,
   days 1 through 4*
   Doxorubicin 9 to 12 mg/m²/day continuous IV infusion, days 1
   through 4*
   Dexamethasone 40 mg/day PO, days 1 through 4, days 9 through
   12, and days 17 through 20
   *Note: Vincristine and doxorubicin may be mixed and administered in
   the same infusion bag, if diluted with 0.9% sodium chloride.

---

Use:    Wilm tumor (pediatrics). *Cycle:* 1 year. Give 1 cycle only.

Regimen 1:    Vincristine 1.5 mg/m² (2 mg maximum dose) IV, weekly for first 10 to
   11 weeks then every 3 weeks for 15 more weeks
   *with*
   Dactinomycin 1.5 mg/m² IV every 6 weeks, starting week 1, for 9
   doses
   Doxorubicin 40 mg/m² IV every 6 weeks for 26 weeks, starting week
   4, for 9 doses

Regimen 2:    Vincristine 1.5 mg/m² (2 mg maximum dose) IV, given every 6 weeks
   for 6 to 15 months
   Dactinomycin 0.015 mg/kg/day IV for 5 doses, given every 6 weeks
   for 6 to 15 months

---

*(continued on next page)*

**Common Chemotherapy Regimens by Diagnosis**

---

**VAD** *(continued)*

*or*
Dactinomycin 0.06 mg/kg IV, given every 6 weeks for 6 to 15 months
*may or may not give with*
Doxorubicin 20 mg/m$^2$ IV, given every 6 weeks for 6 to 15 months

---

**VAD-Liposomal (VLAD)**

Use: Multiple myeloma. *Cycle:* 28 days

Regimen: Vincristine 2 mg IV, day 1
Liposomal doxorubicin 30 to 40 mg/m$^2$ IV, day 1
Dexamethasone 40 mg/day PO, days 1 through 4, days 9 through
12, and days 17 through 20

---

**VATH**

Use: Breast cancer. *Cycle:* 21 days

Regimen: Vinblastine 4.5 mg/m$^2$ IV, day 1
Doxorubicin 45 mg/m$^2$ IV, day 1
Thiotepa 12 mg/m$^2$ IV, day 1
Fluoxymesterone 30 mg/day PO in 3 divided doses, throughout
entire course

---

**VBAP**

Use: Multiple myeloma. *Cycle:* 21 days

Regimen: Vincristine 1 mg/m$^2$ (2 mg maximum dose) IV, day 1
Carmustine 30 mg/m$^2$ IV, day 1
Doxorubicin 30 mg/m$^2$ IV, day 1
Prednisone 60 mg/m$^2$/day PO, days 1 through 4

---

**VBMCP**

Use: Multiple myeloma. *Cycle:* 35 days

Regimen: Vincristine 1.2 mg/m$^2$ (2 mg maximum dose) IV, day 1
Carmustine 20 mg/m$^2$ IV, day 1
Melphalan 8 mg/m$^2$/day PO, days 1 through 4
Cyclophosphamide 400 mg/m$^2$ IV, day 1
Prednisone 40 mg/m$^2$/day PO, days 1 through 7 of all cycles
*with*
Prednisone 20 mg/m$^2$/day PO, days 8 through 14 of first 3 cycles only

*(continued on next page)*

**Common Chemotherapy Regimens by Diagnosis**

---

**VC**

Use: Lung cancer (non-small cell).

Regimen: Vinorelbine 30 mg/m$^2$ IV, weekly
Cisplatin 120 mg/m$^2$ IV, days 1 and 29, then give 1 dose every 6 weeks

---

**VCAP**

Use: Multiple myeloma. *Cycle:* 21 days

Regimen: Vincristine 1 mg/m$^2$ (2 mg maximum dose) IV, day 1
Cyclophosphamide 125 mg/m$^2$/day PO, days 1 through 4
Doxorubicin 30 mg/m$^2$ IV, day 1
Prednisone 60 mg/m$^2$/day PO, days 1 through 4

---

**VCMP-see VMCP**

---

**VD** 99

Use: Breast cancer. *Cycle:* 21 days

Regimen: Vinorelbine 25 mg/m$^2$ IV, days 1 and 8
Doxorubicin 50 mg/m$^2$ IV, day 1

---

**VeIP**

Use: Genitourinary cancer, testicular cancer. *Cycle:* 21 days

Regimen: Vinblastine 0.11 mg/kg/day IV, days 1 and 2
Cisplatin 20 mg/m$^2$/day IV, days 1 through 5
Ifosfamide 1,200 mg/m$^2$/day IV, days 1 through 5
Mesna 1,200 mg/m$^2$/day continuous IV infusion, days 1 through 5

---

**VIC–see CVI**

---

**Vinorelbine-Cisplatin (see also Cisplatin-Vinorelbine)**

Use: Lung cancer (non-small cell). *Cycle:* 42 days

Regimen: Vinorelbine 30 mg/m$^2$ IV, weekly
Cisplatin 120 mg/m$^2$ IV, days 1 and 29 for first cycle; then day 1 of
subsequent cycles

---

**Vinorelbine-Doxorubicin**

Use: Breast cancer. *Cycle:* 21 days

Regimen: Vinorelbine 25 mg/m$^2$ IV, days 1 and 8
Doxorubicin 50 mg/m$^2$ IV, day 1

---

*(continued on next page)*

▬▬▬▬▬▬▬▬▬▬▬▬▬▬▬▬▬▬▬▬▬▬▬▬▬▬▬▬▬▬

**Common Chemotherapy Regimens by Diagnosis**

---

**Vinorelbine-Gemcitabine**

| | |
|---|---|
| Use: | Lung cancer (non-small cell). *Cycle:* 28 days for up to 6 cycles |
| Regimen: | Vinorelbine 20 mg/m$^2$ IV, days 1, 8, and 15 |
| | Gemcitabine 800 mg/m$^2$ IV, days 1, 8, and 15 |

---

**VIP**

| | |
|---|---|
| Use: | Genitourinary cancer, testicular cancer. *Cycle:* 21 days |
| Regimen: | Cisplatin 20 mg/m$^2$/day IV, days 1 through 5 |
| | Etoposide 75 mg/m$^2$/day IV, days 1 through 5 |
| | Ifosfamide 1,200 mg/m$^2$/day IV, days 1 through 5 |
| | Mesna 1,200 mg/m$^2$/day continuous IV infusion, days 1 through 5 |

---

| | |
|---|---|
| Use: | Lung cancer (small cell). *Cycle:* 21 to 28 days |
| Regimen: | Ifosfamide 1,200 mg/m$^2$/day IV, days 1 through 4 |
| | Cisplatin 20 mg/m$^2$/day IV, days 1 through 4 |
| | Mesna 120 to 300 mg/m$^2$ IV, day 1 (give before ifosfamide started) |
| | Mesna 1,200 mg/m$^2$/day continuous IV infusion, days 1 through 4 |
| |    (after mesna bolus given) |
| | *with* |
| | Etoposide 37.5 mg/m$^2$/day PO, days 1 through 14 |
| | *or* |
| | Etoposide 75 mg/m$^2$/day IV, days 1 through 4 |

**100**

---

| | |
|---|---|
| Use: | Lung cancer (non-small cell). *Cycle:* 28 days |
| Regimen: | Ifosfamide 1,000 to 1,200 mg/m$^2$/day IV, days 1 through 3 |
| | Cisplatin 100 mg/m$^2$ IV, days 1 and 8 |
| | Etoposide 60 to 75 mg/m$^2$/day IV, days 1 through 3 |
| | *with* |
| | Mesna 300 mg/m$^2$/dose IV every 4 hours, days 1 through 4 |
| | *or* |
| | Mesna 20% of ifosfamide dose IV before, 4 and 8 hours after |
| |    ifosfamide, days 1 through 4 |

---

**VLAD (see VAD-Liposomal)**

---

**VM**

| | |
|---|---|
| Use: | Breast cancer. *Cycle:* 6 to 8 weeks |
| Regimen: | Mitomycin 10 mg/m$^2$ IV, days 1 and 28 for 2 cycles, then day 1 only |
| | Vinblastine 5 mg/m$^2$ IV, days 1, 14, 28, and 42 for 2 cycles, then |
| |    days 1 and 21 only |

▬▬▬▬▬▬▬▬▬▬▬▬▬▬▬▬▬▬▬▬▬▬▬▬▬▬▬▬▬▬

*(continued on next page)*

**Common Chemotherapy Regimens by Diagnosis**

**VMCP**

Use: Multiple myeloma. *Cycle:* 21 days

Regimen: Vincristine 1 mg/m² (2 mg maximum dose) IV, day 1
Melphalan 6 mg/m²/day PO, days 1 through 4
Cyclophosphamide 125 mg/m²/day PO, days 1 through 4
Prednisone 60 mg/m²/day PO, days 1 through 4

**VP**

Use: Lung cancer (small cell). *Cycle:* 21 days

Regimen: Etoposide 100 mg/m²/day IV, days 1 through 4
Cisplatin 20 mg/m²/day IV, days 1 through 4

**V-TAD**

Use: Acute myelocytic leukemia (AML; induction). *Cycle:* 7 days. Give 1
cycle. Up to 3 cycles have been given, but time between cycles is
not specified.

Regimen: Etoposide 50 mg/m²/day IV, days 1 through 3
Thioguanine 75 mg/m²/dose PO every 12 hours for 10 doses, days
     1 through 5
Daunorubicin 20 mg/m²/day IV, days 1 and 2
Cytarabine 75 mg/m²/day continuous IV infusion, days 1 through 5

**X + T (see Capecitabine-Docetaxel)**

*Reprinted with permission from Drug Facts and Comparisons; 2004,
a Wolters Klewer Company.*

**Combination Chemotherapy Regimens**

### Adenocarcinoma

CaT
Carbo-Tax
CF
EP
FAM
Paclitaxel-Carboplatin-Etoposide
PVB

### Brain

CDDP/VP-16
COPE
MOP
MOPP
PCV
POC
"8 in 1"

### Breast

AC
AC(e)
AC/Paclitaxel, Sequential
AT
CAF
Capecitabine-Docetaxel
CEF
CFM (see CNF)
CMF
CMF-IV
CMFP
CMFVP
CNF
Cooper Regimen
CY/A (see AC)
Dox ⟶ CMF, Sequential
FAC
FEC
FNC
HEC
ICE-T
MF
MV
NA (see Vinorelbine-Doxorubicin)
NFL
Paclitaxel-Herceptin
Paclitaxel-Vinorelbine
TAC

### Breast *(continued)*

Tamoxifen-Epirubicin
Trastuzumab-Paclitaxel
VATH
VD
Vinorelbine-Doxorubicin
VM
X + T (see Capecitabine-Docetaxel)

### Colorectal

F-CL
Fle
FOLFOX-4
FU-LV see F-CL
FU/LV/CPT-11

### Esophageal

TCF
TIP

### Gastric

EAP
ECF
EFP
ELF
FAM
FAMTX
FAP
FUP
MCF
PFL
TC

### Genitourinary-Bladder

CISCA
Cisplatin-Docetaxel
CMV
Gemcitabine-Cisplatin
M-VAC
PC

### Genitourinary-Cervical

BIP
BOMP
Cisplatin-Fluorouracil
Cisplatin-Vinorelbine
CLD-BOMP
MOBP

*(continued on next page)*

## Combination Chemotherapy Regimens

### Genitourinary-Ovarian or Endometrial

AP
Carbo-Tax
CaT
Carbo-Tax
CC
CHAP
CP
CT
Hexa-CAF
PAC
PAC-I (Indiana Protocol)

### Genitourinary-Prostate

Bicalutamide + LHRH-A
Docetaxel-Estramustine
EM-V (see Estramustine/Vinblastine)
Estramustine/Vinblastine
FL
FZ
MP
PE
TEC

### Genitourinary-Renal Cell

Biochemotherapy
    (see Interleukin2-Interferon alfa 2)
Interleukin 2-Interferon alfa 2

### Genitourinary-Testicular or Germ Cell

BEP
CISCA II/VB IV
EP
PVB
TIP
VAB-6
VelP
VIP

### Gestational Trophoblastic Neoplasm

CHAMOCA (modified Bagshawe)
MAC III

### Head and Neck

CABO
CF
CF*
COB
MBC
PFL
TIP

### Hepatoblastoma

IPA
PA-CI

### Kaposi Sarcoma

ABV

### Leukemia-Acute Lymphocytic (ALL), Advanced-Stage Burkitt Protocol, or B-Cell ALL Pediatric Protocol

CAL-G
DVP
Hyper-CVAD/HD MTX Ara-C
IDMTX
IDMTX/6-MP
Linker Protocol
MTX/6-MP
MTX/6-MP/VP
PVA
PVDA
TIT
VAD

### Leukemia-Acute Myelocytic (AML)

5+2
7+3
7+3+7
ARAC-DNR
ATRA + CT see DA + ATRA
CA
DA
DA + ATRA
DAT
DAV
DCT
EMA 86
FLAG-Ida

**103**

(continued on next page)

**Combination Chemotherapy Regimens**

**Leukemia-Acute Myelocytic (AML)** *(cont.)*
Hi-C DAZE
Idarubicin, Cytarabine, Etoposide
  (IDA based BF12)
Idarubicin, Cytarabine, Etoposide
  (ICE protocol)
MC
MV
TAD
V-TAD

**Leukemia-Chronic Lymphocytic (CLL)**
CP
CVP
Cyclophosphamide-Fludarabine
Fludarabine-Cyclophosphamide

**Leukemia-Chronic Myelogenous (CML)**
Interferon-Cytarabine-Hydroxyurea

**Lung-Non-Small Cell**
CAMP
CAP
CaT
CT
CVI
Docetaxel-Cisplatin
EC
EP
FED
G+V
Gemcitabine-Carboplatin
Gemcitabine-Cis
Gemcitabine-Vinorelbine
ICE (see MICE)
ICE-T
MACC
MICE
MVP
PC
VC
VIC (see CVI)
Vinorelbine-Cisplatin
Vinorelbine-Gemcitabine
VIP

**Lung-Small Cell**
ACE
AVE (see CA-VP 16)
CAE (see ACE)
CAV
CAVE
CAV/EP
CA-VP16
CEV
CODE
COPE
EC
EP
ICE (see MICE)
MICE
Paclitaxel-Carboplatin-Etoposide
VIP
VP

**Lymphoma-Hodgkin**
ABVD
B-CAVe
BCVPP
BEACOPP
BVCPP (see BCVPP)
CHlVPP
CHlVPP/EVA
C-MOPP (see COPP)
COMP
COPP
CVPP
EVA
Mini-BEAM
MOPP
MOPP/ABV
MOPP/ABVD
MVPP
NOVP
OPA
OPPA
Stanford V

104

*(continued on next page)*

## Combination Chemotherapy Regimens

### Lymphoma-Non-Hodgkin

Advanced-Stage Burkitt Protocol
    or B-Cell
ALL Pediatric Protocol
CDE
CEPP(B)
CHOP
CHOP-BLEO
CHOP + Rituximab
C-MOPP (see COPP)
CNOP
CODOX-M/IVAC
COMLA
COP
COPP
CVP
DHAOx
DHAP
ESHAP
Hyper-CVAD/HD MTX Ara-C
ICE + Autologous Stem Cell
    Transplantation
MACOP-B
m-BACOD
m-BACOD (reduced dose)
M-BACOD
MINE
MINE-ESHAP
ProMACE
ProMACE/cytaBOM
ProMACE/MOPP
R-CHOP see CHOP + Rituximab

### Melanoma

CDB
CDB + Tamoxifen
CVD
CVD-IL-2I
Dartmouth regimen
    (see CDB + Tamoxifen)
DTIC/Tamoxifen

### Multiple Myeloma

M-2
MP
VAD
VAD-Liposomal
VBAP
VBMCP
VCAP
VCMP see VMCP
VLAD
VMCP

### Neuroblastoma

AC
Pt/VM

### Pancreatic

Gemcitabine-Irinotecan
SMF

### Renal Cell

Interleukin 2-Interferon alfa 2

### Sarcoma

AC
AD
CYVADIC
DI
HDMTX
ICE (see MICE)
ICE-T
IE
IfoVP
MAID
MICE
MTX-CDDPAdr
Topo/CTX
VAC Pediatric
VAC Pulse
VAC Standard
VACAdr

### Wilm Tumor

VAD

# 4

## Common Side Effects of Chemotherapy

Management of the oncology patient requires an in-depth knowledge of the toxicities caused by cancer treatment. Anticipation of toxicities can possibly prevent them or perhaps lessen the effect. This section provides an overview of the common toxicities (nausea/vomiting, alopecia, stomatitis, myelosuppression, peripheral neuropathy, cardiac, pulmonary and gonadal toxicity) caused by cancer treatment. Some are listed by level of severity as well as potential for occurrence. This information was gathered from a variety of oncology texts and formatted into a table for quick reference.

The primary table is followed by several smaller tables with further details on cardiac, pulmonary and hepatic toxicities. This section also includes a sample risk assessment tool, to evaluate pretreatment risk for multiple common symptoms.

# Section 4: Table 1

## Toxicities

| Chemo Agent | Category | N & V | Vesicant | Alopecia | Stomatitis | Myelosuppression | Peripheral Neuropathy | Pulmonary Toxicity | Cardiac Toxicity | Gonadal Toxicity |
|---|---|---|---|---|---|---|---|---|---|---|
| Aminoglutethimide | H | +1 | PO | O | O | O | | | | |
| Anastrozole | H | +1 | PO | O | O | | | | | |
| Arsenic Trioxide | | +1 | | | O | O | | 0/+1 | | |
| Asparaginase | O | +2 | | O | | O | ✓ | | | |
| Azacytidine | AM | +3 | | +3 | | +3 | | | | |
| Bleomycin | AB | +1 | | +2 | +3 | O | | +3 | | |
| Busulfan | AA | +1 | | +1 | +3 | +3 | | +1 | | ✓ |
| Capecitabine | O | +1 | PO | O | +1 | +1/2 | | | | ✓ |
| Carboplatin | AA | +2 | | O | O | +2/3 | ✓ | | | |
| Carmustine | AA | +3 | – | +1 | +2 | +3 | | +2 | | ✓ |
| Chlorambucil | AA | 0/+1 | PO | O | O | +1/2 | | 0/+1 | | ✓ |
| Cisplatin | AA | +3 | | +1 | O | +2 | ✓✓ | | | |
| Cladribine | O | +1 | | O | O | +1/2 | | | | |
| Cyclophosphamide | AA | +2 | | +3 | +3 | +3 | ✓ | +1 | | ✓ |
| Cytarabine | AM | +3 | | +1 | +2 | +3 | | +1 | ✓ | ✓ |
| Dacarbazine | AA | +3 | – | +1 | O | +2 | | | | ✓ |
| Dactinomycin | AB | +3 | > | +2 | +3 | +2/3 | | | | ✓ |
| Daunorubicin | AB | +2 | > | +3 | +3 | +3 | | | | ✓ |
| Docetaxel | AL | +1 | | +2 | +3 | +2/3 | | | | |
| Doxorubicin | AB | +2 | > | +3 | +3 | +3 | | | ✓ | ✓ |
| Epirubicin | AB | +2 | > | +3 | +3 | +3 | | | | |
| Estramustine | H | +1 | PO | O | O | +2 | | | | |
| Etoposide | AL | +1 | – | +2 | +2/3 | +2 | ✓✓ | 0/+1 | | |
| Fludarabine | AM | +1 | | +1 | +2 | +2/3 | ✓ | +1 | | |
| 5-Fluorouracil | AM | +1 | – | +1 | +3 | +1/2 | | | ✓ | ✓ |
| Flutamide | H | +1 | PO | O | O | O | | | | |
| Gemcitabine | AM | +2 | | +1 | +2 | +2/3 | | | | ✓ |
| Goserelin | H | +1 | PO | O | O | O | | | | |
| Hexalen | AA | +3 | PO | O | O | +1 | | | | |
| Hexamethylmelamine | AA | +3 | | O | O | +1 | | | | |
| Hydroxyurea | AM | +1 | PO | O | O | +2 | | | | |
| Idarubicin | AB | +2 | > | +3 | +2 | +3 | | | | |
| Ifosfamide | AA | +2 | | +3 | 0/+1 | +2/3 | | | | |
| Irinotecan | O | +2 | | +3 | +1 | +3 | ✓ | | | |
| Letrozole | HO | +1 | PO | O | O | O | | | | |

(continued on next page)

# Section 4: Table 1 *(continued)*

## Toxicities

| Chemo Agent | Category | N & V | Vesicant | Alopecia | Stomatitis | Myelosuppression | Peripheral Neuropathy | Pulmonary Toxicity | Cardiac Toxicity | Gonadal Toxicity |
|---|---|---|---|---|---|---|---|---|---|---|
| Leuprolide | H | 0 | PO | 0 | 0 | 0 | | | | ✓ |
| Levamisole | O | +1 | | 0 | +1 | 0 | | | | |
| Liposomal doxorubicin | O | +1 | – | +1 | 0 | +1 | | | ✓ | ✓ |
| Lomustine | AA | +2 | PO | +1 | +2 | +2/3 | | +1 | | ✓ |
| Melphalan | AA | +1 | | 0 | 0 | +2/3 | | 0/+1 | | ✓ |
| 6 Mercaptopurine | AM | +2 | PO | 0 | +1 | +2/3 | | | | |
| Methotrexate | AM | +1/2 | | 0 | +3 | +2/3 | | +1 | | ✓ |
| Mithramycin | AB | +1 | V/I | 0 | +2 | +1 | | | | ✓ |
| Mitomycin C | AB | +1/2 | V | 0 | +2 | 2 | | +2 | | ✓ |
| Mitoxantrone | AB | +1 | – | +1 | +2 | +3 | | | | |
| Nitrogen Mustard | AA | +3 | V | +1 | 0 | +2 | | | | ✓ |
| Paclitaxel | AL | +1 | – | +3 | +2 | +2/3 | ✓ | | ✓ | |
| Pentostatin | AM | +1 | | 0 | 0 | +1 | | | | |
| Plicamycin | AB | +1 | V/I | 0 | +2 | +1 | | | | |
| Procarbazine | AA | +2 | PO | 0 | +1 | +2 | ✓ | 0/+1 | | ✓ |
| Streptozotocin | AA | +3 | – | 0 | 0 | +1 | | | | |
| Suramin | O | +1 | PO | +1 | 0 | +2 | ✓ | | | |
| Tamoxifen | H | +1 | PO | 0 | 0 | 0 | | | | |
| Thioguanine | AM | +1 | PO | 0 | +2 | +2 | | | | |
| Thiotepa | AL | +1 | | 0 | +1 | +2/3 | ✓ | | | ✓ |
| Topotecan | O | +2 | | +3 | +2 | +2/3 | | | | |
| Triptorelin Pamoate | HO | +1 | | +1 | +1 | +1 | | | | ✓ |
| Vinblastine | AL | +1 | V | +1 | +2 | +2/3 | ✓ | | | ✓ |
| Vincristine | AL | +1 | V | +2 | +2 | 0/+1 | ✓ | | | ✓ |
| Vindesine | AL | +1 | V | +2 | 0 | +2 | ✓ | | | |
| Vinorelbine | AL | +2 | V | +2 | +2 | +2 | ✓ | | | ✓ |

AntiAng = Anti-angiogenesis, AF = Anti-folate, MA = Monoclonal antibody, MA/TKI = Monoclonal antibody/tyrosine kinase inhibitor, PI = Protease inhibitor

*(continued on next page)*

**Section 4: Table 1** *(continued)*

## Toxicities

| Biotherapy Agent | Category | N & V | Vesicant | Alopecia | Stomatitis | Myelosuppression | Peripheral Neuropathy | Pulmonary Toxicity | Cardiac Toxicity | Gonadal Toxicity |
|---|---|---|---|---|---|---|---|---|---|---|
| Alemtuzumab | MA/TKI | +1 | | 0 | +1 | +2/3 | 0 | √ | +1 | 0 |
| Arsenic trioxide | AntiAng | +1/2 | | | | +2 | | √ | +1 | |
| Bevacizumab | MA | +1/2 | | | | +1 | | +1 | | |
| Bortezomib | PI | +1 | | | | +1 | √ | | | |
| Cetuximab | MA/TKI | +1 | | | | +1 | | +1 | | |
| Gefitinib | TKI | 0 | PO | | +1 | | | +1 | | |
| Gemtuzumab | MA | | | | +1 | +2 | | | | |
| Ibritumomab | MA | +1 | | | | +2 | | | | |
| Imatinib mesylate | MA/TKI | +2 | PO | | | +2 | | √ | +1 | |
| Pemetrexed | AF | +1 | | | +1 | +2/3 | | | | |
| Rituximab | MA | +1 | | | | +2 | | | | |
| Thalidomide | AntiAg | +1 | PO | | | +1 | √ | +1 | √ | √ |
| Tositumomab | MA | +1 | | | | +2 | | | | |
| Trastuzumab | MA/TKI | +1 | | | | | | | √ | |

AntiAng = Anti-angiogenesis, AF = Anti-folate, MA = Monoclonal antibody, MA/TKI = Monoclonal antibody/tyrosine kinase inhibitor, PI = Protease inhibitor

Bacquiran DC. Lippincott's Cancer Chemotherapy Handbook. Philadelphia, Pa: Lippincott, Williams and Wilkins; 2001.
Casciato DA, ed. Manual of Clinical Oncology. 5th ed. Philadelphia, Pa: Lippincott, Williams and Wilkins; 2004.
Skeel RT, ed. Handbook of Cancer Chemotherapy. 6th ed. Philadelphia, Pa: Lippincott, Williams and Wilkins; 2003.

**Section 4: Table 2**

## Cardiotoxicity of Chemotherapeutic Drugs

| Classification | Drug | Incidence | Characteristic Effects | Comments |
|---|---|---|---|---|
| Antitumor antibiotic (anthracycline) | Doxorubicin | If total dose <550 mg/m² incidence is 0.1% - 1.2% (Kaszyk, 1986; Von Hoff et al, 1979). If total dose >550 mg/m² incidence rises exponentially (Von Hoff et al, 1979). If total dose is 1,000 mg/m² incidence is nearly 50% (Carlson, 1992; Von Hoff et al, 1979). Incidence may manifest during therapy for months to years afterward (Mead Johnson Oncology Products, 2001). Late effects for pediatric patients; in one study, some relevant cardiac impairments (12% of 129 patients) occurred, three of which required cardiac drug therapy (Langer et al, 2004) | ECG changes; nonspecific ST-T wave changes; premature ventricular and atrial contraction; low-voltage QRS changes; sinus tachycardia (Kaszyk, 1986) Decreased ejection fraction, sinus tachycardia, premature ventricular and atrial contractions, cardiomyopathy with symptom of CHF (Carlson, 1992). | Chronic effects seen with cumulative doses may result in CHF. Concomitant administration of other antineoplastics (eg, cyclophosphamide) has been implicated as a risk factor, although exact synergism is unclear (Burns, 1992). Cardiotoxicity at lower doses may occur in mediastinally irradiated patients and/or patients with preexisting heart disease (Adams et al, 2003). |
| | Doxorubicin liposomal Pegylated liposomal doxorubicin | Effects on the myocardium have not been confirmed. In studies of patients with AIDS-related Kaposi's sarcoma, 4.3% experienced cardiac-related adverse effects possibly related to Doxil® (Ortho Biotech, 2004). Irreversible toxicity may occur as the total dose nears 550 mg/m²; patients receiving mediastinal radiotherapy or previous or concomitant cardiotoxic therapy may experience heart failure at 400 mg/m² (Ortho Biotech, 2004). | Nonspecific arrhythmia, tachycardia, cardiomyopathy, and/or CHF. Acute left ventricular failure can occur with high doses. CHF may be unresponsive to treatment. At cumulative doses at or above 450 mg/m², a seven-fold greater mean percent decrease in LVEF was observed with doxorubicin versus Doxil (-17.2% versus -2.3%; mean percent change from baseline in LVEF in doxorubicin-treated patients and Doxil-treated patients, respectively). Ten Doxil-treated patients developed protocol-defined cardiac events, compared with 48 doxorubicin-treated patients (O'Brien et al, 2004). | Because experience with large cumulative doses is limited, consider the cardiac risk posed by doxorubicin hydrochloride liposomal to be comparable to that of conventional doxorubicin formulation. Doxil (pegylated liposomal doxorubicin), although categorized as an anthracycline, is believed to be associated with less risk of cardiotoxicity than the other anthracyclines (Escobar et al, 2003; Rivera et al, 2003). Irreversible cardiac damage is dose-limiting. Cardiotoxicity of Doxil is indicated to be lower than with conventional doxorubicin. Long-term cardiac safety is unknown (Safra, 2003). |
| | Daunorubicin | If total dose <600 mg/m², incidence is 0% - 41% (Kaszyk, 1986). If total dose 1,000 mg/m², incidence is 12% (Kaszyk, 1986). | Nonspecific arrhythmia, tachycardia, cardiomyopathy, and/or CHF. Acute left ventricular failure can occur with high doses. CHF may be unresponsive to treatment. Acute toxicity unrelated to dose may occur within hours. Although rare, myocarditis-pericarditis syndrome may be fatal (Wilkes & Burke, 2004). | Chronic effects are similar to those of doxorubicin, but higher cumulative doses may be tolerated (Von Hoff et al. 1977). Liposomal form (see below) is less cardiotoxic. |

111

*(continued on next page)*

**Cardiotoxicity of Chemotherapeutic Drugs**

| Classification | Drug | Incidence | Characteristic Effects | Comments |
|---|---|---|---|---|
| Antitumor antibiotic (anthracycline) *(continued)* | Daunorubicin citrate liposomal | Chronic therapy >300 mg/m$^2$ has increased the incidence of cardiomyopathy and CHF. In a phase III study, 13.8% of patients reported a triad of back pain, flushing, and chest tightness (Nextar Pharmaceuticals, 1999). | Cardiomyopathy associated with a decrease in LVEF, especially in patients with prior anthracycline disease experience or preexisting cardiac disease (Nextar Pharmaceuticals, 1999). | Ensure that the patient undergoes a cardiac exam before each course and at total cumulative doses of 320 mg/m$^2$ (160 g/m$^2$ for higher risk patients) and at every 160 mg/m$^2$ thereafter. Triad usually occurs during the first five minutes of infusion, subsides with infusion interruption, and generally does not recur if the infusion is resumed at a slower rate (Nextar Pharmaceuticals, 1999). |
| | Dactinomycin | Incidence is rare (Kaszyk, 1986) | – | Assessment is complicated by concomitant combination chemotherapy (including anthracyclines) or prior mediastinal radiation. Monitor vital signs before, during, and four hours after infusion. |
| | Epirubicin hydrochloride | The probability of developing clinically evident CHF is estimated as approximately 0.9% at a cumulative dose of 550 mg/m$^2$, 1.6% at 700 mg/m$^2$, and 3.3% at 900 mg/m$^2$. The total cumulative dose has been established at 400 mg/m$^2$. The risk of developing CHF increases rapidly with increasing total cumulative doses in excess of 900 mg/m$^2$; cumulative dose only should be exceeded with extreme caution (Berchem et al, 1996; Pfizer, 2003a). | Myocardial toxicity, manifested in its most severe form by potentially fatal CHF, may occur either during therapy with epirubicin or months to years after termination of therapy (Pfizer, 2003a). | Active or dormant cardiovascular disease, prior or concomitant radiotherapy to the mediastinal / pericardial area, previous therapy with other anthracyclines or anthracenediones, or concomitant use of other cardiotoxic drugs may increase the risk of cardiac toxicity. In the adjuvant treatment of breast cancer, the maximum cumulative dose used in clinical trials was 720 mg/m$^2$. Cardiac toxicity with Ellence® may occur at lower cumulative doses whether or not cardiac risk factors are present (Pfizer, 2003a). |
| Alkylating agent | Estramustine (estradiol and nonitrogen mustard) | CHF occurred in 3 in 93 patients. MI occurred in 3 in 93 patients. The recommended daily dose is 14 mg per kg of body weight (ie, one 140 mg capsule for each 10 kg or 22 lb of body weight) given in three or four divided doses. Most patients in studies in the United States have been treated at a dosage range of 10 - 16 mg/kg/day (Pfizer, 2003b). | General fluid retention; exacerbation of preexisting or incipient peripheral edema or CHF has been seen in some patients. Men receiving estrogens for prostatic cancer are at increased risk for thrombosis, including fatal and nonfatal myocardial infarction (Pfizer, 2003b). | Emcyt® capsules should be used with caution in patients with a history of cerebral vascular or coronary artery disease. Because hypertension may occur, blood pressure should be monitored periodically (Pfizer, 2003b). |

112

*(continued on next page)*

## Cardiotoxicity of Chemotherapeutic Drugs

| Classification | Drug | Incidence | Characteristic Effects | Comments |
|---|---|---|---|---|
| High-dose therapy | Cyclophosphamide | Toxicity is rare with cumulative or standard doses. Some reports of increased frequency with high-dose therapy, >180–200 mg/kg/day x four days (Allen, 1992; Bristol-Myers Squibb Oncology/Immunology, 2000). Pediatric patients with thalassemia have been shown to have a potential for cardiac tamponade when cyclophosphamide is given with busulfan (FDA, 1998). | ECG: Diminished QRS complex ECG: Diminished QRS complex ac tamponade in children often is preceded by complaints of abdominal pain and vomiting (FDA, 1998). | May result in acute lethal pericarditis, pericardial effusion, cardiac tamponade, and hemorrhagic myocardial necrosis (Mills & Roberts, 1979; Wujcik & Downs, 1992). Cardiotoxicity usually is related to high doses for short intervals prior to BMT (Allen, 1992). Cases of cardiomyopathy with subsequent death have been reported following experimental high-dose therapy with cytarabine in combination with cyclophosphamide when used for BMT preparation (FDA, 1998). |
| | 5-fluorouracil | Incidence is 1.6% (Labianca et al, 1982). One death was reported from myocardia ischemia (Soe et al, 1996). | Angina, palpitations, sweating, and/or syncope (Akhtar et al, 1993). Severe but reversible cardiogenic shock (Akhtar et al, 1996) | May be treated prophylactically or therapeutically with long-acting nitrates or calcium channel blockers (Eskilsson et al, 1988). |
| | Capecitabine | Incidence is rare; incidence of cardiotoxicity associated with fluorinated pyrimidine therapy is 1% (Bertolini et al, 2001; Roche Pharmaceuticals, 2004; Van Cutsem et al, 2002). | Myocardial infarction, angina, dysrhythmias, cardiogenic shock, sudden death, and electrocardiograph changes | These adverse events may be more common in patients with a prior history of coronary artery disease. Interrupt drug if grade II or III adverse reactions occur; discontinue drug if grade IV (FDA, 2001; Roche Pharmaceuticals, 2004). |
| Taxane | Paclitaxel | Asymptomatic bradycardia occurred in almost 30% of patients with ovarian cancer; cardiac ischemia occurred in 5% (Rowinsky et al, 1991). Other disturbances: 5% (not associated with clinical symptoms. Significant cardiac events occurred in 3% of all cases (Bristol-Myers Squibb Oncology/Immunology, 2000). It has been reported that Cremophor EL® activates histamine receptors. Rare reports of MI. CHF has been reported in cases of patients receiving other chemotherapy agents. (Bristol-Myers Squibb, 2000; D'Incalci et al, 1998; Patel et al, 2000). | Asymptomatic bradycardia, hypotension, asymptomatic ventricular tachycardia, atypical chest pain. | Toxicity has been documented as asymptomatic bradycardia (40–60 bpm), hypotension, asymptomatic ventricular tachycardia, and atypical chest pain. Obtain a baseline ECG, patient history, and cardiac assessment before treatment; however, routine cardiac monitoring during infusion is not recommended (Arbuck et al, 1992; Fischer et al, 1993; Rowinsky at al, 1991). |

*(continued on next page)*

**Section 4: Table 2** *(continued)*

## Cardiotoxicity of Chemotherapeutic Drugs

| Classification | Drug | Incidence | Characteristic Effects | Comments |
|---|---|---|---|---|
| Taxane | Docetaxel | Few reports<br>Hypotension is 2.8% (1.8% required treatment).<br>Incidence related to high-dose treatment is unknown (Aventis Pharmaceuticals, 2003). | CHF occurred in patients also treated with doxorubicin (>360 mg/m$^2$) (Sparano, 1999). Heart failure, sinus tachycardia, atrial flutter, dysrhythmia, unstable angina, pulmonary edema, and/or hypertension (Aventis Pharmaceuticals, 2003) | Well tolerated in elderly patients with non-small cell lung cancer (Hainsworth et al, 2000) |
| Monoclonal antibody | Gemtuzumab ozogamicin | Effects are infrequent and acute infusion related at 9 mg/m$^2$ (all grade incidents): hypertension, 16% of participants; hypotension, 20%; and tachycardia, 11% (often in the first 24 hours of infusion) (Wyeth Pharmaceuticals, 2004). | Hypertension, tachycardia, hypotension | Monitor vital signs before, during, and four hours after infusion.<br>See comments about dactinomycin. |
| | Trastuzumab | Incidence with Herceptin® as a single agent: 7%<br>Incidence with paclitaxel: 11%<br>When combined with anthracycline and cyclophosphamide: 28%<br>The data suggest that advanced age may increase the probability of cardiac dysfunction (Genentech, Inc., 2003). | Signs and symptoms of cardiac dysfunction observed in patients treated with Herceptin include dyspnea, increased cough, paroxysmal nocturnal dyspnea, peripheral edema, S$_3$ gallop, or reduced ejection fraction (Genentech, Inc., 2003). Reducing the rate decreased infusion-related events for first infusion by 80%; 40% for subsequent infusions (Genentech, Inc., 2003). | CHF has been associated with disabling cardiac failure, death, and mural thrombosis leading to stroke.<br>Discontinuation of therapy is strongly considered for those with significant CHF or asymptomatic ejection fraction decreases.<br>Extreme caution should be exercised in treating patients with preexisting cardiac dysfunction.<br>Patients receiving Herceptin should undergo frequent monitoring for deteriorating cardiac function (Genentech, Inc., 2003).<br>Some severe reactions have been treated successfully with interruption of the Herceptin infusion and administration of supportive therapy including oxygen, IV fluids, beta agonists, and corticosteroids (Genentech, Inc., 2003). |
| | Rituximab | Cardiac toxicity when used as a single agent is unknown.<br>Infusion-related deaths within 24 hours: 0.04%–0.07% (Genentech/IDEC Pharmaceuticals, 1999)<br>Incidence of mild to moderate hypotension requiring treatment interruption: 10%<br>Incidence of angioedema: 13% | Hypotension and angioedema<br>Infusion-related complex includes these cardiac events: myocardial infarction, ventricular fibrillation, or cardiogenic shock (Genentech/IDEC Pharmaceuticals, 1999). | Nearly all fatalities have occurred on first infusion.<br>Discontinue and medically treat patients who develop clinically significant cardiopulmonary reactions.<br>After symptoms resolve, resume treatment by reducing the infusion rate by 50% (eg, reduce an initial infusion rate of 100 mg/hour to 50 mg/hour). |

*(continued on next page)*

114

**Section 4: Table 2** (continued)

## Cardiotoxicity of Chemotherapeutic Drugs

| Classification | Drug | Incidence | Characteristic Effects | Comments |
|---|---|---|---|---|
| Antimetabolite | Gemcitabine hydrochloride | CHF and MI have been reported rarely with the use of gemcitabine. Arrhythmias, predominantly supraventricular in nature, have been reported very rarely. Incidence of hypotension is 11% when given with cisplatin. Hypotension study of Gemza® maximum tolerated dose above 1,000 mg/m² on a daily x 5 dose schedule showed that patients developed significant hypotension (Eli Lilly & Co., 2004). | Hypotension, myocardial infarction, arrhythmia, hypertension (Eli Lilly & Co., 2004) | Age, gender, and infusion time factors: Lower clearance in women and the elderly results in higher concentrations of gemcitabine for any given dose. Increased toxicity when administered more frequently than once weekly or with infusions longer than 60 minutes (Eli Lilly & Co., 2004) |
| | Cladribine | Serious side effects are rare (Bryson & Sorkin, 1993). Incidence of edema and tachycardia is 6%. Incidence of chest pain has been reported (Ortho Biotech, 2002; Wilkes & Burke, 2004). | Tachycardia, edema, chest pain | Most events occurred in patients with a history of cardiovascular disease or chest tumors (Bryson & Sorkin, 1993). |
| Plant alkaloid | Vinorelbine tartrate | There have been rare reports of MI with Navelbine®. Chest pain was reported in 5% of patients (GlaxoSmithKline, 2002). | Hypertension, hypotension, vasodilation, tachycardia, and pulmonary edema have been reported (GlaxoSmithKline, 2002). | Most reports of chest pain were in patients who had either a history of cardiovascular disease or tumor within the chest (GlaxoSmithKline, 2002). |
| Interleukin | Interleukin-2 | Side effects following the use of Proleukin® IL-2 (aldesleukin) appear to be dose-related. Risk increases with doses >100,000 U/kg (Wilkes & Burke, 2004). Average dose is 600,000 IU/kg (Chiron Corporation, 2004). Most adverse reactions are self-limiting and usually, but not invariably, reverse or improve within two to three days of discontinuation of therapy. Aldesleukin administration has been associated with CLS. The rate of drug-related deaths in the 255 patients with metastatic renal cell carcinoma who received single-agent aldesleukin was 4% (11/255); the rate of drug-related deaths in the 270 patients with metastatic melanoma who received single-agent aldesleukin was 2% (6/270). | Alteration in cardiac output resulting from CLS (loss of vascular tone and extravasation of plasma proteins and fluid into the extravascular space). CLS results in hypotension and reduced organ perfusion, which may be severe and can result in death. CLS may be associated with cardiac arrhythmias (supraventricular and ventricular), CHF, angina, pleural and pericardial effusion, myocarditis, chest pain, and (rarely) MI (Chiron Corporation, 2004; Wilkes & Burke, 2004). CLS begins immediately after aldesleukin treatment starts. In most patients, this results in a concomitant drop in mean arterial blood pressure within 2 - 12 hours after the start of treatment. With continued therapy, clinically significant hypotension (systolic blood pressure 90 mmHg or a 20 mmHg drop from baseline systolic pressure) and hypoperfusion will occur (Chiron Corporation, 2004). | Aldesleukin administration should be withheld in patients developing moderate to severe lethargy or somnolence; continued administration may result in coma. Should adverse events that require dose modification occur, dosage should be withheld rather than reduced. Patients should have normal cardiac, pulmonary, hepatic, and CNS function at the start of therapy. Medical management of CLS begins with careful monitoring of the patient's fluid and organ perfusion status; this is achieved by frequent determination of blood pressure and pulse and by monitoring organ function, which includes assessment of mental status and urine output. Hypovolemia is assessed by catheterization and central pressure monitoring. Dose modification for toxicity should be accomplished by withholding or interrupting a dose rather than reducing the dose to be given. |

**115**

BMT = bone marrow transplant; CHF = congestive heart failure; CLS = capillary leak syndrome; CNS = central nervous system; ECG = electrocardiogram;

LVEF = left ventricular ejection fraction; MI = myocardial infarction

Chemotherapy and Biotherapy Guidelines and Recommendations for Practice. 2nd ed. Pittsburgh, Pa: Oncology Nursing Press; 2005. Reprinted with permission.

**Section 4: Table 3**

## Pulmonary Toxicity of Chemotherapeutic Drugs

| Classification | Drug | Incidence | Characteristic Effects and Comments |
|---|---|---|---|
| Alkylating agents | Busulfan | Incidence is rare but serious. Busulfan is associated with pulmonary damage and pneumonitis. It occurs in between 2.5% and 11.5% of patients, usually those on long-term treatment, although it can occur more acutely. A progressive and often untreatable pneumonitis is an important complication of therapy. Bronchopulmonary dysplasia with pulmonary fibrosis occurs with chronic therapy (GlaxoSmithKline, 2004). | Insidious onset cough, dyspnea, and low-grade fever; bronchodysplasia progressing to interstitial pulmonary fibrosis ("busulfan lung") (Wilkes & Burke, 2004) Bronchopulmonary dysplasia with pulmonary fibrosis is a rare but serious complication following chronic busulfan therapy. The average onset of symptoms is four years after therapy; delayed onsets have occurred (range = 4 months - 10 years) (GlaxoSmithKline, 2004). Chest x-rays show diffuse linear densities, sometimes with reticular nodular or nodular infiltrates or consolidation. Pleural effusions have occurred (GlaxoSmithKline, 2004; Smalley & Wall, 1966). |
| | Chlorambucil | Incidence is low. Respiratory dysfunction is reported at high doses (GlaxoSmithKline, 2003c). | Pulmonary fibrosis; bronchopulmonary dysplasia in patients receiving long-term therapy (GlaxoSmithKline, 2003c) |
| | Cyclophosphamide | The incidence of cyclophosphamide pulmonary toxicity is rare. Diffuse alveolar damage is the most common manifestation of cyclophosphamide-induced lung disease (Rossi et al, 2000). There is no relationship between development of lung injury and dose or duration of administration (Erasmus, 2000). | Edema, fibrosis, alveolar hemorrhage, and fibrin deposition (Twohig & Matthay, 1990); onset can be six months or longer. Interstitial pneumonitis has been reported as part of the postmarketing experience. Interstitial pulmonary fibrosis has been reported in patients receiving high doses of cyclophosphamide over a prolonged period (Mead Johnson Oncology, 2000). Anaphylactic reactions and death also have been reported in association with this event. Possible cross-sensitivity with other alkylating agents has been reported (Mead Johnson Oncology, 2000). Treatment is discontinuation of the agent, and steroids have good to variable response (Mead Johnson Oncology, 2000). |
| | Melphalan | Reports of bronchopulmonary dysplasia (GlaxoSmithKline, 2003a) Acute hypersensitivity reactions including anaphylaxis were reported in 2.4% of 425 patients receiving the injected drug for myeloma (GlaxoSmithKline, 2003a). | Pulmonary fibrosis, interstitial pneumonia, bronchospasm, and dyspnea also may be a sign of rare hypersensitivity, not pulmonary toxicity. These patients appeared to respond to antihistamine and corticosteroid therapy. If a hypersensitivity reaction occurs, IV or oral melphalan should not be readministered because hypersensitivity reactions also have been reported with oral melphalan (GlaxoSmithKline, 2003a). |
| | Oxaliplatin | Associated with pulmonary fibrosis (<1% of study patients), which may be fatal Incidence of events increase with combined therapy. An acute syndrome of pharyngolaryngeal dysesthesia seen in 1% - 2% (grade 3 or 4) of patients previously untreated for advanced colorectal cancer. Previously treated patients experienced subjective sensations of dysphagia or dyspnea, without laryngospasm or bronchospasm (no stridor or wheezing) (Sanofi-Synthelabo, Inc., 2004). | Anaphylactic-like reactions are treatable with epinephrine, corticosteroids, and antihistamines. The combined incidence of cough, dyspnea, and hypoxia was 43% (any grade) and 7% (grades 3 and 4) in the oxaliplatin plus 5-FU/LV arm compared to 32% (any grade) and 5% (grades 3 and 4) in the irinotecan plus 5-FU/LV arm of unknown duration for patients with previously untreated colorectal cancer. In case of unexplained respiratory symptoms such as nonproductive cough, dyspnea, crackles, or radiologic pulmonary infiltrates, oxaliplatin should be discontinued until further pulmonary investigation excludes interstitial lung disease or pulmonary fibrosis (Sanofi - Synthelabo, Inc., 2004). |

. (continued on next page)

## Pulmonary Toxicity of Chemotherapeutic Drugs

| Classification | Drug | Incidence | Characteristic Effects and Comments |
|---|---|---|---|
| Alkylating agents *(continued)* | Temozolomide | Upper respiratory tract infection: 8%<br>Pharyngitis: 8%<br>Sinusitis: 6%<br>Coughing: 5%<br>(Schering Corporation, 2004) | Allergic reactions, including rare cases of anaphylaxis; used with nitrosoureas and procarbazine (Schering Corporation, 2004) |
| Anticancer cytokines | Aldesleukin (IL-2) | Life-threatening grade IV:<br>• Dyspnea: 1%<br>• Respiratory disorders: 3% (acute respiratory distress syndrome [ARDS], respiratory failure, intubation); 1% (apnea)<br>Adverse events occurring in ≥10% of patients (N = 525) (Chiron Corporation, 2002)<br>• Dyspnea: 43%<br>• Lung disorder: 24% (physical findings associated with pulmonary congestion, rales, rhonchi)<br>• Respiratory disorder: 11% (ARDS, chest x-ray infiltrates, unspecified pulmonary changes)<br>• Increased cough: 11%<br>• Rhinitis: 10% | Pulmonary congestion, dyspnea, pulmonary edema, respiratory failure, tachypnea, pleural effusion, wheezing, apnea, pneumothorax, hemoptysis (Chiron Corporation, 2002) |
| | Interferon alfa-2b | Rare (Schering Corporation, 2002) | Fever, cough, dyspnea, pulmonary infiltrates, pneumonitis, pneumonia |
| | Oprelvekin (IL 11) | Dyspnea: 48%<br>Increased cough: 29%<br>Pharyngitis: 25%<br>Pleural effusions: 10%<br>(Wyeth Pharmaceuticals, 2004b) | Peripheral edema, dyspnea; preexisting fluid collections, including pericardial effusions or ascites, should be monitored. Fluid retention is reversible within several days following discontinuation of the oprelvekin.<br>Fluid balance should be monitored, and appropriate medical management is advised.<br>Closely monitor fluid and electrolyte status in patients receiving chronic diuretic therapy (Wyeth Pharmaceuticals, 2004b).<br>Patients should be advised to immediately seek medical attention if any of the following signs or symptoms develop: swelling of the face, tongue, or throat; difficulty breathing, swallowing, or talking; shortness of breath; wheezing (Wyeth Pharmaceuticals, 2004b). |
| Antimetabolites | Capecitabine | Dyspnea: 14% (Roche Pharmaceuticals, 2003)<br>Not considered a major toxicity but has demonstrated these side effects: 0.1% cough; 0.1% epistaxis and hemoptysis and respiratory distress; 0.2% asthma | Manage toxicities with symptomatic treatment, dose interruptions, and dose adjustment. Once dose has been adjusted, it should not be increased at a later time (Roche Pharmaceuticals, 2003). |
| | Cytarabine | "Cytarabine syndrome" in doses >5 g/m² (6 - 12 hours after dose) (Castleberry et al, 1981; Spratto & Woods, 2004)<br>Cytarabine liposomal: No pulmonary data (Chiron Corporation, 2000). | A syndrome of sudden respiratory distress, rapidly progressing to pulmonary edema, capillary leak syndrome, respiratory failure, and adult respiratory disease (Haupt et al, 1981) |

*(continued on next page)*

117

**Section 4: Table 3** *(continued)*

## Pulmonary Toxicity of Chemotherapeutic Drugs

| Classification | Drug | Incidence | Characteristic Effects and Comments |
|---|---|---|---|
| Antimetabolites *(continued)* | Fludarabine phosphate | Cough: 10%*; 44%**<br>Pneumonia: 16%*; 22%**<br>Dyspnea: 9%*; 22%**<br>Sinusitis: 5%*; 0%**<br>Pharyngitis: 0%*; 9%**<br>Upper respiratory infection: 2%*; 16%**<br>Allergic pneumonitis: 0%*; 6%**<br>*N = 101; **N = 32 (Berlex Laboratories, 2003) | Pulmonary hypersensitivity reactions such as dyspnea, cough, and interstitial pulmonary infiltrate have been observed.<br>In a clinical investigation using fludarabine phosphate injection in combination with pentostatin for the treatment of refractory chronic lymphocytic leukemia in adults, there was an unacceptably high incidence of fatal pulmonary toxicity. Therefore, this combination is not recommended (Berlex Laboratories, 2003). |
| | Gemcitabine hydrochloride | Dyspnea: 23% (severe dyspnea in 3%) (Eli Lilly & Co., 2004)<br>Parenchymal lung toxicity, including interstitial pneumonitis, pulmonary fibrosis, pulmonary edema, and adult respiratory distress syndrome, has been reported rarely (Eli Lilly & Co., 2004). | Dyspnea, cough, bronchospasm, and parenchymal lung toxicity (rare) may occur. If such effects develop, gemcitabine should be discontinued. Early use of supportive care measures may help to ameliorate these conditions (Eli Lilly & Co., 2004).<br>Prolonged infusion time beyond 60 minutes and doses more than once weekly increase toxicities (Castleberry et al, 1981; Spratto & Woods, 2004).<br>Respiratory failure and death occurred very rarely in some patients despite discontinuation of therapy (Pavlakis et al, 1997).<br>Some patients experienced the onset of pulmonary symptoms up to two weeks after the last dose (Eli Lilly & Co., 2004). |
| | Methotrexate | Pulmonary edema: 1% - 2% (Immunex, 1999)<br>The incidence of pulmonary toxicity in patients receiving methotrexate is 5% - 10% (Rossi et al, 2000). The toxicity is not dose related, although patients who receive treatment more frequently may be more susceptible to lung injury (Aronchick & Gefter, 1991). | Fever, dyspnea, cough (especially dry nonproductive), nonspecific pneumonitis, or a chronic interstitial obstructive pulmonary disease (deaths have been reported); pulmonary infiltrates (Immunex, 1999) |
| Antitumor antibiotics | Bleomycin sulfate | 10% of treated patients (Bristol-Myers Squibb Oncology/Immunology, 1999). Nonspecific pneumonitis in approximately 1% progresses to pulmonary fibrosis and death.<br>More common in patients older than 70 years of age receiving more than 400 units total dose. Toxicity is unpredictable and has been seen occasionally in young patients receiving low doses (Bristol-Myers Squibb Oncology/Immunology, 1999).<br>Possible lower toxicity if not given IV bolus (Bristol-Myers Squibb Oncology/Immunology, 1999; Chisholm et al, 1992) | The characteristics of bleomycin-induced pneumonitis include dyspnea and fine rales. Bleomycin-induced pneumonitis produces patchy x-ray opacities usually of the lower lung fields that look the same as infectious bronchopneumonia or even lung metastases in some patients.<br>Early toxicity may be self-resolving. Monitor for early warning signs of toxicity to avoid irreversible pulmonary damage.<br>Chest x-rays should be taken every one to two weeks. If pulmonary changes are noted, treatment should be discontinued. Conflicting studies regarding exposure to increasing concentrations of oxygen-increasing toxicity warrants prudently maintaining oxygen levels at room air (25%) (Bristol-Myers Squibb Oncology/Immunology, 1999).<br>Carbon monoxide diffusion capacity may be abnormal before other symptoms appear (Sleijfer et al, 1995). |

*(continued on next page)*

**Section 4: Table 3** *(continued)*

## Pulmonary Toxicity of Chemotherapeutic Drugs

| Classification | Drug | Incidence | Characteristic Effects and Comments |
|---|---|---|---|
| Antitumor antibiotics *(continued)* | Doxorubicin hydrochloride liposome | Serious and sometimes life-threatening or fatal allergic/anaphylactoid-like infusion reactions have been reported (Ortho Biotech Corporation, 2003). | Acute infusion-related pulmonary reactions include shortness of breath and tightness of the throat (other reactions include, but are not limited to, flushing, facial swelling, headache, chills, back pain, tightness in the chest, and/or hypotension). In most patients, these reactions resolve over the course of several hours to a day once the infusion is terminated. In some patients, the reaction has resolved with slowing of the infusion rate. Doxil® should be administered at an initial rate of 1 mg/minute to minimize the risk of infusion reactions (Ortho Biotech Corporation, 2003). |
| | Mitomycin | Pulmonary toxicity has been reported with both single-agent therapy and combination chemotherapy, 3% - 36%, 6 - 12 months after therapy.<br>Prior treatment with mitomycin, cumulative doses >30 mg/m², and other anticancer drugs may increase risk of toxicity (Bristol-Myers Squibb Oncology, 2000). | Dyspnea, nonproductive cough, diffuse alveolar damage, capillary leak, and pulmonary edema; severe bronchospasm has been reported following administration of vinca alkaloids in patients who previously or simultaneously received mitomycin. Acute respiratory distress occurred within minutes to hours after the vinca alkaloid injection. The total doses for each drug varied considerably (Bristol-Myers Squibb Oncology, 2000).<br>Signs and symptoms of pneumonitis associated with mitomycin may be reversed if appropriate therapy is instituted early. Drug may be discontinued if dyspnea occurs even with normal chest radiograph (Luedke et al., 1985).<br>Caution should be exercised using oxygen, because oxygen itself is toxic to the lungs.<br>Pay careful attention to fluid balance and avoid overhydration (Bristol-Myers Squibb Oncology, 2000). |
| | Mitoxantrone | Reports of pulmonary toxicity (Immunex, 2000) | Interstitial pneumonitis |
| Miscellaneous antineoplastic agents | Arsenic trioxide | Incidence of respiratory events (all grades, N = 40):<br>• Cough: 65%<br>• Dyspnea: 53%<br>• Epistaxis: 25%<br>• Hypoxia: 23%<br>• Pleural effusion: 20%<br>• Wheezing: 13%<br>Grade 3 and 4:<br>• Dyspnea: 10%<br>• Hypoxia: 10%<br>• Pleural effusion: 3%<br>(Cell Therapeutics, 2004) | These adverse effects have not been observed to be permanent or irreversible, nor do they usually require interruption of therapy (Cell Therapeutics, 2004). |

*(continued on next page)*

119

**Section 4: Table 3** *(continued)*

## Pulmonary Toxicity of Chemotherapeutic Drugs

120

| Classification | Drug | Incidence | Characteristic Effects and Comments |
|---|---|---|---|
| Miscellaneous antineoplastic agents *(continued)* | Gefitinib | Cases of interstitial lung disease have been observed in patients at an overall incidence of about 1%. Approximately one-third of the cases have been fatal. Reports indicated that interstitial lung disease has occurred in patients who have received prior radiation therapy (31%), prior chemotherapy (57%), and no previous therapy (12%) (AstraZeneca Pharmaceuticals, 2004). | Interstitial pneumonia, pneumonitis, and alveolitis. Patients often present with the acute onset of dyspnea, sometimes associated with cough or low-grade fever, often becoming severe within a short time and requiring hospitalization. If acute onset or worsening pulmonary symptoms (dyspnea, cough, fever) occurs, therapy should be interrupted and promptly investigated. If interstitial lung disease is confirmed, discontinue Iressa®. Increased mortality has been observed in patients with concurrent idiopathic pulmonary fibrosis whose condition worsens while receiving gefitinib (AstraZeneca Pharmaceuticals, 2004). |
| | Imatinib mesylate | Severe superficial edema and severe fluid retention (pleural effusion, pulmonary edema, and ascites) were reported in 1% - 6% of patients taking imatinib for gastrointestinal stromal tumors. 14% - 15% reported dyspnea. Interstitial pneumonitis and pulmonary fibrosis are rare (Novartis Pharmaceuticals, 2004). | 54% - 74% of patients (two studies) had fluid retention, making pulmonary events difficult to identify. Other fluid retention events include pleural effusion, ascites, pulmonary edema, pericardial effusion, anasarca, edema aggravated, and fluid retention not otherwise specified. The overall safety profile of pediatric patients (39 children studied) was similar to that found in studies with adult patients treated with imatinib; however, no peripheral edema has been reported (Novartis Pharmaceuticals, 2004). |
| | Irinotecan hydrochloride | Severe pulmonary events are rare, 4% grades 3 and 4; dyspnea (Pharmacia & Upjohn, 2002). | Dyspnea, increased coughing, rhinitis, and pneumonia Actual toxicity caused by the drug alone is unknown because more than half of patients had malignant or preexisting lung disease, and many were on combination therapy (Pharmacia & Upjohn, 2002). Irinotecan should not be used in combination with the "Mayo Clinic" regimen of 5-FU/leucovorin (administration for four to five consecutive days every four weeks) because of reports of increased toxicity, including toxic deaths (Pharmacia & Upjohn, 2002). |
| | Topotecan hydrochloride | The incidence of grades 3 and/or 4 dyspnea was 4% in patients with ovarian cancer and 12% in patients with small cell lung cancer. All grades, dyspnea: 22% (GlaxoSmithKline, 2003b) | Dyspnea, coughing, and pneumonia are the main pulmonary side effects (GlaxoSmithKline, 2003b). |
| Monoclonal antibodies | Alemtuzumab | Infusion rate-related dyspnea: 17% Acute infusion-related events were most common during the first week of therapy. Incidence (N = 149)<br>• Dyspnea: 26%<br>• Cough: 25%<br>• Bronchitis/pneumonitis: 21%<br>• Pneumonia: 16%<br>• Pharyngitis: 12%<br>• Bronchospasm: 9%<br>• Rhinitis: 7%   (Berlex Laboratories, 2002) | Alemtuzumab has been associated with infusion-related events, including hypotension, rigors, fever, shortness of breath, bronchospasm, chills, and/or rash. To ameliorate or avoid infusion-related events, patients should be premedicated with an oral antihistamine and acetaminophen prior to dosing and monitored closely for infusion-related adverse events. Side effects include asthma, bronchitis, chronic obstructive pulmonary disease, hemoptysis, hypoxia, pleural effusion, pleurisy, pneumothorax, pulmonary edema, pulmonary fibrosis, pulmonary infiltration, respiratory depression, respiratory insufficiency, sinusitis, stridor, and throat tightness (Berlex Laboratories, 2002). |

*(continued on next page)*

# Section 4: Table 3 *(continued)*

## Pulmonary Toxicity of Chemotherapeutic Drugs

| Classification | Drug | Incidence | Characteristic Effects and Comments |
|---|---|---|---|
| Monoclonal antibodies *(continued)* | Gemtuzumab ozogamicin | Hypoxia: 5%<br>Pharyngitis: 12%<br>Pneumonia: 13%<br>Increased cough: 17%<br>Epistaxis: 28%<br>Dyspnea: 32% (often during the first 24 hours)<br>Severe pulmonary events leading to death have been reported infrequently (Wyeth Pharmaceuticals, 2004a). | Signs, symptoms, and clinical findings include dyspnea, pulmonary infiltrates, pleural effusions, noncardiogenic pulmonary edema, pulmonary insufficiency and hypoxia, and ARDS. These events occur as sequelae of infusion reactions.<br>Monitor for increased cough, dyspnea, pharyngitis, and pneumonia, and check vital signs before, during, and four hours after infusion.<br>Patients with white cell counts >30,000 µL may be at increased risk; also, patients with symptomatic intrinsic lung disease may have more severe pulmonary reactions.<br>Do not administer as an IV push or bolus (Wyeth Pharmaceuticals, 2004a). |
| | Rituximab | 38% (N = 135) experienced pulmonary events in clinical trials.<br>Infusion-related deaths involving pulmonary function: 0.04% - 0.07%.<br>Bronchospasm: 8% (Genentech, Inc., 2003b) | Most common respiratory system adverse events experienced were increased cough, rhinitis, bronchospasm, dyspnea, and sinusitis.<br>Infusion-related symptom complex includes pulmonary effects: hypoxia, bronchospasm, dyspnea, pulmonary infiltrates, and ARDS (Genentech, Inc., 2003b).<br>There have been reports of bronchiolitis obliterans presenting up to six months postinfusion and a limited number of reports of pneumonitis (including interstitial pneumonitis) presenting up to three months postinfusion, some of which resulted in fatal outcomes.<br>Treatment should be interrupted for severe reactions and resumed at 50% reduced infusion rate when symptoms resolve. The safety of resuming or continuing administration of rituximab in patients with pneumonitis or bronchiolitis obliterans is unknown (Genentech, Inc., 2003b). |
| | Trastuzumab | As a single agent:<br>Increased cough: 26%<br>Dyspnea: 22%<br>Pharyngitis: 12%<br>In the postmarketing setting, severe hypersensitivity reactions (including anaphylaxis), infusion reactions, and pulmonary adverse events have been reported (Severe pulmonary events leading to death have been reported rarely). (Genentech, Inc., 2003a). | Increased cough, dyspnea, rhinitis, pharyngitis, pulmonary infiltrates, pleural effusions, noncardiac edema, pulmonary insufficiency, hypoxia, and ARDS (Genentech, Inc., 2003a)<br>Other severe events reported rarely in the postmarketing setting include pneumonitis and pulmonary fibrosis (Genentech, Inc., 2003a).<br>Patients with symptomatic intrinsic lung disease or with extensive tumor involvement of the lungs, resulting in dyspnea at rest, may be at greater risk for severe reactions. Adverse effects increase with combined drug therapy (Genentech, Inc., 2003a). |
| Nitrosoureas | Carmustine | Although rare, cases of fatal pulmonary toxicity have been reported. Most of these patients were receiving prolonged therapy with total doses of carmustine greater than 1,400 mg/m². However, there have been reports of pulmonary fibrosis in patients receiving lower total doses (Bristol-Myers Squibb Oncology, 1998a).<br>In a long-term study of carmustine, all those initially treated at younger than five years of age died of delayed pulmonary fibrosis (Bristol-Myers Squibb Oncology, 1998a). | Pulmonary infiltrates and/or fibrosis have been reported to occur from 9 days to 43 months after treatment and appear to be dose-related. Fibrosis may be slowly progressive (Bristol-Myers Squibb Oncology, 1998a).<br>When used in high doses (300 - 600 mg/m²) prior to bone marrow transplantation, pulmonary toxicity may occur and may be dose limiting. The pulmonary toxicity of high-dose carmustine may manifest as severe interstitial pneumonitis, which occurs most frequently in patients who have had recent radiation to the mediastinum.<br>Perform baseline and regular pulmonary function tests, especially in patients with risk factors or who have received > 800 mg/m². There is a linear relationship between total dose and pulmonary toxicity at doses >1,000 mg/m², with 50% of patients developing pulmonary toxicity at total cumulative doses of 1,500 mg/m². Risk factors include preexisting lung disease, smoking, cyclophosphamide therapy, and recent (within months) thoracic radiation. Patients with baseline forced vital capacity and/or pulmonary diffusion capacity for carbon monoxide that are less than 70% of the predicted value are at high risk (Bristol-Myers Squibb Oncology, 1998a). |

*(continued on next page)*

**Pulmonary Toxicity of Chemotherapeutic Drugs**

| Classification | Drug | Incidence | Characteristic Effects and Comments |
|---|---|---|---|
| Nitrosoureas *(continued)* | Lomustine | Rare, usually in doses >1,100 mg/m² (one reported case at a dose of 600 mg) (Bristol-Myers Squibb Oncology, 1998b) There appeared to be some late reduction of pulmonary function of all long-term survivors. This form of lung fibrosis may be slowly progressive and has resulted in death in some cases (Bristol-Myers Squibb Oncology, 1998b). | Pulmonary toxicity characterized by pulmonary infiltrates and/or fibrosis has been reported rarely with lomustine. Onset of toxicity has occurred after an interval of six months or longer from the start of therapy with cumulative doses of lomustine usually >1,100 mg/m² (Bristol-Myers Squibb Oncology, 1998b). Delayed onset pulmonary fibrosis occurring up to 17 years after treatment has been reported in patients who received nitrosoureas in childhood and early adolescence (1-16 years) combined with cranial radiotherapy for intracranial tumors (Bristol-Myers Squibb Oncology, 1998b). |
| Plant alkaloids | Docetaxel | Unknown if drug is actual cause of toxicity (Aventis Pharmaceuticals, 2003; Merad et al, 1997) | Pulmonary infiltrates, pleural effusion, pulmonary edema Reversible with diuretics (Aventis Pharmaceuticals, 2003) |
| | Etoposide | Reported cases of pulmonary events have been infrequently reported: interstitial pneumonitis/pulmonary fibrosis; anaphylactic-like reactions characterized by chills, fever, tachycardia, bronchospasm, dyspnea, and/or hypotension have been reported to occur in 0.7% - 2% of patients receiving IV etoposide and in less than 1% of patients treated with the oral capsules (Bristol Laboratories, 1998). | Anaphylactic-like reactions have occurred during the initial infusion of etoposide. Facial/tongue swelling, coughing, diaphoresis, cyanosis, tightness in throat, laryngospasm, back pain, and/or loss of consciousness have sometimes occurred in association with the above reactions. In addition, an apparent hypersensitivity-associated apnea has been reported rarely. Higher rates of anaphylactic-like reactions have been reported in children who received infusions at concentrations higher than those recommended. The role that concentration of infusion (or rate of infusion) plays in the development of anaphylactic-like reactions is uncertain. Treatment is symptomatic. The infusion should be terminated immediately, followed by the administration of pressor agents, corticosteroids, antihistamines, or volume expanders at the discretion of the physician (Bristol Laboratories, 1998). |
| | Paclitaxel | Rare for single agent: 2% dyspnea Rare reports of interstitial pneumonia, lung fibrosis, and pulmonary embolism (Bristol-Myers Squibb Oncology, 2003) 8.5% - 9% combined therapy Events occur usually in high doses or in combined therapy (Bristol-Myers Squibb Oncology, 2003; Dunsford et al, 1999). | Hypersensitivity pneumonitis (Dunsford et al, 1999) Rare reports of radiation pneumonitis have been received in patients receiving concurrent radiotherapy (Bristol-Myers Squibb Oncology, 2003). |
| | Vinorelbine tartrate | Shortness of breath was reported in 3% of patients; it was severe in 2% receiving vinorelbine. Rare but <u>severe</u>: Reported cases of interstitial pulmonary changes and ARDS, most of which were fatal, occurred in patients treated with single-agent vinorelbine (GlaxoSmithKline, 2002). | Acute shortness of breath and severe bronchospasm, most commonly when vinorelbine was used in combination with mitomycin. These adverse events may require treatment with supplemental oxygen, bronchodilators, and/or corticosteroids, particularly when there is preexisting pulmonary dysfunction. The mean time to onset of these symptoms after vinorelbine administration was one week (range = 3 - 8 days). Patients with alterations in their baseline pulmonary symptoms or with new onset of dyspnea, cough, hypoxia, or other symptoms should be evaluated promptly (GlaxoSmithKline, 2002). |

*Chemotherapy and Biotherapy Guidelines and Recommendations for Practice, 2nd ed. Oncology Nursing Press, 2005. Reprinted with permission.*

## Hepatotoxicity of Chemotherapeutic and Biotherapeutic Drugs

| Medication Name | Incidence | Comments |
|---|---|---|
| 6-mercaptopurine | – | If daily dose is >2 mg/kg, hepatocellular or cholestatic liver effects may occur (Perry, 1992). Hepatotoxicity usually is mild and reversible. Elevated transaminases and cholestatic jaundice may occur. |
| Asparaginase | 42% - 87% (Capizzi et al, 1970) Asparaginase increases the indicators of hepatic function (transaminases, alkaline phosphatase, and hyperbilirubinemia). These changes rarely reach critical significance (Muller & Boos, 1998). 50% experience abnormal serum alkaline phosphatase, transaminases, or bilirubin (Oettgen et al, 1970). Up to 87% develop fatty infiltration of the liver (Pratt & Johnson, 1971; Sahoo & Hart, 2003). | – |
| Bleomycin | 10%; more common in patients older than age 70 who receive a total dose >400 units. Toxicity is unpredictable and occasionally has occurred in young patients receiving low doses (Bristol-Myers Squibb Oncology/Immunology, 1999). | – |
| Busulfan | Rare; at high doses, veno-occlusive disease (VOD) may occur (Hassan, 1999). The risk of VOD may be lowered by adjusting the dose to achieve a safe systemic drug exposure (Balis et al, 1997). | – |
| Capecitabine | 17%; 21% for patients with hepatic malignancy. At 2,500 mg/m$^2$ daily for two weeks, grade III or IV hyperbilirubinemia may occur. 20% - 40% elevation in serum bilirubin, alkaline phosphatase, and transaminases (Chu & DeVita, 2002). | If grade II - IV elevations in bilirubin occur, interrupt capecitabine treatment immediately (Roche Laboratories, 1999). |
| Carmustine | Transient elevations in serum transaminases in up to 90% of patients within one week of therapy (Chu & DeVita, 2002) | Effects usually are not clinically significant (DeVita et al, 1965); however, carmustine may be associated with severe VOD when used during bone marrow transplant (BMT) (McDonald et al, 1993). |
| Cisplatin | Rare | Hepatotoxicity may increase with higher doses (Cavalli et al, 1978; Pollera et al, 1987). |
| Cyclophosphamide | Rare; less than 1% with high doses (>120 mg/kg/day for four days). Risk increases at cumulative doses >400–500 mg. | – |
| Cytarabine | – | Dose-related; elevation of transaminases bilirubin (Katz & Cassileth, 1977; Kummar et al, 2005) |
| Dactinomycin | >15%; hepatic toxicity may be dose-related. Severe hepatotoxicity is associated with the single-bolus dose schedule (Balis et al, 1997). | Elevation of serum transaminases; dose and schedule dependent |
| Denileukin diftitox | 15% - 20% experienced elevation of serum transaminases and hypoalbuminemia (albumin <2.3g/dL) (Chu & DeVita, 2002). | Usually seen in first course and resolved within two weeks |
| Doxorubicin | Rare (Perry, 1992) | Extensively metabolized in liver; reduce dose for altered hepatic function (Sifton, 2002) |
| Floxuridine | Intra-arterial hepatic infusion produced hepatitis in 50% of patients | 90% of drug is extracted by hepatocytes (Hohn et al, 1989). |

**123**

*(continued on next page)*

## Hepatotoxicity of Chemotherapeutic and Biotherapeutic Drugs

| Medication Name | Incidence | Comments |
|---|---|---|
| Gemcitabine | Transient elevation of serum transaminases (10% - 20% develop grade III - IV), elevation of alkaline phosphatase (15% - 20%), and elevation of serum bilirubin (Abratt et al, 1994) | Consider dose modification in patients with abnormal liver function because of potential for increased toxicity. |
| Gemtuzumab ozogamicin | Hepatotoxicity with elevation of serum bilirubin and liver function tests (LFTs) was observed in up to 20% of patients (Chu & DeVita, 2002). | – |
| Ifosfamide | Transient hepatic dysfunction: rare | – |
| Interleukin-2 | Elevated bilirubin: 40% (2% progress to grade IV) Interleukin-2 therapy is associated with elevated LFT results (23% serum glutamic-oxaloacetic transaminase increase) (Chiron Corporation, 1998). | Typically normalize within five to six days (Schwartz et al, 2002) |
| Melphalan | Transient hepatic elevation in LFTs at high doses used in autologous BMT | – |
| Methotrexate (MTX) | Transient elevation of serum transaminases. High-dose MTX combined with leucovorin rescue associated with transaminases greater than 20 times baseline and elevation of serum bilirubin up to 3 mg/dl (Locasciulli et al, 1992). | Returns to normal within 10 days (Kummar et al, 2005) |
| Mitoxantrone | Transient, reversible elevation of liver enzymes | Dose modification required in patients with liver dysfunction |
| Paclitaxel | 7% - 22% (Bristol-Myers Squibb Oncology, 2003) Events usually occur at high doses or in combination therapy (Bristol-Myers Squibb Oncology, 2003); patients with liver dysfunction are at increased risk of toxicity secondary to delayed clearance. Dose reduction is recommended for these patients. | The toxicity of paclitaxel is greater for patients with elevated liver enzymes (Bristol-Myers Squibb Oncology, 2003). |
| Thioguanine | – | Elevation of serum bilirubin and transaminases VOD (rare) |
| Vincristine | Rare | Hepatotoxicity does not tend to occur at standard doses. Consider dose modification for patients with hepatic dysfunction. |
| Vinorelbine | Transient elevation in LFTs (Chu & DeVita, 2002) | Metabolized in liver by cytochrome P450 microsomal system |

**Section 4: Table 5**

## Alterations in Renal Function of Selected Chemotherapeutic Drugs

| Drug | Alteration | Risk factors | Abnormalities | Management |
|---|---|---|---|---|
| Cisplatin | Damage to proximal and distal tubules<br>Decreased renal tubular reabsorption | Concurrent use of other nephrotoxic drugs<br>Existing renal dysfunction | Azotemia<br>↑ BUN<br>↑ Serum creatinine<br>↑ Uric acid<br>↓ Creatinine clearance<br>↓ Serum magnesium<br>↓ Serum calcium<br>Proteinuria<br>↓ Potassium | Prevention: hydration (2-3 L) and diuresis (> 100 mL/hr)<br>Magnesium supplement (Evans et al, 1995)<br>Supportive: electrolyte replacement, dose adjustment, discontinuation of drug therapy |
| Cyclophosphamide | SIADH | High dose and hydration with free water (ie, D₅W) | Hyponatremia<br>↑ Urine output<br>↑ Urine osmolality<br>↓ Serum osmolality | Prevention: monitor electrolytes, hydration with normal saline<br>Supportive: discontinue drug therapy |
| Ifosfamide | Proximal tubular defect | High-dose administration<br>Existing renal dysfunction | ↑ BUN<br>↑ Serum creatinine<br>↓ Creatinine clearance<br>Proteinuria | Prevention: adequate hydration, monitor for early signs of toxicity; may be reversible |
| Methotrexate | Injury to proximal and distal convoluted tubules | High-dose therapy<br>Dehydration<br>Existing renal dysfunction<br>Concurrent use of other nephrotoxic drugs<br>Existing effusions or ascites<br>Prior treatment with cisplatin | ↑ BUN<br>↑ Serum creatinine<br>↓ Creatinine clearance<br>Hematuria<br>Azotemia<br>Oliguria<br>Hypokalemia<br>Aminoaciduria<br>Electrolyte abnormalities | Prevention (high dose): hydration, adequate urine output, alkalinization to maintain pH ≥7.0<br>Supportive: hydration<br>Administer leucovorin if serum methorexate levels are elevated |

(continued on next page)

**Section 4: Table 5** *(continued)*

## Alterations in Renal Function of Selected Chemotherapeutic Drugs

| Drug | Alteration | Risk factors | Abnormalities | Management |
|---|---|---|---|---|
| Mitomycin | Mild, reversible renal insufficiency<br>Hemolytic-uremic syndrome (uncommon) | Prolonged therapy<br>Cumulative doses >50-100 mg | ↑ BUN<br>↑ Serum creatinine<br>↓ Platelets<br>Anemia<br>Proteinuria<br>Hematuria<br>Hypertension | Prevention: none<br>Supportive: ? Plasma pheresis |
| Nitrosureas | Glomerular and tubular damage | Cumulative doses ≥1.2 g/m² | ↑ BUN<br>↑ Serum creatinine | Prevention: adjust dose for renal impairment<br>Supportive: monitor cumulative dose and renal function |
| Plicamycin | Damage to proximal and distal tubules | Daily schedule with cumulative doses > 25-50 µg/kg | ↑ BUN<br>↑ Serum creatinine<br>Proteinuria<br>Azotemia<br>↓ Serum electrolytes | Prevention: avoid high doses:<br>monitor for early signs of toxicity |
| Streptozocin | Damage to renal tubules | Doses >1-1.5 g/m²/wk<br>Concurrent use of other nephrotoxic drugs<br>Existing renal dysfunction | ↑ BUN<br>↑ Serum creatinine<br>Proteinuria<br>↓ Creatinine clearance<br>Glucosuria<br>Hypokalemia<br>Renal tubular acidosis<br>Hypophosphatemia | Prevention: monitor early signs of toxicity; protein, amino acids in urine, phosphate, potassium in serum<br>Adequate hydration |

*Fischer DS, Knobf MT, Durivage HJ, Beaulieu NJ. The Cancer Chemotherapy Handbook. 6th ed. Philadelphia, Pa: Mosby; 2003. Reprinted with permission.*

A useful resource for oncology clinicians is the National Cancer Institute's Common Terminology Criteria for Adverse Events (CTCAE v3.0).

The CTCAE v3.0 is a reference "library" of definitions for grading the effects of cancer treatment. The purpose of the CTCAE v3.0 is to facilitate the evaluation of new therapies, treatment modalities and supportive measures and to standardize reporting of Adverse Events across groups and modalities without regard to chronicity. A major focus of v3.0 was the development of a more complete characterization of both early and persistent events of surgery and radiation.

The length of this document prohibits its inclusion in this publication. To access the latest version of this document, go to:

**http://ctep.cancer.gov/reporting/index.html**

which pulls up all the reports, then select:

**CTCAEv3.pdf**

from the list.

An example of common toxicity criteria for stomatitis/pharyngitis (oral/pharyngeal mucositis) is:

**Common Toxicity Criteria (CTC)**

| | | | Grade | | |
|---|---|---|---|---|---|
| **Adverse Event** | **0** | **1** | **2** | **3** | **4** |
| Stomatitis pharyngitis (oral/pharyngeal mucositis) | none | painless ulcers, erythema, or mild soreness in the absence of lesions | painful erythema, edema, or ulcers, but can eat or swallow | painful erythema, edema or ulcers requiring IV hydration | severe ulceration or requires parenteral or enteral nutritional support or prophylactic intubation |

## Section 4: Table 6    Sample Risk Assessment Tool

### Pretreatment Risk Assessment

Patient: _____   Diagnosis: _____

Regimen: _____   Date: _____

### Neutropenia

- ☐ Myelosuppressive Chemo Regimen
- ☐ Previous Radiation to Marrow
- ☐ Pre-existing Neutropenia
- ☐ Extensive Prior Chemotherapy
- ☐ Poor Performance Status (ECOG 3 or 4)
- ☐ Serum Albumin <3.5 (NHL)
- ☐ Bone Marrow Involvement
- ☐ ↓Immune Function
- ☐ Hx of Febrile Neutropenia
- ☐ Elevated LDH (NHL)
- ☐ Advanced Cancer
- ☐ Active Infection
- ☐ Open Wounds
- ☐ Age >65
- ☐ Other_____

Risk Identified? _____   Comments: _____

### Chemotherapy Regimens Associated with Increased Toxicity

**BREAST CANCER**
Docetaxel, Doxorubicin
Docetaxel, Doxorubicin, Cyclophosphamide
Doxorubicin, Paclitaxel

**SMALL CELL LUNG CANCER**
Etoposide, Cisplatin
Topotecan, Paclitaxel

**OVARIAN CANCER**
Paclitaxel
Topotecan

**BLADDER CANCER**
MVAC
Paclitaxel, Carboplatin

**NON-SMALL CELL LUNG CANCER**
Cisplatin, Paclitaxel

**COLORECTAL CANCER**
Irinotecan

**NON-HODGKIN'S LYMPHOMA**
CHOP
DHAP

**128**

### Anemia

- ☐ Myelosuppressive Chemo Regimen
- ☐ Bone Marrow Involvement
- ☐ Nutritional Deficiency/Malabsorption
- ☐ Previous Radiation to Marrow
- ☐ Blood Loss – Surgical, GI, GYN
- ☐ Pre-existing Anemia
- ☐ Active Infection
- ☐ Renal Insufficiency
- ☐ Chronic Illness
- ☐ Other_____

Risk Identified? _____   Comments: _____

### Chemotherapy Regimens Associated with Increased Toxicity

CHOP
Paclitaxel, Carboplatin or Cisplatin
Etoposide, Cisplatin
Paclitaxel, Doxorubicin

Cyclophosphamide, Mitoxantrone, Vincristine
Topotecan
Cisplatin, 5FU
Cyclophosphamide, Doxorubicin, 5FU

### Nausea/Vomiting

- ☐ Emetogenic Treatment Regimen
- ☐ Female
- ☐ <50 Years
- ☐ Hx of N/V with Anesthesia/Analgesics
- ☐ Radiation to Abdomen
- ☐ Hx of Hyperemesis with Pregnancy
- ☐ GI Malig – Adv/Lg Tumor Burden
- ☐ Prior Inadequate Control of N/V
- ☐ Hx of Motion Sickness
- ☐ Other_____

Risk Identified? _____   Comments: _____

## Pretreatment Risk Assessment

### Chemotherapy Regimens Associated with Increased Toxicity

**INTERMEDIATE RISK (occurs in at least 30% of patients)**

| | |
|---|---|
| Irinotecan (Camptosar®) | Melphalan (Alkeran®) >50 mg/m$^2$ |
| Teniposide (VM-26) | Arsenic trioxide (Trisenox™) |
| Paclitaxel (Taxol®) | Oxaliplatin (Eloxatin®) >75 mg/m$^2$ |
| Docetaxel (Taxotere®) | Amifostine (Ethyol®) >500 mg/m$^2$ |
| Mitomycin (Mutamycin®) | Interleukin 2 12-15 mil units/m$^2$ |
| Topotecan (Hycamtin®) | Procarbazine (oral) |
| Gemcitabine (Gemzar®) | |
| Etoposide (VP-16, Vepesid®) | |
| Mitoxantrone (Novantrane®) | |

**HIGH RISK (occurs in >30% to 90% patients)**

| | |
|---|---|
| Dacarbazine (DTIC®) | Carmustine (BCNU) |
| Dactinomycin (Cosmegen®) | Daunorubicin (Daunomycin) |
| Lomustine (CCNU®) | Doxorubicin (Adriamycin®) |
| Streptozocin (Zanosar®) | Epirubicin (Ellence®) |
| Hexalmethylmelamine (Hexalen®) | Idarubicin (Idamycin®) |
| Topotecan (Hycamtin®) | Procarbazine (oral) |
| Carboplatin (Paraplatin®) | Cytarabine (Ara-C®) |
| Cyclophosphamide (Cytoxan®) | Ifosfamide (Ifex®) |
| Mechlorethamine (Nitrogen Mustard) | Busulfan >4 mg/day |
| | Methotrexate >1000 mg/m$^2$ |

**129**

**VERY HIGH RISK (occurs in 99% of patients)**
Cisplatin

## Anxiety/Depression

| | | |
|---|---|---|
| ☐ Chemotherapy/Other Rx | ☐ Personal or Family Hx of Anxiety/Depression | ☐ Loss of Social/Emotional Support |
| ☐ Pancreatic, Brain, GYN, Lung, H&N CA | ☐ Drug or Alcohol Abuse | ☐ Loss of Financial Resources |
| ☐ Relapsed/Refractory Disease | ☐ Impaired Sexual Function | ☐ Loss of Functional Abilities |
| ☐ Uncontrolled Pain | ☐ Altered Physical Appearance | ☐ Other_____ |

Risk Identified? _____    Comments: _____

## Chemotherapy Regimens Associated with Increased Toxicity

| | |
|---|---|
| Vincristine | Vinblastine |
| Intrathecal Methotrexate | Procarbazine |
| Interferon | L'asparaginase |
| Tamoxifen | Interleukin |

## Oral Mucositis

| | | |
|---|---|---|
| ☐ Chemotherapy | ☐ ↓ Salivation | ☐ Hx or Presence of Dental Disease |
| ☐ Current or Prior Radiation to H&N | ☐ Elderly | ☐ Other_____ |
| ☐ Hx of Mucositis | ☐ Poor Fitting Oral Prosthesis | |

Risk Identified? _____    Comments: _____

## Chemotherapy Regimens Associated with Increased Toxicity

| | | |
|---|---|---|
| Actinomycin D | Bleomycin | Daunorubicin |
| Docetaxel | Etoposide | 5 FU |
| Methotrexate | Plicamycin | Mitoxantrone |
| Doxorubicin | Cytarabine | Thioguanine |
| Floxuridine | Vinblastine | |

## Pretreatment Risk Assessment

## Constipation

☐ Chemotherapy          ☐ Inactivity             ☐ Elderly
☐ Hx of Constipation     ☐ Current Narcotic Use    ☐ Other_____
☐ Antiemetic Regimen     ☐ Oral Iron

Risk Identified? _____     Comments: _____

## Chemotherapy Regimens Associated with Increased Toxicity

Vinblastine              Thalidomide
Vincristine              Vinorelbine

## Diarrhea

☐ Chemotherapy               ☐ Hx of Diarrhea/Bowel Disease    ☐ Lactose Intolerance
☐ Radiation to Colon/Abd/Pelvis   ☐ Enteral Feedings             ☐ Other_____

Risk Identified? _____     Comments: _____

**Chemotherapy Regimens Associated with Increased Toxicity**

Taxotere                 Camptosar
Oxaliplatin              Avastin
5 FU

**Neurotoxicity** – High-dose Cytarabine, High-dose Cyclophosphamide

**Peripheral Neuropathy** – Cisplatin, Carboplatin, Oxaliplatin, Taxol, Taxotere, Vincristine, Vinblastine, Vinorelbine

**Ototoxicity** – Cisplatin

**Hand and Foot Syndrome** – Capecitabine, Doxil®

**Other Toxicities to Consider:** _____

**Signature:** _____

# 5

# Symptom Management

Cancer symptom management is the hallmark of the specialty of oncology nursing. Symptoms are the patient's unique experience. They may be linked to a physical problem or they may have a strong psychological component. Management and control of the symptoms that result from cancer and its treatment can improve quality of life and alleviate suffering, even if the cancer is not curable.

This section focuses on the most common symptoms associated with cancer and cancer treatment. It includes the possible causes of the symptom as well as the management. More detail is provided on pain, depression, insomnia, fatigue and nausea/vomiting in separate tables at the end of the section. Again, this is a quick reference for experienced clinicians. For novices and for further details on the assessment and management of cancer-related symptoms, consult an oncology text.

This section includes specific drug information for pain, depression and insomnia, in supplemental tables. In addition, more detailed information for nurses on sexuality, fertility, grief and loss is found in this chapter.

The Eastern Cooperative Oncology Group (ECOG)/Karnofsky Performance Scale is found at the end of this section. This highly useful scale measures functional status of the patient—a parameter that is invariably affected when cancer symptoms occur.

**Symptom Management**

| Symptom | Possible Cause | Nonpharmacologic Management | Pharmacologic Management |
|---|---|---|---|
| Anorexia-cachexia | • Decreased caloric intake<br>• Increased metabolic needs<br>• Nausea-vomiting<br>• Altered GI function<br>• Taste changes<br>• Tumor effects<br>• Loss of albumin<br>• Other symptoms (pain, fatigue, etc.) | • Increase caloric intake<br>• Enteral or parenteral nutrition support<br>• Relaxation exercises<br>• Light exercise before meals<br>• Treat other symptoms (pain, etc)<br>• Oral hygiene<br>• Small frequent meals<br>• Encourage rest | • Megestrol acetate (Megace®) 800 mg/day for appetite stimulation (available as pill or liquid form) |
| Cancer pain | • Tumor invasion of bone<br>• Tumor invasion of brain<br>• Tumor invasion of peripheral nervous system<br>• Tumor invasion of abdominal organs or obstruction<br>• Peripheral neuropathy due to chemotherapy<br>• Postsurgical pain syndromes<br>• Postradiation pain syndromes | • Relaxation exercises<br>• Guided imagery<br>• Biofeedback<br>• Distraction<br>• Massage<br>• Heat/cold application<br>• Nerve block<br>• Treatment of the tumor with surgery, radiation or chemotherapy | See Tables 5-2 and 5-3 |
| Constipation | • Obstruction or compression of bowel by tumor<br>• Nerve involvement or cord compression<br>• Dehydration<br>• Hypercalcemia<br>• Hypokalemia<br>• Decreased intake of fiber and fluids<br>• Decreased mobility<br>• Changes in usual bowel patterns<br>• Chemotherapy<br>• Radiation therapy | • Increase dietary fiber<br>• Adequate fluid intake<br>• Exercise<br>• Privacy and comfort<br>• Bowel regimen | • Bulk laxatives increase size and weight of stool, can be preventive, eg, psyllium, methylcellulose<br>• Lubricants coat and soften the stool easing passage, eg, mineral oil<br>• Stool softeners soften the stool easing passage, eg, Colace®<br>• Saline laxatives draw water into the gut, for acute use, eg, magnesium citrate<br>• Osmotic laxatives increase osmotic pressure, eg, lactulose, sorbitol<br>• Detergent laxatives act directly on colon to reduce surface tension, eg, docusate<br>• Stimulant laxatives stimulate motility via local irritation, eg, bisacodyl, senna<br>• Suppositories cause local irritation<br>• Enemas, when no response to regular laxative therapy and dietary measures |

*(continued on next page)*

## Symptom Management

| Symptom | Possible Cause | Nonpharmacologic Management | Pharmacologic Management |
|---|---|---|---|
| Depression | • Medication side effect<br>• Response to cancer diagnosis<br>• Grief response<br>• Genetic predisposition | • Counseling, active listening<br>• Psychotherapy<br>• Cognitive interventions<br>• Adequate pain management, nutrition and rest. | See Table 5-4 |
| Diarrhea | • Partial bowel obstruction<br>• Endocrine-secreting tumor<br>• Fecal impaction<br>• Anxiety<br>• Chemotherapy<br>• Biotherapy<br>• Radiation enteritis<br>• Post-GI surgery | • Low residue diet<br>• Decrease roughage in diet<br>• Smaller frequent meals<br>• Foods at room temperature<br>• Increase fluid intake<br>• Avoid alcohol and caffeine<br>• Consider lactose-free diet | • Loperamide HCl (Imodium AD®) 4 mg po initially followed by 2 mg after each stool, up to 8 pills per day (instructions vary from package insert)<br>• Kaolin/pectate (Kaopectate®) 60-120 mL after each loose stool x 48 hr<br>• Atropine sulfate/diphenoxylate HCl (Lomotil®) 2 to 4 mg po, 3 to 4 times per d, up to 8 pills per day<br>• Octreotide acetate (Sandostatin®) 50-200 mcg SQ 2-3 times per day or IV infusion, for high volume diarrhea or known endocrine or secretory disorder |
| Dyspnea | • Lung tumor<br>• Pleural effusion<br>• Pericardial effusion<br>• Pneumonia<br>• Ascites<br>• Anemia<br>• Pulmonary embolism<br>• Decreased lung capacity<br>• Pulmonary fibrosis<br>• Cardiomyopathy | • Strengthening and conditioning exercises<br>• Pursed lip breathing<br>• Positioning<br>• Oxygen therapy<br>• Relaxation techniques for anxiety | • Morphine sulfate infusion (usually reserved for terminal phase): 1-2 mg every 5 to 10 minutes until relief is noted, then continuous infusion<br>• Nebulized morphine |
| Fatigue | • Deconditioning<br>• Surgery<br>• Chemotherapy<br>• Radiation therapy<br>• Biotherapy<br>• Anemia<br>• Depression<br>• Nutritional status<br>• Sleep disturbances | • Energy conservation tips<br>• Strengthening and conditioning exercises<br>• Relaxation techniques for anxiety<br>• Adequate nutrition<br>• See Table 5-5 for more detail on fatigue | If anemic: erythropoeitin for hemoglobin <10 gm/dL, 40,000 U sq weekly or 10,000 U sq three times per week until Hgb normalizes or darbepoetin alfa 2.25 mcg/kg SQ weekly |
| Insomnia | • Pain<br>• Anxiety<br>• Depression<br>• Medication side effects<br>• Environment<br>• Physical illness (eg, fever, chills) | • Sleep hygiene guidelines<br>• Behavioral relaxation | See Table 5-6 Sedatives and Hypnotics See Table 5-7 Anxiolytics |

**133**

*(continued on next page)*

## Symptom Management

| Symptom | Possible Cause | Nonpharmacologic Management | Pharmacologic Management |
|---|---|---|---|
| Lymphedema | • Lymph node dissection, upper or lower extremity<br>• Radiation therapy<br>• Infection<br>• Aging<br>• Obesity | • Upper or lower extremity exercises<br>• Avoid heavy lifting or venipuncture on affected side<br>• Prevention of infection<br>• Elevation of the extremity<br>• Compression garment<br>• Massage/physical therapy<br>• Complex decongestive physiotherapy (CDP) | None |
| Mucositis | • Oral tumor<br>• Chemotherapy<br>• Radiation therapy<br>• Biotherapy<br>• Bone marrow transplantation | • Meticulous oral hygiene<br>• Mouth rinses: water, saline, sodium bicarbonate and half-strength hydrogen peroxide, chlorhexidine<br>• Research has shown that salt and bicarbonate rinses are the most effective and least costly option for mucositis pain relief and resolution<br>• Adequate hydration<br>• Lip moisturizers<br>• Synthetic saliva | • Pilocarpine (Salagen®) 5 mg TID for radiation induced xerostomia<br>• Pain medications |
| Nausea-vomiting | • Chemotherapy<br>• Radiation therapy<br>• Tumor-induced<br>• Terminal disease | • Relaxation<br>• Guided imagery<br>• Systematic desensitization<br>• Distraction<br>• Acupressure<br>• Dietary modifications | See Table 5-8 |

## Highlights of Pain Management

Cancer pain can be managed effectively through relatively simple means in up to 90% of the 8 million Americans who have cancer or a history of cancer. Unfortunately, pain associated with cancer is frequently under-treated.

Although cancer pain or associated symptoms cannot always be entirely eliminated, appropriate use of available therapies can effectively relieve pain in the great majority of patients. Pain management improves the patient's quality of life throughout all stages of the disease. Patients with advanced cancer experience multiple concurrent symptoms with pain; therefore, optimal pain management necessitates a systematic symptom assessment and appropriate management for optimal quality of life. Despite the wide range of available pain management therapies, data are insufficient to guide their use in children, adolescents, older adults, and special populations.

State and local laws often restrict the medical use of opioids to relieve cancer pain, and third-party payers may not reimburse for noninvasive pain control treatments. Thus, clinicians should work with regulators, state cancer pain initiatives, or other groups to eliminate these health care system barriers to effective pain management. (These and other barriers to effective pain management are listed below.) Changes in health care delivery may create additional disincentives for clinicians to practice effective pain management.

Flexibility is the key to managing cancer pain. As patients vary in diagnosis, stage of disease, responses to pain and interventions, and personal preferences, so must pain management. The recommended clinical approach outlined below emphasizes a focus on patient involvement.

A. Ask about pain regularly. Assess pain and associated symptoms systematically using brief assessment tools. Assessment should include discussion about common symptoms experienced by cancer patients and how each symptom will be treated.

B. Believe patient and family reports of pain and what relieves the pain. (Caveats include patients with significant psychological/existential distress and patients with cognitive impairment.)

C. Choose pain-control options appropriate for the patient, family, and setting.

D. Deliver interventions in a timely, logical, coordinated fashion.

E. Empower patients and their families. Enable patients to control their course to the greatest extent possible.

Effective pain management is best achieved by a team approach involving patients, their families, and health care providers. The clinician should:

- Initiate prophylactic anti-constipation measures in all patients prior to or concurrent with opiate administration.
- Discuss pain and its management with patients and their families.
- Encourage patients to be active participants in their care.
- Reassure patients who are reluctant to report pain that there are many safe and effective ways to relieve pain.
- Consider the cost of proposed drugs and technologies.
- Share documented pain assessment and management with other clinicians treating the patient.
- Know state/local regulations for controlled substances.

*Source: National Cancer Institute, www.cancer.gov. Full references available on web site. Updated 8/20/2004.*

## Pain Assessment Screening Questions

- Are you experiencing pain now?
- Have you experienced persistent/ongoing pain in the past three months?

### Reassessment Questions

- Location – Written description of pain
- Intensity – Use pain scale (rate 0-10, facial expression scale)
        Pain level at present
        Pain level at worst and best
        Acceptable pain level
- Quality – In patient's own words
- Pattern – Onset, constant/intermittent, frequency, duration of episode
- Document response to intervention

### Pain Scale

| | |
|---|---|
| No Pain (0) | |
| Mild Pain (1-3) | Annoying, nagging interfering little with ADLs |
| Moderate Pain (4-6) | Pain that interferes significantly with ADLs |
| Severe Pain (7-10) | Disabling, inability to perform ADLs |

# Section 5: Table 2

## Selected Oral Analgesics for Mild or Moderate Pain: Comparative Doses

| Drug | Common brand name | Duration of analgesia (hr) | Oral dose (mg) | Plasma half-life (hr) | Anti-inflammatory | Platelet problems | Significant adverse effects |
|---|---|---|---|---|---|---|---|
| Aspirin | Many | 3-5 | 550 | 3-5 | Yes | Yes | GI, renal |
| Acetaminophen | Tylenol® | 3-4 | 650 | 1-4 | No | No | Hepatic |
| Sodium salicylate | Generic | 3-4 | 650 | 3-5 | Yes | No | GI |
| Difunisal | Dolobid® | 8-12 | 500 | 8-12 | Yes | Mild | GI |
| Choline magnesium trisalicylate | Trilisate® | 8-12 | 1000 | 9-17 | Yes | No | Tinnitis |
| Salsalate | Disalcid® | 16 | 750 | 1-2 | Yes | Mild | Tinnitis |
| Ibuprofen | Motrin® | 3-5 | 400 | 2-3 | Yes | Yes | GI |
| Fenoprofen | Nalfon® | 4-5 | 300 | 3-4 | Yes | Yes | GI |
| Diclofenac | Voltaren® | 4-6 | 50 | 1-2 | Yes | Yes | GI |
| Flurbiprofen | Ansaid® | 6-8 | 50 | 3-9 | Yes | Yes | GI |
| Ketoprofen | Orudis® | 5-7 | 50 | 1-4 | Yes | Yes | GI |
| Naproxen | Naprosyn® | 2-8 | 250 | 12-15 | Yes | Yes | GI |
| Naproxen sodium | Anaprox® | 7-8 | 275 | 12-15 | Yes | Yes | GI |
| Indomethacin | Indocin® | 3-4 | 25 | 3-11 | Yes | Yes | GI, CNS |
| Tolmetin | Tolectin® | 3-4 | 200-400 | 1-2 | Yes | Yes | GI |
| Sulindac | Clinoral® | 7 | 150 | 7-18 | Yes | Yes | GI |
| Mefenamic acid | Ponstel® | 6 | 250 | 3-4 | Yes | Yes | Marrow, GI |
| Meclofenamate | Meclomen® | 8 | 50 | 1-5 | Yes | Yes | GI |
| Piroxicam | Feldene® | 24 | 20 | 30-88 | Yes | Yes | GI |
| Etodolac | Lodine® | 4-12 | 200 | 7 | Yes | Yes | GI |
| Propoxyphene | Darvon® | 4-6 | 65 | 6-12 | No | No | CNS |
| Propoxyphene napsylate | Darvon-N® | 4-6 | 100 | 6-12 | No | No | CNS |
| Pentazocine | Talwin® Nx | 3-4 | 50 | 2-3 | No | No | CNS |
| Codeine | Many | 3-5 | 32 | 2-3 | No | No | Constipation, CNS |
| Hydrocodone | Many | 3-4 | 5 | 3-4 | No | No | Constipation, CNS |
| Oxycodone | Roxicodone® | 3-6 | 5 | 3-6 | No | No | Constipation, CNS |
| Meperidine | Demerol® | 3-4 | 50 | 3-4 | No | No | CNS |

GI, Gastrointestinal; CNS, central nervous system

*Source: Fischer DS, Knobf MT, Durivage HJ, Beaulieu NJ. The Cancer Chemotherapy Handbook. 6th ed. Philadelphia, Pa: Mosby; 2003. Reprinted with permission.*

137

# Section 5: Table 3

## Opioids for Moderate to Severe Pain: Approximate Equianalgesic Doses

| Drug | Brand name | Parenteral dose (mg) | Oral dose (mg) | Duration of analgesia (hr) | Plasma half-life (hr) |
|---|---|---|---|---|---|
| Morphine | Generic | 10 | 30 | 4-5 | 2-4 |
| Controlled-release morphine | MS Contin®, Oramorph SR® | — | 30 | 6-12 | — |
| Hydromorphone | Dilaudid® | 1.5 | 4 | 3-4 | 2-3 |
| Oxymorphone | Numorphan® | 1.5 | 5 (rectal) | 3-6 | 2-3 |
| Methadone | Dolophine® | 10 | 20 | 5-6 | 30-60 |
| Levorphanol | Levo-Dromoran® | 2 | 4 | 4-6 | 12-18 |
| Meperidine | Demerol® | 100 | 300 | 2-4 | 3-4 |
| Fentanyl | Duragesic® | 0.1 | 0.025/hr patch | 1-2* | 1.5-6 |
| Oxycodone | Roxicodone® | — | 5 | 3-6 | 3-6 |
| Controlled-release oxycodone | OxyContin® | — | 10 | 12 | — |
| Ketorolac+ | Toradol® | 30 | 10 | 5-6 | 5 |
| Codeine | Generic | 120 | 200 | 2-4 | 3-4 |
| Tramadol | Ultram® | — | 50-100 | 4-6 | 7 |

* IV     +Nonopiate, nonsteroidal anti-inflammatory inhibitor

*Source: Fischer DS, Knobf MT, Durivage HJ, Beaulieu NJ. The Cancer Chemotherapy Handbook. 6th ed. Philadelphia, Pa: Mosby; 2003. Reprinted with permission.*

## Section 5: Table 4

**Antidepressants**

| Class Drug | Generic/Brand | Usual daily Dosage | Common, Frequent SE |
|---|---|---|---|
| SSRIs | Citalopram/Celexa® | 40 mg QD | Nausea, headache, |
| | Fluoxetine/Prozac® | 20 mg QD | Diarrhea, agitation |
| | Paroxetine/Paxil® | 20 mg QD | Insomnia, dizziness, |
| | Sertaline/Zoloft® | 100 mg QD | tremor, fatigue, sexual dysfunction, sweating |
| Tricyclics | Amitriptyline/Elavil® | 150 mg QD | Anticholinergic effects |
| | Desipramine/Norpramine® | 150 mg QD | Orthostatic hypotension, |
| | Imipramine/Tofranil® | 150 mg QD | drowsiness, weight gain, |
| | Nortriptyline/Pamelor® | 75 mg QD | tachycardia |
| MAOIs | Phenelzine/Nardil® | 30 mg BID | Postural hypotension |
| | Tranylcypromine/Parnate® | 20 mg BID | Restlessness, insomnia, daytime sleepiness |
| Other | Bupropion/Wellbutrin® | 100 mg TID | Rash, anxiety, agitation |
| | Wellbutrin SR® | 150 mg BID | Insomnia, tremor, HA, anorexia, constipation, nausea, dry mouth |
| | Mirtazapine/Remeron® | 15 mg QD | Somnolence, weight gain, increased appetite, dizziness, dry mouth |
| | Nefazodone/Serzone® | 200 mg BID | Somnolence, dizziness, dry mouth, nausea, HA |
| | Trazodone/Desyrel® Desyrel Dividose® | 300 mg Div. | Drowsiness, headache GI upset |
| | Venlafaxine/Effexor® | 75 mg BID | Nausea, somnolence |
| | Effexor XR® | 150 mg QD | HA, dizziness, sweating, anorexia, insomnia, nervousness, anxiety, sexual dysfunction |

*Source:* Drug Facts and Comparisons (2003-2004). *Wolters-Kluwer Health, Inc. Reprinted with permission.*

## Section 5: Table 5

**Fatigue in the Cancer Patient**

| Symptoms of Fatigue | |
| --- | --- |
| Physical | Tired, weak, no energy |
| Emotional | Impatient, irritable, lack of motivation |
| Behavioral | Withdraws from social environment, requires more effort to accomplish tasks |
| Mental/Cognitive | Inability to think clearly, poor memory, inability to concentrate |

**Physiologic Mechanisms of Fatigue**

A decrease in activity can quickly lead to irreversible decline in energy and function that affects every organ system

Changes in cardiorespiratory and musculoskeletal systems decrease energy-producing capacity and mechanical efficiency

Decreased muscle contractility

**Keys to Fatigue Management**

Minimizing unnecessary bed rest

Balancing the energy expenditure with energy conservation

Ensuring uninterrupted quiet and rest

Minimizing emotional drains and maximizing priorities

Maintain or increase current levels of functioning

Prioritizing and pacing activities is crucial

Planning and energy conservation ensure that energy is available for activities of importance

Energy-saving devices can help patients use energy more effectively

## Section 5: Table 6

**Sedatives and Hypnotics**

| Drug | Adult oral dose | Half-life (hours) |
| --- | --- | --- |
| Zolpidem (Ambien®) | 10 mg | 2.5 |
| Ethchlorvynol (Placidyl®) | 500 mg | 10-20 |
| Estazolam (ProSom®) | 1-2 mg | 10-24 |
| Flurazepam (Dalmane®) | 15-30 mg | 50-100 |
| Quazepam (Doral®) | 15 mg | 25-41 |
| Temazepam (Restoril®) | 15-30 mg | 10-17 |
| Triaxolam (Halcion®) | 0.125-0.5 mg | 1.5-5.5 |
| Chloral hydrate | 0.5-1 g | 7-10 |

*Source:* Drug Facts and Comparisons (2003-2004). *Wolters-Kluwer Health, Inc. Reprinted with permission.*

**Anxiolytics**

| Drug | Dosage range (mg/d) | Speed of onset | Elimination t 1/2 (hrs) |
|------|---------------------|----------------|--------------------------|
| Alprazolam (Xanax®) | 0.75 - 4 | Intermediate | 6.3 – 26.9 |
| Chlordiazepoxide (Librium®) | 15 - 100 | Intermediate | 5 - 30 |
| Clonazepam ( Klonopin®) | 1.5 - 20 | Intermediate | 18 - 50 |
| Clorazepate (Tranzene®) | 15 - 60 | Fast | 40 - 50 |
| Diazepam (Valium®) | 4 - 40 | Very fast | 20 - 80 |
| Lorazepam (Ativan®) | 2 - 4 | Intermediate | 10 - 20 |
| Oxazepam (Serax®) | 30 - 120 | Slow | 5 - 20 |

Drug Facts and Comparisons. *St. Louis, Mo: A Wolters Klewer Company; 2004.*
*Reprinted with permission.*

# Antiemetic Therapy: Select Pharmacologic Agents for the Control of Chemotherapy-Induced Nausea and Vomiting

| Classification | Medication Name | Dose and Schedule | Indications | Comments | Side Effects |
|---|---|---|---|---|---|
| Serotonin antagonist | Ondansetron | 8-32 mg IV once; infuse over 15 minutes; give 30 minutes before chemotherapy<br>Oral doses vary, ranging from 8-24 mg/day<br>With moderately emetogenic therapy; administer 8 mg bid 30 minutes before chemotherapy and continuing for 1-2 days after chemotherapy<br>With highly emetogenic chemotherapy, administer 24 mg po 30 minutes before chemotherapy<br>Orally disintegrating tablet formulation: 8 mg | Prevention of nausea and vomiting associated with single-day highly emetogenic chemotherapy in adults | Ondansetron and dexamethasone can be combined | Headache, diarrhea, fever, constipation, transient increase in serum SGOT, SGPT, hypotension |
| | Granisetron | 2 mg po up to 1 hour before chemotherapy; 1 mg po or 0.01 mg/kg IV 30 minutes before chemotherapy | Prevention of nausea and vomiting during chemotherapy at initial and repeated cycles.<br>Approved for use with high-dose cisplatin | Granisetron can be administered by rapid bolus | Headache, asthenia, diarrhea, constipation, fever, somnolence |
| | Dolasetron | 100 mg po, or 100 mg IV, 30 minutes before chemotherapy | Prevention of chemotherapy-induced nausea and vomiting | Dolasetron will precipitate with dexamethasone in D5W | Headache, diarrhea, dizziness, fatigue, abnormal liver function |
| | Palonosetron | 0.25 mg fixed IV dose; infuse over 30 seconds<br>Give 30 minutes prior to chemotherapy | Prevention of acute nausea associated with initial and repeated courses of moderately and highly emetogenic chemotherapy and the prevention of delayed nausea and vomiting associated with initial and repeat courses of moderately emetogenic chemotherapy | Mean terminal elimination half-life is approximately 40 hours<br>First 5HT$_3$ to be approved for delayed nausea and vomiting<br>Repeat dosing within a seven-day interval is not recommended until further evaluated<br>Not currently used for pediatric patients | Headache, constipation |
| NK-1 antagonist | Aprepitant | Capsules 125 mg po day one of chemotherapy and then 80 mg po days two and three | Prevention of acute and delayed chemotherapy-induced nausea and vomiting in combination with other antiemetics<br>Approved for initial and repeated courses of highly emetogenic chemotherapy | Drug is given in combination with corticosteroid and 5HT$_3$ antagonists on day one and a corticosteroid on days two and three<br>Use with caution in patients receiving chemotherapy that is primarily metabolized through CYP3A4<br>The efficacy of oral contraceptives during administration of aprepitant may be compromised<br>Co-administration of aprepitant and warfarin may decrease NR; monitor closely | Constipation, hiccups, loss of appetite, diarrhea, fatigue |

(continued on next page)

# Section 5: Table 8

## Antiemetic Therapy: Select Pharmacologic Agents for the Control of Chemotherapy-Induced Nausea and Vomiting *(continued)*

| Classification | Medication Name | Dose and Schedule | Indications | Comments | Side Effects |
|---|---|---|---|---|---|
| Corticosteroid | Dexamethasone | Doses vary; 20 mg IV or po before chemotherapy; 4 mg po bid or tid for 2–4 days | Prevention of nausea and vomiting caused by moderately emetogenic chemotherapy. Prevention of delayed nausea and vomiting | Adding a corticosteroid increases the efficacy of antiemetic regimens by 15%–25%. Add dexamethasone to $5HT_3$ regimens. Use is contraindicated with most biotherapy agents | Administer slowly over at least 10 minutes to prevent perianal burning or itching. Insomnia, anxiety, acne |
| Dopamine antagonists | Metoclopramide | 20–40 mg po q 4–6 hours. 10 mg IV q 4 hours; IV dose can be given up to 2 mg/kg q 4 hours | Prevention of nausea and vomiting caused by moderately emetogenic chemotherapy. Prevention of delayed nausea or vomiting | Incidence of drowsiness is greater with high doses. May cause diarrhea | Sedation, extrapyramidal symptoms, dystonia, dizziness, or thostasis |
| | Prochlorperazine | Doses vary; 10 mg IV q 4 hours; 10–20 mg po q 4 hours | Prevention of nausea and vomiting caused by moderately emetogenic chemotherapy. Prevention of delayed nausea or vomiting | Not used for pediatric patients. Highly sedating | |
| | Haloperidol | 1–4 mg IV/po or IM q 2–6 hours | Prevention of acute or delayed nausea or vomiting | Administering haloperidol with diphenhydramine 25–50 mg po or IV prevents extrapyramidal symptoms; more common in younger patients; highly sedating | |
| Cannabinoids | Dronabinol | 5 mg po tid or qid | Prevention of nausea and vomiting caused by moderately emetogenic chemotherapy | Incidence of paranoid reactions of abnormal thinking increases with maximum doses | Sedation, euphoria, dysphoria, drymouth, orthostasis |
| Anxiolytic | Lorazepam | 1–3 mg po sublingual; 0.5–2 mg IV q 4–6 hours | Prevention of anticipatory nausea and vomiting. In combination with other antiemetics as needed for acute or delayed nausea and vomiting | Use with caution in elderly patients or those with hepatic or renal dysfunction | Sedation |

Chemotherapy and Biotherapy Guidelines and Recommended for Practice. *2nd edition.* Pittsburgh, Pa: Oncology Nursing Society; 2005. *Reprinted with permission.*

## Section 5: Table 9

**Emetogenic Potential for Commonly Used Chemotherapeutic Agents**

| Very high (>90%) | High (60-90%) | Moderate (30-60%) | Low (10-30%) |
|---|---|---|---|
| Carmustine* | Azacitidine | Altretamine | Cytarabine |
| Cisplatin | Carboplatin | Daunorubicin | Docetaxel |
| Cyclophosphamide* | Carmustine | Doxorubicin | Etoposide |
| Cytarabine* | Cyclophosphamide | Epirubicin | 5-Fluorouracil |
| Mechlorethamine | Dacarbazine | Idarubicin | Gemcitabine |
| Melphalan* | Dactinomycin | Ifosfamide | Irinotecan |
| Streptozocin | Lornustine | Mitomycin | Paclitaxal |
| | | Mitoxantrone | Trioktepa |
| | | Oxaliplatin | Topatecan |
| | | Plicamycin | |
| | | Procarbazine | |

*High dose*

*Fischer DS, Knobf MT, Durivage HJ, Beaulieu NJ. The Cancer Chemotherapy Handbook. Philadelphia, Pa: Mosby; 2003. Reprinted with permission.*

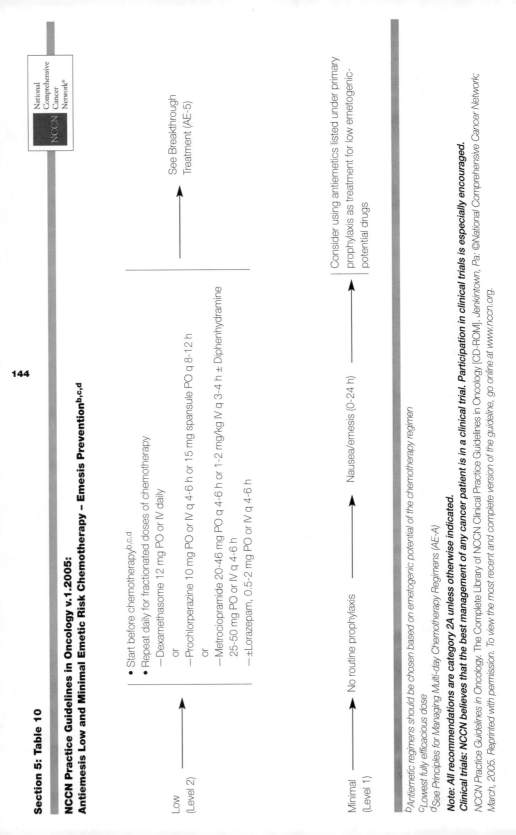

**Section 5: Table 10**

**NCCN Practice Guidelines in Oncology v.1.2005:**
**Antiemesis Low and Minimal Emetic Risk Chemotherapy – Emesis Prevention[b,c,d]**

National
Comprehensive
Cancer
Network®
NCCN

Low
(Level 2)

• Start before chemotherapy[b,c,d]
• Repeat daily for fractionated doses of chemotherapy
  – Dexamethasone 12 mg PO or IV daily
    or
  – Prochlorperazine 10 mg PO or IV q 4-6 h or 15 mg spansule PO q 8-12 h
    or
  – Metroclopramide 20-46 mg PO q 4-6 h or 1-2 mg/kg IV q 3-4 h ± Diphenhydramine
    25-50 mg PO or IV q 4-6 h
  – ±Lorazepam, 0.5-2 mg PO or IV q 4-6 h

→ See Breakthrough
Treatment (AE-5)

Minimal
(Level 1)

→ No routine prophylaxis

Nausea/emesis (0-24 h) →

Consider using antiemetics listed under primary prophylaxis as treatment for low emetogenic-potential drugs

[b]Antiemetic regimens should be chosen based on emetogenic potential of the chemotherapy regimen
[c]Lowest fully efficacious dose
[d]See Principles for Managing Multi-day Chemotherapy Regimens (AE-A)

**Note: All recommendations are category 2A unless otherwise indicated.**
**Clinical trials: NCCN believes that the best management of any cancer patient is in a clinical trial. Participation in clinical trials is especially encouraged.**

*NCCN Practice Guidelines in Oncology. The Complete Library of NCCN Clinical Practice Guidelines in Oncology [CD-ROM]. Jenkintown, Pa: ©National Comprehensive Cancer Network; March, 2005. Reprinted with permission. To view the most recent and complete version of the guideline, go online at www.nccn.org.*

# Section 5: Table 11

## NCCN Practice Guidelines in Oncology v.1.2005: Antiemesis Moderate Emetic Risk Chemotherapy – Emesis Prevention

National Comprehensive Cancer Network®

**Moderate[h]**
**(Level 3-4)**

### Day 1

- Start before chemotherapy[b,c,d] and
  - Dexamethasone 12 mg PO or IV and
  - 5-HT3 antagonist:[f]
    Palonosetron 0.25 mg IV[e,g] (category 1)
    (preferred)
    or
    Ondansetron 16-24 mg PO or 8-12 mg (maximum 32 mg) IV
    or
    Granisetron 1-2 mg PO or 1 mg PO bid (category 1) or 0.01 mg/kg (maximum 1 mg) IV (category 1)
    or
    Dolasetron 100 mg PO or 1.8 mg/kg or 100 mg IV
  and
  - ±Lorazepam 0.5-2 mg PO or IV or sublingual q 6 h
  - Consider adding Aprepitant 125 mg PO in select patients[i]

### Day 2-4

- Dexamethasone 8 mg PO or IV daily or 4 mg PO or IV bid (preferred)
- 5-HT3 antagonist:[f]
  Ondansetron 8 mg PO bid or 16 mg PO daily or 8 mg (maximum 32 mg) IV
  or
  Granisetron 1-2 mg PO daily or 1 mg PO bid or 0.01 mg/kg (maximum 1 mg) IV.
  or
  Dolasetron 108 mg PO daily or 1.8 mg/kg IV or 180 mg IV
  or
- Metoclopramide 0.5 mg/kg PO or IV q 6 h or 20 mg PO 4 times daily ± Diphenhydramine 25-50 mg PO or IV q 4-6 h prn
  or
- Aprepitant 80 mg PO days 2-3 if used on Day 1[e]
  and
- Dexamethasone 8 mg PO or IV daily
- ±Lorazepam 0.5-2 mg PO or IV or sublingual q 6 h

See Breakthrough Treatment (AE-5)

---

[b]Antiemetic regimens should be chosen based on emetogenic potential of the chemotherapy regimen

[c]Lowest fully efficacious dose

[d]See Principles for Managing Multi-day Emetogenic Chemotherapy Regimens (AE-A)

[e]See New Antiemetic Agents for Treating Nausea and Vomiting (AE-B)

[f]Order of listed antiemetics does not reflect preference

[g]Palonosetron is administered on day 1 only; no follow up 5-HT3 antagonist or dosing needed.

[h]Data for post-carboplatin ≥300 mg/m², cyclophosphamide ≥600-1000 mg/m², doxorubicin ≥50 mg/m² emesis prevention are category 1.

[i]Aprepitant may be considered for patients receiving the following chemotherapy: carboplatin, cyclophosphamide, doxorubicin, epirubicin, ifosfamide, irinotecan or methotrexate

**Note: All recommendations are category 2A unless otherwise indicated.**
**Clinical trials: NCCN believes that the best management of any cancer patient is in a clinical trial. Participation in clinical trials is especially encouraged.**

*NCCN Practice Guidelines in Oncology. The Complete Library of NCCN Clinical Practice Guidelines in Oncology [CD-ROM]. Jenkintown, Pa: ©National Comprehensive Cancer Network; March, 2005. Reprinted with permission. To view the most recent and complete version of the guideline, go online at www.nccn.org.*

## NCCN Practice Guidelines in Oncology v.1.2005: Antiemesis High Emetic Risk Chemotherapy – Emesis Prevention[b,c,d]

146

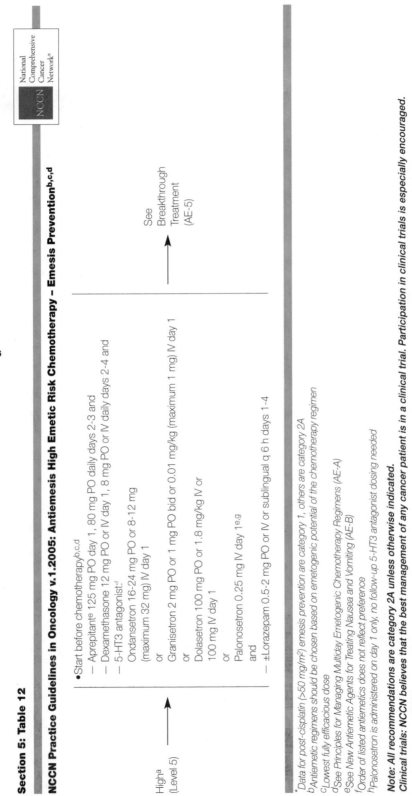

High[a]
(Level 5)

- Start before chemotherapy[b,c,d]
  - Aprepitant[e] 125 mg PO day 1, 80 mg PO daily days 2-3 and
  - Dexamethasone 12 mg PO or IV day 1, 8 mg PO or IV daily days 2-4 and
  - 5-HT3 antagonist:[f]
    Ondansetron 16-24 mg PO or 8-12 mg
    (maximum 32 mg) IV day 1
    or
    Granisetron 2 mg PO or 1 mg PO bid or 0.01 mg/kg (maximum 1 mg) IV day 1
    or
    Dolasetron 100 mg PO or 1.8 mg/kg IV or
    100 mg IV day 1
    or
    Palonosetron 0.25 mg IV day 1[e,g]
  and
  - ±Lorazepam 0.5-2 mg PO or IV or sublingual q 6 h days 1-4

See
Breakthrough
Treatment
(AE-5)

*Data for post-cisplatin (>50 mg/m²) emesis prevention are category 1, others are category 2A
[b]Antiemetic regimens should be chosen based on emetogenic potential of the chemotherapy regimen
[c]Lowest fully efficacious dose
[d]See Principles for Managing Multiday Emetogenic Chemotherapy Regimens (AE-A)
[e]See New Antiemetic Agents for Treating Nausea and Vomiting (AE-B)
[f]Order of listed antiemetics does not reflect preference
[h]Palonosetron is administered on day 1 only; no follow-up 5-HT3 antagonist dosing needed

**Note: All recommendations are category 2A unless otherwise indicated.**
**Clinical trials: NCCN believes that the best management of any cancer patient is in a clinical trial. Participation in clinical trials is especially encouraged.**

## NCCN Practice Guidelines in Oncology v.1.2005:
## Antiemesis Breakthrough Treatment for Chemotherapy Induced Nausea/Vomiting[c,d,j]

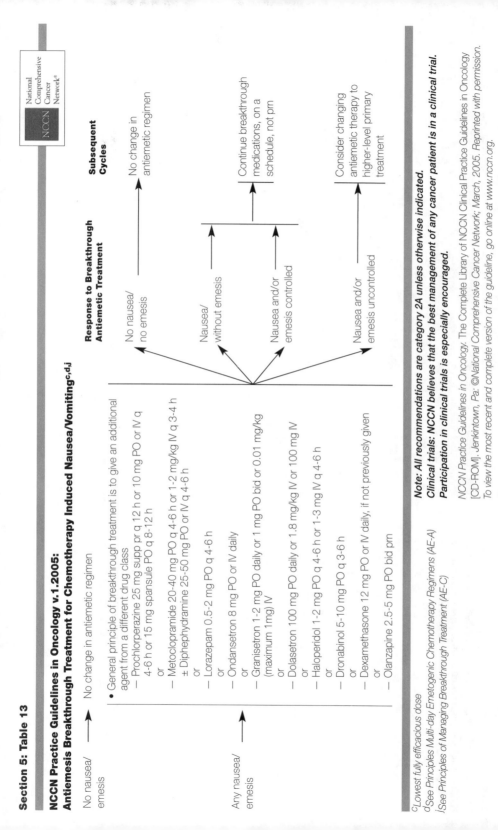

No nausea/ emesis ⟶ No change in antiemetic regimen

• General principle of breakthrough treatment is to give an additional agent from a different drug class
  — Prochlorperazine 25 mg supp pr q 12 h or 10 mg PO or IV q 4-6 h or 15 mg spansule PO q 8-12 h
  or
  — Metoclopramide 20-40 mg PO q 4-6 h or 1-2 mg/kg IV q 3-4 h ± Diphephydramine 25-50 mg PO or IV q 4-6 h
  or
  — Lorazepam 0.5-2 mg PO q 4-6 h
  or
Any nausea/ emesis ⟶
  — Ondansetron 8 mg PO or IV daily
  or
  — Granisetron 1-2 mg PO daily or 1 mg PO bid or 0.01 mg/kg (maximum 1mg) IV
  or
  — Dolasetron 100 mg PO daily or 1.8 mg/kg IV or 100 mg IV
  or
  — Haloperidol 1-2 mg PO q 4-6 h or 1-3 mg IV q 4-6 h
  or
  — Dronabinol 5-10 mg PO q 3-6 h
  or
  — Dexamethasone 12 mg PO or IV daily, if not previously given
  or
  — Olanzapine 2.5-5 mg PO bid prn

**Response to Breakthrough Antiemetic Treatment**

No nausea/ no emesis

Nausea/ without emesis

Nausea and/or emesis controlled

Nausea and/or emesis uncontrolled

**Subsequent Cycles**

No change in antiemetic regimen

Continue breakthrough medications, on a schedule, not prn

Consider changing antiemetic therapy to higher-level primary treatment

[c]Lowest fully efficacious dose

[d]See Principles of Multi-day Emetogenic Chemotherapy Regimens (AE-A)

[j]See Principles of Managing Breakthrough Treatment (AE-C)

*Note: All recommendations are category 2A unless otherwise indicated.*
*Clinical trials: NCCN believes that the best management of any cancer patient is in a clinical trial.*
*Participation in clinical trials is especially encouraged.*

NCCN Practice Guidelines in Oncology: The Complete Library of NCCN Clinical Practice Guidelines in Oncology [CD-ROM]. Jenkintown, Pa: ©National Comprehensive Cancer Network; March, 2005. *Reprinted with permission. To view the most recent and complete version of the guideline, go online at www.nccn.org.*

# NCCN Practice Guidelines in Oncology v.1.2005:
## Anticipatory Emesis Prevention/Treatment

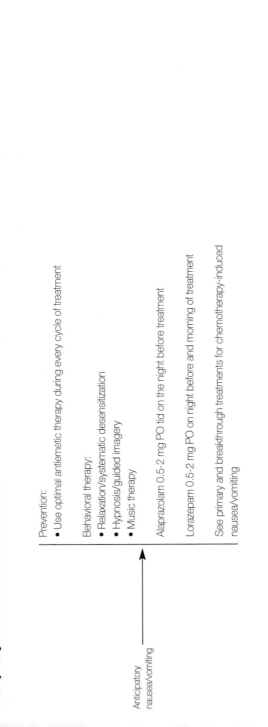

**Anticipatory nausea/vomiting** →

Prevention:
- Use optimal antiemetic therapy during every cycle of treatment

Behavioral therapy:
- Relaxation/systematic desensitization
- Hypnosis/guided imagery
- Music therapy

Alaprazolam 0.5-2 mg PO tid on the night before treatment

Lorazepam 0.5-2 mg PO on night before and morning of treatment

See primary and breakthrough treatments for chemotherapy-induced nausea/vomiting

*Note: All recommendations are category 2A unless otherwise indicated.*
*Clinical trials: NCCN believes that the best management of any cancer patient is in a clinical trial.*
*Participation in clinical trials is especially encouraged.*

*NCCN Practice Guidelines in Oncology. The Complete Library of NCCN Clinical Practice Guidelines in Oncology [CD-ROM]. Jenkintown, Pa: ©National Comprehensive Cancer Network; March, 2005. Reprinted with permission. To view the most recent and complete version of the guideline, go online at www.nccn.org.*

**Performance Scale (Karnofsky and ECOG)**

| ECOG | | Karnofsky | |
|---|---|---|---|
| 0 | Fully active, able to carry on all predisease performance without restriction. | 100% | Normal, no complaints, no evidence of disease. |
| | | 90% | Able to carry on normal activity; minor signs or symptoms of disease. |
| 1 | Restricted in physically strenuous activity but ambulatory and able to carry out work of a light or sedentary nature, eg, light housework, office work. | 80% | Normal activity with effort; some signs or symptoms of disease. |
| | | 70% | Cares for self; unable to carry on normal activity or to do active work |
| 2 | Ambulatory and capable of all self-care but unable to carry out any work activities; up and about more than 50% of waking hours. | 60% | Requires occasional assistance, is mostly able to care for him or herself. |
| | | 50% | Requires considerable assistance and frequent medical care. |
| | | 40% | Disabled, requires special care assistance. |
| 3 | Capable of only limited self-care, and confined to bed or chair more than 50% of waking hours. | 30% | Severely disabled, hospitalization indicated; death not imminent. |
| | | 20% | Very sick, hospitalization necessary; active supportive treatment necessary. |
| 4 | Completely disabled; cannot carry on any self-care; totally confined to bed or chair. | 10% | Moribund, fatal processes progressing rapidly. |
| 5 | Dead | 0% | Dead |

149

*Modified from Karnofsky DA et al. The use of the nitrogen mustards in the palliation treatment of carcinoma with particular reference to bronchogenic carcinoma. Cancer. 1948;1:634-656.*

*Oken MM et al. Toxicity and response criteria of the Eastern Cooperative Oncology Group.* Am J Clin Oncol. 1982;5:649-655.

*Source: Casciato D, ed. Manual of Clinical Oncology. 5th ed. Philadelphia, Pa: Lippincott, Williams and Wilkins; 2004. Reprinted with permission.*

## Sexuality and Fertility

## The Prevalence and Types of Sexual Dysfunction in People With Cancer

Sexuality is a complex, multidimensional phenomenon that incorporates biologic, psychologic, interpersonal, and behavioral dimensions. It is important to recognize that a wide range of normal sexual functioning exists. Ultimately, sexuality is defined by each patient and his/her partner within a context of factors such as gender, age, personal attitudes, and religious and cultural values.

Many types of cancer and cancer therapies are frequently associated with sexual dysfunction. Across sites, estimates of sexual dysfunction after various cancer treatments have ranged from 40% to 100% posttreatment. Research suggests that about 50% of women who have had breast cancer experience long-term sexual dysfunction as do a similar proportion of women who have had gynecologic cancer. For men with prostate cancer, erectile dysfunction (erections inadequate for intercourse) has been the primary form of sexual dysfunction investigated. Prevalence rates of erectile dysfunction have varied. For Hodgkin's lymphoma and testicular cancer, 25% of people who have had these cancers are left with long-term sexual problems.

An individual's sexual response can be affected in a number of ways, and the causes of sexual dysfunction are often both physiological and psychological. The most common sexual problems for people with cancer are loss of desire for sexual activity in men and women, erectile dysfunction in men, and dyspareunia (pain with intercourse) in women. Men may also experience anejaculation (absence of ejaculation), retrograde ejaculation (ejaculation going backward to the bladder), or the inability to reach orgasm. Women may experience changes in genital sensations due to pain or a loss of sensation and numbness, as well as a decreased ability to reach orgasm. Loss of sensation can be as distressing as painful sensation for some individuals. In women, premature ovarian failure as a result of chemotherapy or pelvic radiation therapy is a frequent antecedent to sexual dysfunction, particularly when hormone replacement is contraindicated because the malignancy is hormonally sensitive. Most often, orgasm remains intact for men and women, although it may be delayed secondary to medications and/or anxiety.

Unlike many other physiological side effects of cancer treatment, sexual problems do not tend to resolve within the first year or two of disease-free survival. Rather, they may remain constant and fairly severe. Although it is unclear the extent that sexual problems influence a survivor's rating of overall health-related quality of life, these problems are clearly bothersome to many patients and interfere with a return to normal post-treatment life. Assessment, referral, intervention, and follow-up are important for maximizing quality of life and survival.

## Fertility Issues

Adjuvant radiation therapy and/or chemotherapy introduce higher risks of infertility in the treatment of cancer. Sterility from these therapies may be temporary or permanent. The occurrence of this toxicity is related to a number of factors including the individual's gender, age at the time of treatment, type of therapeutic agent, total dose, single versus multiple agents, and length of time since treatment.

With regard to chemotherapy, patient age is an important factor and the possibility of gonadal recovery improves with the length of time off chemotherapy. The germinal epithelium of the adult testis is more susceptible to damage than that of the prepubertal testis. The evidence to date (largely from adjuvant studies) suggests that patients older than 35 to 40 years of age are most susceptible to the ovarian effects of chemotherapy. The ovaries of younger women can tolerate greater doses. Predicting the outcome for any individual patient is difficult as the course of ovarian functioning following chemotherapy is variable. Relative risk of ovarian failure and testicular damage from cytotoxic agents has been studied, and the alkylating agents have subsequently been shown to be damaging to fertility. The following agents have been shown to be gonadotoxic: busulfan, melphalan, cyclophosphamide, nitrosoureas, cisplatin, chlorambucil, mustine, carmustine, lomustine, cytarabine, ifosfamide and procarbazine.

Chemotherapy regimens for the treatment of non-Hodgkin's lymphoma are generally less gonadotoxic than those used for Hodgkin's lymphoma. The effects of chemotherapy on testicular function has also been widely studied in patients with testicular cancer. A recent review reported that more than half of the patients with testicular germ-cell cancer showed impaired spermatogenesis before undergoing cytotoxic treatment. Permanent infertility is ultimately defined by dose of cisplatin in these patients. At doses below 400 mg/m$^2$, long-term effects on endocrine function and sperm production are unlikely to occur. Higher doses should be expected to cause long-term endocrine-gonadal dysfunction.

When the testes are exposed to radiation, sperm count begins to decrease and, depending on the dosage, may result in temporary or permanent sterility. Men who receive radiation to the abdominal or pelvic region may still regain partial or full sperm production depending on the amount of injury to the testes. For patients with testicular germ-cell cancer, using modern radiation techniques—radiation doses to the paraaortic field <30 Gy) and testis shielding providing testis scatter radiation (<30 Gy)—radiation-induced impairment of fertility is very unlikely. For men, gonadal toxicity can be evidenced by the following 3 measurements: testicular biopsy, serum hormone assays (levels), and semen analysis. When male infertility is the result of abnormal hormone production, the use of hormone manipulation may lead to the return of sperm production.

For women, a dose of 5 Gy to 20 Gy administered to the ovary is sufficient to completely impair gonadal function regardless of the patient's age; a dose of 30 Gy provokes premature menopause in 60% of women younger than 26 years of age. Measurement of gonadal toxicity in women is more difficult to assess due to the relative inaccessibility of the ovary to biopsy (which would require laparoscopy). Therefore, menstrual and reproductive history, measurements of serum hormone levels, and clinical evidence of ovarian function are the criteria most commonly used to determine ovarian failure.

### Preventive Strategies

**152**  For women, studies have shown that movement of the ovaries out of the field of radiation (ovariopexy), either laterally, toward the iliac crest, or behind the uterus may help preserve fertility when high doses of radiation therapy are being applied. By relocating the ovaries laterally it is possible to shield them during radiation of the paraaortic and femoral lymph nodes. Pelvic radiation, however, still provokes an irradiation of the ovary of 5% to 10%, even if transposed outside the irradiation area. Similar prevention strategies are available for men. When possible, lead shields are used to protect the testes.

### Procreation Alternatives

When feasible and relative to the necessity of treatment, oncology professionals should discuss reproductive cell and tissue banking with patients, referring to a reproductive endocrinologist prior to chemotherapy and/or radiation. Men can store sperm from semen ejaculate, epididymal aspirate, testicular aspirate, and testicular biopsy. Women can store ovarian tissue, ovarian follicles, and embryos. In oocyte cryopreservation, which is still experimental, reproductive cells/tissue are cryopreserved for future use in artificial insemination for patients who wish to protect their reproductive capacity. Reviews of indications for cryopreservation of ovarian tissue and current reproductive-assisted technologies are available.

These options may not be appropriate for all patients. Counseling is an important part of the decision making process for patients. Thinking through these decisions at a time when patients are struggling with issues of life and potential death is often difficult. Patients need to consider costs, stress, time, emotions, and potential inclusion of another individual in the pregnancy process (ie, a surrogate). For many patients, the financial costs associated with in vitro fertilization and subsequent embryo cryopreservation is cost prohibitive.

Consideration also needs to be given to the current rate of failure for in vitro fertilization procedures and the potential adverse effect of malignancy on sperm parameters. A retrospective analysis, with a limited sample size, reported that the oocytes from patients with malignant disorders were of a poorer quality and exhibited a significantly-impaired fertilization rate compared with age-matched controls. Importantly, data on the outcome of pregnancies have not shown any increase in genetically-mediated birth defects, birth-weight effects, and sex ratios. Based on the evidence thus far, individuals treated with cytotoxic chemotherapy who remain fertile are not at an increased risk of having children with genetic abnormalities. For all patients who wish to be parents and have permanent infertility, adoption should be presented as a choice.

*Source: National Cancer Institute, www.cancer.gov.*
*Full references available on web site. Updated 4/22/2004.*            **153**

## Loss, Grief and Bereavement

Health care providers will encounter grieving individuals throughout their personal and professional lives. The progression from the final stages of cancer to the death of a loved one is experienced in different ways by different individuals. In fact, one may find that the cancer experience, although it is difficult and trying, has led to significant personal growth. Coping with death is usually not an easy process and cannot be dealt with in a cookbook fashion. The way in which a person will grieve depends on the personality of the grieving individual and his or her relationship with the person who died. The cancer experience, the manner of disease progression, one's cultural and religious beliefs, coping skills and psychiatric history, the availability of support systems, and one's socioeconomic status also affect how a person will cope with grief.

Distinguishing between the terms grief, mourning, and bereavement is important.

**Grief:** The normal process of reacting both internally and externally to the perception of loss. Grief reactions may be seen in response to physical or tangible losses (eg, a death) or in response to symbolic or psychosocial losses (eg, divorce, losing a job). Each type of loss implies experience of some type of deprivation. As a family goes through a cancer illness many losses are experienced and each prompts its own grief reaction. Grief reactions can be psychological, emotional, physical, or social. Psychological/emotional reactions can include anger, guilt, anxiety, sadness, and despair. Physical reactions can include sleep difficulties, appetite changes, somatic complaints, or illness. Social reactions can include feelings about taking care of others in the family, the desire to see or not to see family or friends, or the desire to return to work. As with bereavement, grief processes are dependent on the nature of the relationship with the person lost, the situation surrounding the loss, and one's attachment to the person.

**Mourning:** The process by which people adapt to a loss. Different cultural customs, rituals, or rules for dealing with loss that are followed and influenced by one's society are also a part of mourning.

**Bereavement:** The period after a loss during which grief is experienced and mourning occurs. The length of time spent in a period of bereavement is dependent upon the intensity of the attachment to the deceased, and how much time was involved in anticipation of the loss.

**154** Grief work includes three tasks for a mourner. These tasks include freedom from ties to the deceased, readjustment to the environment from which the deceased is missing, and formation of new relationships. To emancipate from the deceased, a person must modify the emotional energy invested in the lost person. This does not mean that the deceased was not loved or is forgotten, but that the mourner is able to turn to others for emotional satisfaction. In readjustment, the mourner's roles, identity, and skills may have to be modified in order to live in the world without the deceased. In modifying emotional energy, the energy that was once invested in the deceased is invested in other people or activities.

Since these tasks usually require significant effort, it is not uncommon for those who are grieving to experience overwhelming fatigue. The grief experienced is not just for the person who died, but also for the unfulfilled wishes, plans, and fantasies that were held for the person or the relationship. Death often awakens emotions of past losses or separations. One author describes three phases of mourning:

1. The urge to recover the lost person.
2. Disorganization and despair.
3. Reorganization.

These phases grew out of the attachment theory of human behavior, which postulates people's need to attach to others in order to improve survival and reduce risk of harm.

*Source: National Cancer Institute, www.cancer.gov.*
*Full references available on web site. Updated 7/21/2004.*

# 6

# Oncology Care Essentials

This section contains miscellaneous but important information for the oncology clinician. Care of central venous access devices (CVADs), anticoagulation dosing, and contents of a chemotherapy spill kit are all essential to the care of the oncology patient. Clinical trial information and definitions are included as well as commonly used interpretation charts for documenting lab results. This section includes laboratory reference values for hematology, coagulation studies, chemistry and serum tumor markers. The section concludes with chemotherapy drugs with a low, moderate or high risk of hypersensitivity reaction as well as a list of emergency drugs and equipment for use in case of hypersensitivity reaction.

## 1. Central Venous Access Devices (CVADs)

Central venous access devices are single or multi-lumen catheters that are inserted into a major vein, usually in the arm, chest or neck. They are available in various sizes and are constructed of a radio-opaque material so that appropriate placement can be confirmed. Categories of CVADs include percutaneous catheters, tunneled catheters, implanted ports and peripherally inserted central catheters (PICCs).

Routine care of CVADs includes irrigation, cap changes and skin care. Due to lack of scientific evidence for definitive standards of catheter care, individual institutions vary in guidelines for care of these devices. The basic principles are as follows:

**Skin Care** — Consider sterile technique initially following insertion of the device, continuing for 3 to 4 weeks. A sterile technique is also used in immunocompromised patients and commonly used in inpatient settings. Patients can be taught a clean technique for home use. Assess the site daily for signs of infection such as erythema, irritation, swelling, drainage or tenderness. The site can be cleaned with an antiseptic solution (chlorohexidine is currently recommended), using a circular motion moving outward from the insertion site. Dressings are usually applied initially following insertion of the device. A clear occlusive dressing is usually preferred so that the site can be monitored. Dressing change policies vary from daily to three times per week to weekly.

**Cap Changes** — Lumen caps can be changed weekly during infrequent use and daily to three times per week for routine use.

**Irrigation and Flushing** — If blood is drawn from the catheter, the first 5 – 10 mL are discarded, unless the specimens are to be used for blood cultures. After blood withdrawal, the CVAD should be flushed with 10 – 20 mL of normal saline, followed by a Heparin® flush. Heparin flush (10 units/mL or 100 units/mL) dosages vary from 2 to 5 mL. Each lumen of a multi-lumen catheter should be flushed with heparin when not in use. Institutional policies vary on heparinization of unused catheters, from daily to weekly for percutaneous and tunneled catheters. Ports are usually flushed after use and monthly when not used. Groshong type catheters have a closed tip end with a slit valve that prevents the backflow of blood into the catheter. These types do not require irrigation with heparin.

### References

*Camp-Sorrell D.* ONS Access Device Guidelines: Recommendations for Nursing Practice and Education. *Pittsburgh, Pa: Oncology Nursing Press; 2004.*

Chemotherapy and Biotherapy Guidelines and Recommendations for Practice. *3rd ed. Pittsburgh, Pa: Oncology Nursing Press. 2001 Reprinted with permission.*

*Bacquiran DC.* Lippincott's Cancer Chemotherapy Handbook. *2nd ed. Philadelphia, Pa: Lippincott; 2001.*

*Fischer DS, Knobf MT, Durivage HJ, Beaulieu NJ.* The Cancer Chemotherapy Handbook. *6th ed. Philadelphia, Pa: Mosby; 2003.*

*Wyrick S. Central line care: Chlorhexadine vs. Betadine.* Oncology Nursing Forum. *2005;32(2):450.*

### 2. Anticoagulation Dosing

Anticoagulants are used in treating clotting complications. Most commonly in the cancer patient, this includes deep vein thrombosis (DVT) and pulmonary embolism (PE). Heparin prevents new clots but does not dissolve existing clots. It has a short half life (90 minutes). Monitoring the partial thromboplastin time (PTT) assesses the efficacy of the anticoagulation heparin provides. Heparinization usually begins with a bolus of 5000 units IV followed by an infusion to maintain the PTT at 1.5 to 2.0 times the normal value. During the early stages of IV heparin infusion, the PTT should be checked every 4 hours and at appropriate intervals thereafter.

Another option for initiating anticoagulant therapy is low molecular weight heparin (LMWH), which can be given outside the hospital setting without the need for monitoring clotting tests.

## Section 6: Figure 1

**Peripherally inserted catheter (PICC) placement**

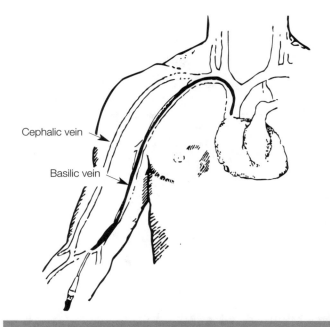

Cephalic vein

Basilic vein

*Reyman PW. Chemotherapy: principles of administration. In: Groenwald S, Frogge M, Goodman M, Yarbo C, eds. Cancer Nursing Principles and Practice. 3rd ed. Boston, Mass: Jones & Bartlett; 1993:314. Reprinted with permission.*

## Section 6: Figure 2

**Placement of tunneled central venous access catheter**

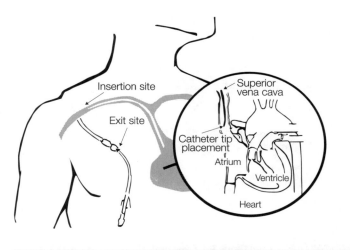

Insertion site

Exit site

Superior vena cava

Catheter tip placement

Atrium

Ventricle

Heart

*Courtesy of Bard Access Systems, Salt Lake City, Utah. Reprinted with permission.*

## Section 6: Figure 3

**Port design**

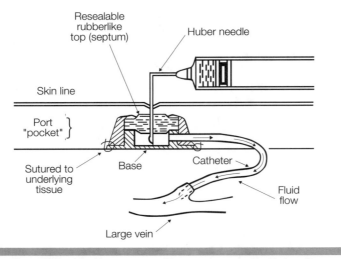

Resealable rubberlike top (septum)

Huber needle

Skin line

Port "pocket" }

Sutured to underlying tissue

Base

Catheter

Fluid flow

Large vein

*Camp-Sorrell D. Implantable ports: everything you always wanted to know.*
*J Intrav Nurs. 1992;15(5):264. Reprinted with permission.*

For patients in which there is a concern for bleeding, low dose warfarin may be used. Warfarin (Coumadin®) is an oral anticoagulant that suppresses clotting factors but has no effect on platelets. Its half-life is 1.2 to 2.5 ds. The PT (prothrombin time) can be used to measure warfarin's effectiveness. The INR (International Normalized Ratio) is a more reliable, standardized measurement for oral anticoagulants. The INR provides a consistent ratio that can be used universally. An INR of 2.0:3.0 is generally accepted for prophylaxis and treatment of deep venous thrombosis (DVT) and for pulmonary embolism prophylaxis. Once anticoagulation has been established with heparin, oral anticoagulants are initiated at anticipated maintenance dose or a slightly higher loading dose (eg, 5 to 10 mg/d of Coumadin for 2 to 4 ds). Daily dosage is adjusted based on the results of the PT or INR determination.

### References

*Casciato DA, ed.* Manual of Clinical Oncology. *5th ed. Philadelphia, Pa: Lippincott, Williams, Wilkins; 2004.*

Drug Facts and Comparisons 2004. *St. Louis, Mo: A Wolters Kluwer Company.*

*Blinder M, Behl R. Coagulation disorders in cancer. In: L Govindan R, ed.* The Washington Manual of Oncology. *Philadelphia, Pa: Lippincott, Williams and Wilkins; 2002.*

## Section 6: Table 1

### Clinical Trials: Phases

| Phase | Objective |
| --- | --- |
| Phase I | Determine the maximum tolerated dose at a given dose, route and schedule. Define toxicities. Investigate pharmacokinetic activities of the agent. These are the first studies in people, and they test safety. |
| Phase II | Determine antitumor activity at a given dose and schedule. Validate toxicities. Focuses on a particular type of cancer, tests safety and begins to evaluate how well it works. |
| Phase III | Compare with standard therapies using randomized trials. Make recommendations for general use. |
| Phase IV | Conduct post-marketing studies to identify other clinical applications for the drug. Generate information about added benefits and risks. |

*Baquiran D. Clinical trials. In: Lippincott's Cancer Chemotherapy Handbook. 2nd ed. Philadelphia, Pa: Lippincott; 2001.*

## Section 6: Table 2

### Clinical Trials: Measurement of Response to Treatment

| Response | Description |
| --- | --- |
| Complete response (CR) | Disappearance of all clinical evidence of tumor by physical examination or radiologic studies with no appearance of new lesions. The response must last for a minimum of four weeks. The patient must be free of all cancer-related symptoms and all abnormal biochemical parameters must return to normal. |
| Partial response (PR) | Fifty percent or greater decrease in the sum of the product of the diameters of the measured lesions. No new lesions may appear. This improvement must continue for at least four weeks during which there is no cancer-associated deterioration in weight, performance status, or symptoms. If there is no change in tumor size but the biochemical parameters decline by 80% or more, the patient will be considered stable. |
| Stable disease (STAB) | Patients who do not meet the criteria for partial response without signs and symptoms of progressive disease for a minimum of three months. |
| Progressive disease (PROG) | A greater than 25% increase in the total area of the bidimensionally measurable lesion(s). The appearance of new lesions or greater or significant deterioration that cannot be attributed to treatment or medical conditions will be considered disease progression. |

*Baquiran D. Clinical trials. In: Lippincott's Cancer Chemotherapy Handbook. 2nd ed. Philadelphia, Pa: Lippincott; 2001.*

## Section 6: Table 3

**Laboratory Data: Interpretation of Charts**

### Complete Blood Count

WBC = white blood count
HGB = hemoglobin
HCT = hematocrit
PLT = platelets

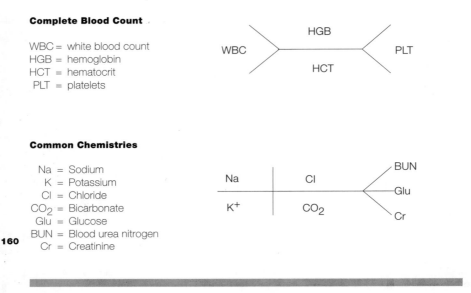

### Common Chemistries

Na = Sodium
K = Potassium
Cl = Chloride
$CO_2$ = Bicarbonate
Glu = Glucose
BUN = Blood urea nitrogen
Cr = Creatinine

## Section 6: Table 4

**Temperature Conversion Chart**

| Fahrenheit | Celsius |
| --- | --- |
| 94.0 | 34.4 |
| 95.0 | 35.0 |
| 96.0 | 35.5 |
| 97.0 | 36.1 |
| 98.0 | 36.6 |
| 98.6 | 37.0 |
| 99.0 | 37.2 |
| 100.0 | 37.7 |
| 101.0 | 38.3 |
| 102.0 | 38.8 |
| 103.0 | 39.4 |
| 104.0 | 40.0 |
| 105.0 | 40.5 |
| 106.0 | 41.1 |
| 107.0 | 41.6 |
| 108.0 | 42.2 |

**Contents of an Antineoplastic Spill Kit**

| Number | Item |
| --- | --- |
| 1 | Gown with cuffs and back closure (made of nonpermeable fabric) |
| 1 pair | Shoe covers |
| 2 pair | Gloves |
| 1 pair | Utility gloves |
| 1 pair | Chemical splash goggles |
| 1 | Rebreather mask approved by National Institute of Occupational Safety and Health (NIOSH) |
| 1 | Disposable dustpan (to collect broken glass) |
| 1 | Plastic scraper (to scoop materials into dustpan) |
| 2 | Plastic-backed absorbent towels |
| 1 each | 250 mL and 1 liter spill-control pillows |
| 2 | Disposable sponges (one to clean up spill, one to clean up floor after removal of spill) |
| 1 | "Sharps" container |
| 2 | Large, heavy-duty waste-disposal bags |
| 1 | Hazardous waste label |

*Occupational Health and Safety Administration (OSHA).* Controlling Occupational Exposure to Hazardous Drugs. *Washington, DC: Occupational Health and Safety Administration; 1995:21-1- 21-34. OSHA Instruction CPL 2-2.20B.*

## Laboratory Reference Values (Adults)

*These values will vary, depending on the individual laboratory as well as the methods and instruments used. These tables are intended as a reference.*

**Hematology**

| Hemoglobin | Males:<br>Females: | 13.5 – 19 gm/dL<br>12.5 – 16 gm/dL | |
|---|---|---|---|
| Hematocrit | Males:<br>Females: | 42 – 52%<br>37 – 47% | |
| MCV | | 78 – 100 fL | |
| MCH | | 27 – 31 pg | |
| RDW | | 11.5 – 14 % | |
| Reticulocyte count | | 0.5 – 1.85 % of erythrocytes | |
| Erythropoeitin | Males:<br>Females: | 17.2 mU/mL (mean)<br>18.8 mU/mL (mean) | |
| Ferritin | Males:<br>Females: | 20 – 300 ng/mL<br>15 – 120 ng/mL | |
| Iron | Males:<br>Females: | 75 – 175 mcg/dL<br>65 – 165 mcg/dL | |
| Iron binding capacity<br>% saturation | | 250 – 450 mcg/dL<br>20 – 50 % | |
| Transferrin | | 240 – 480 mg/dL | |
| Folate,<br>serum | | >3.5 mcg/L | |
| Vitamin $B_{12}$,<br>serum | | 190 – 900 ng/mL | |
| WBC | | 4.0 – 10.5 x1000 $mm^3$ | (100%) |
| | Total neutrophils<br>Segs<br>Bands<br>Lymphocytes<br>Monocytes<br>Eosinophils<br>Basophils | 1.5 – 6.6<br>1.3 – 6.0<br><1.0<br>1.5 – 3.5<br><1.0<br><0.7<br><0.1 | (segs + bands)<br>(40 – 60%)<br>(3%)<br>(20 – 40%)<br>(4 – 8%)<br>(1 – 3%)<br>(0 –1%) |
| Platelets | | 150,000 – 350,000 $mm^3$ | |

*(continued on next page)*

162

## Laboratory Reference Values (Adults)

### Blood Coagulation Tests

| | | |
|---|---|---|
| Bleeding Time | | 3.0 – 9.5 minutes |
| Fibrinogen | Males:<br>Females: | 180 – 340 mg/dL<br>190 – 420 mg/dL |
| Partial thromboplastin time (aPTT) | | 25 – 38 seconds |
| Prothrombin time (PT), one stage | | +/- 2 seconds of control<br>(control should be 11 – 16 seconds) |
| Thrombin time (TT) | | +/- 5 seconds of control |

### Blood Chemistries

| | | |
|---|---|---|
| Albumin | | 3.7 – 5.6 gm/dL |
| Amylase (total) | | 35 – 115 units/L |
| Bicarbonate | | 21 –29 mEq/L |
| Bilirubin | Total<br>Direct | < 1.0 mg/dL<br>< 0.6 mg/dL |
| BUN | | 8 – 21 mg/dL |
| Calcium | | 8.9 – 10.7 mg/dL |
| Carbon dioxide | | 17 – 31 mEq/L |
| Chloride | | 96 – 109 mEq/L |
| Creatinine | | 0.8 – 1.2 mg/dL |
| GGT | Males:<br>Females: | 11 – 34 units/L<br>11 – 28 units/L |
| Glucose (fasting) | | 60 – 100 mg/dL (depends on method) |
| LDH | | 340 – 670 units/L |
| Lipase | | 56 – 239 units/L |
| Magnesium | | 1.7 – 2.3 mg/dL |

**163**

*(continued on next page)*

**Laboratory Reference Values (Adults)**

| | | | |
|---|---|---|---|
| Phosphate | | | 2.8 – 4.6 mg/dL |
| Potassium | | | 3.6 – 4.8 mEq/L |
| Protein, serum | | | 6.3 – 8.6 gm/dL |
| Sodium | | | 135 – 145 mEq/L |
| Transaminase | AST | Males: | 15 – 45 units/L |
| | | Females: | 5 – 30 units/L |
| | ALT | Males: | 10 – 40 units/L |
| | | Females: | 5 – 35 units/L |
| Uric acid | | Males: | 4.0 – 8.6 mg/dL |
| | | Females: | 3.0 – 5.9 mg/dL |

*Wallach J.* Interpretation of Diagnostic Tests. *7th ed. Philadelphia, Pa: Lippincott, Williams, Wilkins; 2000.*

**Section 6: Table 7**

**Serum Tumor Markers**

| Marker | Upper limit | Tumor |
|---|---|---|
| Alpha feto-protein | 25 mcg/L | Testis, hepatoma |
| Beta HCG | <1 ng/mL | Testis, trophoblastic neoplasia |
| Calcitonin | 0.1 ng/mL | Thyroid (medullary carcinoma) |
| CA 15-3 | 32 U/mL | Breast |
| CA 19-9 | 37 U/mL | Pancreas, colorectal |
| CA 125 | 35 U/mL | Ovary |
| CEA | 5 ng/mL | Colorectal, lung (sm. cell), breast |
| PSA | 2.5 – 4.0 ng/mL | Prostate |
| Paraproteins | varies | Myeloma, lymphoma |
| Thyroglobulin | 10 ng/mL | Thyroid |

*Lowitz BB, Casciato DA. Principles of cancer medicine. In:* Manual of Clinical Oncology. *5th ed. Philadelphia, Pa: Lippincott, Williams and Wilkins; 2004.*

## Section 6: Table 8

### Immediate Hypersensitivity Reactions: Predicted Risk of Chemotherapy

| High Risk | Low to Moderate Risk | Rare Risk |
|---|---|---|
| Asperaginase* | Anthracyclines | Cytarabine |
| Murine monoclonal | Bacillus Calmais-Guérin | Cyclophosphamide |
| antibodies | Biomycin | Chlorambucil |
| (eg, rituximab) | Carboplatin | Dacarbazine |
| Pacitaxel | Chimeric and human | 5-Fluorouracil |
| | monoclonal antibodies | Ifosfamide |
| | Cisplatin | Interferons |
| | Cyclosporin | Mitoxantrone |
| | Docetaxel | |
| | Etoposide | |
| | Melphalan* | |
| | Procarbazine | |
| | Teniposide | |

*Significantly increased risk with IV route
Chemotherapy and Biotherapy Guidelines and Recommendations for Practice. 3rd ed. Pittsburgh, Pa: Oncology Nursing Press; 2001. Reprinted with permission.

## Section 6: Table 9

### Emergency Drugs and Equipment for Use in Case of Hypersensitivity or Anaphylactic Reaction*

| Drug | Strength | Usage |
|---|---|---|
| Epinephrine | Adults: 0.1 mg-0.5 mg IV push every 10 min. as needed Pediatric dose: 0.01 mg/kg IV or SC or 0.1 mg-0.3 mg every 10-15 min | Administer by inhalation, SC, IM, or IV in anaphylaxis or allergic reaction |
| Diphenhydramine hydrochloride | 25-50 mg Pediatrics: 1 mg/kg (maximum 50 mg) | Administer IV to block further antigen-antibody reaction |
| Aminophylline | 50 mg/kg Not used for pediatric patients | Administer IV over 30 min. to enhance bronchodilation |
| Dopamine | 2-20 mcg/kg/min. Pediatrics: 5=20 mcg/kg/min. Adjust to patient's response. | Administer IV to counter hypotension |
| Steroids Solu-Medrol® Solu-Cortef® | 30-60 mg Pediatrics: 0.3-0.5 mg/kg 100-500 mg Pediatrics: 1-2 mg/kg | Administer IV to ease bronchoconstriction and cardiac dysfunction |
| Dexamethasone | 10-20 mg Pediatrics: 0.1-0.2 mg/kg | |

*Additional emergency medication (eg, sodium bicarbonate, furosemide, lidocaine, naloxone hydrochloride, or sublingual nitroglycerine) and emergency supplies (eg, oxygen, suction machine with catheters and ambu bag) should be available in case of medical emergency.
Chemotherapy and Biotherapy Guidelines and Recommendations for Practice. 3rd ed. Pittsburgh, Pa: Oncology Nursing Press; 2001. Reprinted with permission.

# 7

# Oncologic Emergencies

The oncologic emergencies are a group of potentially life-threatening conditions that may occur at the time of initial cancer diagnosis or at the time of cancer recurrence. Clinicians must be aware of the risk factors for these emergencies, the signs and symptoms as well as the corrective measures needed to treat them. When promptly recognized and treated, permanent disabling side effects can be avoided in many cases.

Oncologic emergencies can present as obstructive emergencies, metabolic conditions or infiltrative emergencies. The following table is a quick reference for experienced clinicians, intended as a review of the topic. For more detailed information, consult an oncology text. The table identifies the type and classification of oncologic emergency, predisposing factors, signs and symptoms, and treatment methods.

**Section 7: Table 1**

## Oncologic Emergencies

| Type | Classification | Common Predisposing Oncologic Factors | Common Signs and Symptoms | Treatment |
|------|----------------|----------------------------------------|----------------------------|-----------|
| Superior vena cava syndrome | Obstructive | • Lung cancer, most often small cell<br>• Lymphoma<br>• Rarely breast, testicular, or sarcoma | • Shortness of breath<br>• Facial and neck swelling<br>• Trunk and upper extremity edema<br>• Headache<br>• Thoracic and neck vein distention | • Correction of airway obstruction<br>• Oxygen for hypoxia<br>• Corticosteroids<br>• Radiation therapy to tumor mass<br>• Chemotherapy if indicated for tumor |
| Intestinal obstruction | Obstructive | • GI tumors<br>• Ovarian cancer<br>• Vinca alkaloid neurotoxicity<br>• Radiation injury of small bowel | • Abdominal pain<br>• Abdominal distention<br>• Alternating diarrhea and constipation<br>• Vomiting<br>• Fever<br>• Leukocytosis<br>• High pitched, hyperactive bowel sounds proximal to obstruction, absent distal to obstruction | • NG tube decompression<br>• Surgical intervention<br>• Hydration to correct fluid imbalance<br>• Chemo or radiation therapy may be helpful in carcinomatosis |

*(continued on next page)*

**Section 7: Table 1** *(continued)*

## Oncologic Emergencies

| Type | Classification | Common Predisposing Oncologic Factors | Common Signs and Symptoms | Treatment |
|---|---|---|---|---|
| Syndrome of Inappropriate Antidiuretic Hormone (SIADH) | Metabolic (water intoxication) | • Lung cancer, esp. small cell<br>• Brain masses or infection<br>• GI, prostate, ovary, leukemia, Hodgkin's | • Lethargy<br>• Nausea<br>• Anorexia, N/V<br>• Generalized weakness<br>• Confusion<br>• Absence of edema<br>• Sluggish DTRs<br>• Weight gain<br>• Hyponatremia<br>• Low BUN/cr<br>• Decreased serum osm., increased urine osm.<br>• Increased urinary excretion of sodium<br>• Hypokalemia<br>• Hypocalcemia | • Treat the underlying cancer cause<br>• Severe hyponatremia: aggressive management with IV NaCl, diuretics, monitor CVP and electrolytes<br>• Moderate hyponatremia: fluid restriction, demeclocycline po to induce renal resistance to ADH and facilitate free water excretion |
| Hypercalcemia | Metabolic | • Usually results from excessive bone resorption relative to bone formation<br>• Bone metastases<br>• Squamous cell lung and head/neck cancers<br>• Breast cancer<br>• Renal cancer<br>• Multiple myeloma<br>• Lymphoma | • Polyuria, polydipsia, nocturia<br>• Anorexia<br>• Easy fatiguability<br>• Profound muscle weakness<br>• Irritability, apathy<br>• Depression<br>• N/V, constipation, obstipation<br>• Pruritis<br>• Shortened Q-T interval, prolonged P-R interval on ECG | • Hydration and saline diuresis<br>• Bisphosphonates to inhibit osteoclast activity (Pamidronate IV)<br>• Less commonly used drugs include Mithramycin IV, Calcitonin, gallium<br>• Dialysis rarely used |

*(continued on next page)*

**Section 7: Table 1** *(continued)*

## Oncologic Emergencies

| Type | Classification | Common Predisposing Oncologic Factors | Common Signs and Symptoms | Treatment |
|------|----------------|----------------------------------------|----------------------------|-----------|
| Septic Shock | Metabolic | • Leukemia<br>• Lymphoma<br>• Neutropenia following chemotherapy<br>• Prolonged hospitalization | • Fever and chills<br>• Change in mental status, confusion<br>• Hypotension, tachycardia, tachypnea<br>• Decreased $PO_2$<br>• Oliguria<br>• Metabolic acidosis<br>• Risk of infection increases slightly with WBC <1000/mcL, increases sharply with WBC <500 | • Oxygen for hypoxia, mechanical ventilation may be required<br>• IV hydration to maintain blood pressure<br>• Vasopressors to maintain cardiac output and renal perfusion<br>• Broad spectrum antibiotics |
| Disseminated Intravascular Coagulation | Metabolic | • Overwhelming viral or bacterial sepsis and shock<br>• Release of thrombin from malignant cells, esp. AML, melanoma, lung, stomach, colon, breast, ovary and prostate cancers<br>• Transfusion reaction | • Diffuse clotting occurring simultaneously with hemorrhage<br>• Petechiae<br>• Ecchymosis<br>• Prolonged bleeding from injection sites<br>• Hemolysis<br>• Hypotension<br>• Oliguria<br>• Renal failure<br>• Hematuria<br>• Change in mental status<br>• Acrocyanosis | • Remove precipitating factor if possible<br>• Heparin infusion to inactivate thrombin and inhibit clotting<br>• Platelet transfusions and fresh frozen plasma infusions<br>• Amicar® IV to inhibit fibrinolysis if necessary<br>• Antiplatelet drugs (aspirin, dipyridamole) for chronic DIC, not bleeding |

*(continued on next page)*

**Oncologic Emergencies**

| Type | Classification | Common Predisposing Oncologic Factors | Common Signs and Symptoms | Treatment |
|------|----------------|---------------------------------------|---------------------------|-----------|
| Cardiac Tamponade | Infiltrative | • Malignant pericardial effusion<br>• Breast and lung cancer most common<br>• Melanoma, leukemia, lymphoma | • Signs and symptoms extremely variable<br>• Neck vein distention that increases on inspiration<br>• Pulsus paradoxus (fall in SBP of >10 mm Hg at the end of inspiration)<br>• Distant heart sounds<br>• Pulmonary rales<br>• Hepatosplenomegaly<br>• Ascites<br>• Extreme anxiety and agitation<br>• Dyspnea and tachypnea<br>• N/V, hiccups<br>• Dysphagia<br>• Perfuse perspiration | • Pericardiocentesis to remove fluid<br>• Oxygen<br>• IV hydration<br>• Vasopressors<br>• When stable, may need pericardial window placed<br>• Radiation therapy for short and long term control of malignant effusion<br>• Pericardial sclerosing agents |
| Spinal Cord Compression | Infiltrative | • Metastases to the spine<br>• Lung cancer, breast cancer, prostate cancer, myeloma, lymphoma, unknown primary, kidney, melanoma, GI cancers | • Midline or paravertebral back pain which worsens on movement<br>• Tenderness over site<br>• Motor weakness followed by sensory changes<br>• Bowel and bladder dysfunction<br>• Hyperactive DTRs<br>• Babinski response<br>• Decreased anal sphincter tone | • Rapid intervention is essential<br>• Steroids (dexamethasone) to alleviate symptoms and control pain<br>• Radiation therapy is primary treatment<br>• Surgery: emergent decompression by laminectomy for rapidly progressing symptoms |

171

*(continued on next page)*

## Oncologic Emergencies

| Type | Classification | Common Predisposing Oncologic Factors | Common Signs and Symptoms | Treatment |
|------|---------------|----------------------------------------|----------------------------|-----------|
| Anaphylaxis | Allergic | • Transfusion reaction – infusion of IgA proteins to IgA deficient recipient who has developed IgA antibodies<br>• Chemotherapy reaction – believed to be antigen/antibody reaction, a type 1 hypersensitivity reaction that is IgE mediated<br>• High risk: L-asparaginase, paclitaxel<br>• Low to moderate risk: anthracyclines, bleomycin, carboplatin, cisplatin, cyclosporine, docetaxel, etoposide, melphalan, methotrexate, procarbazine, teniposide | • Urticaria<br>• Localized or generalized itching<br>• Shortness of breath with or without wheezing<br>• Agitation or uneasiness<br>• Chest tightness<br>• Periorbital or facial edema<br>• Abdominal cramping or nausea<br>• Chills<br>• Cardiovascular collapse, shock | • Transfusion reaction: stop transfusion, keep vein open, notify MD and blood bank, emergency equipment at bedside<br>• Localized reaction: diphenhydramine and/or corticosteroids<br>• Flare reaction in vein: stop drug and flush with saline followed by hydrocortisone IV, slowly resume infusion, consider premeds for future doses<br>• Generalized reaction: stop chemo, maintain M, emergency drugs as needed |
| Tumor Lysis Syndrome | Metabolic | • Massive release into the blood of breakdown products of dying tumor cells<br>• Acute leukemia<br>• Burkitt's lymphoma<br>• Rare in solid tumors | • Hyperkalemia<br>• Hypocalcemia<br>• Hyperphosphatemia<br>• Hyperuricemia<br>• Oliguria<br>• Acute renal failure<br>• Tetany<br>• Cardiac arrhythmias or cardiopulmonary arrest | • Aggressive hydration<br>• Alkalization of urine<br>• Allopurinol to decrease uric acid levels<br>• Correction of electrolyte imbalances<br>• Hemodialysis may be necessary for those who do not respond or develop renal insufficiency |

*Casciato DA, ed. Manual of Clinical Oncology. 5th ed. Philadelphia, Pa: Lippincott, Williams and Wilkins; 2004.*

Myelosuppression is the most common dose-limiting toxicity of chemotherapy. Most chemotherapy drugs are myelosuppressive. The primary manifestations of myelosuppression are anemia, thrombocytopenia, and neutropenia. This section will address each of these problems separately.

## 1. Cancer-Related Anemia

Anemia has been defined as a reduction in either the red blood cell (RBC) volume or the concentration of hemoglobin in the blood. It is a common condition among cancer patients. It may be due to the disease process or may be a side effect of treatment regimens. Anemia may reveal a more aggressive underlying disease or it may play a direct role in terms of response to therapy.

There are many different types of anemia; some are more common in the cancer patient. The causes of anemia in cancer patients require distinctly different management, therefore determining the cause of the anemia is critical in these patients, as it is in the general population. It cannot be merely considered a side effect of cancer. Aggressive treatment of cancer-related anemia has been shown to improve quality of life.

The RBC originates in the bone marrow as an undifferentiated stem cell. The stem cell is differentiated into a red blood cell when a feedback system, initiated by decreased oxygen tension at the level of the kidney, causes an increased release of erythropoietin from the kidney. Erythropoietin is a hormone found naturally in humans, which triggers the bone marrow to differentiate stem cells into erythrocytes or RBCs. Once the bone marrow responds and increased levels of RBCs are pushed into the circulation, the kidney senses an increase in oxygen tension. Erythropoietin levels decrease and RBC levels are maintained. This feedback system serves to maintain a normal hemoglobin level. However, multiple areas of the system can be affected by cancer, including the bone marrow that can be infiltrated by tumor or decimated by chemotherapy. The kidney can be affected as well as erythropoietin levels.

## 2. Laboratory Assessment of Anemia

The complete blood count (CBC) is the basic screening test for anemia. Normal values for CBC and other labs are found in Section 7. Table 8-1 details the results of laboratory tests for many of the common types of anemia. This table is intended as a quick reference in determining the type of anemia, based on laboratory results.

**Hemoglobin:** determines the amount of hemoglobin or the oxygen carrying capacity of the peripheral blood.

**Hematocrit:** determines the space or volume occupied by red blood cells in relation to the total blood volume, it is expressed as a percentage of the total.

**The Red Cell Indices:**

> **MCV (mean corpuscular volume):** indicates the average volume or size of a single RBC in a given blood sample.

> **MCH (mean corpuscular hemoglobin):** indicates the average weight of hemoglobin in each RBC.

> **MCHC (mean corpuscular hemoglobin concentration):** indicates the average hemoglobin concentration or color of the RBC.

> **RDW (red cell distribution width):** an automated calculation of variation in size, which provides a measure of homogeneity (normal RDW) or heterogeneity (high RDW).

**Reticulocyte Count:** measures newly released RBCs; reticuloctyes circulate for 24 hours before maturing into erythrocytes, therefore they reflect erythropoeitic activity of the marrow (increased or decreased in response to anemic state).

**Ferritin:** measures the body's storage of iron, first test to become abnormal in iron deficiency.

**Transferrin:** regulates iron transport in the blood.

**Total Iron Binding Capacity (TIBC):** measures transferrin indirectly.

**Serum Iron:** measures the amount of iron bound to the transferrin.

**Coomb's Test:** detects immunoglobulin antibodies and/or complement on the red cell membrane, used to evaluate for hemolytic anemias.

**Serum B$_{12}$ and Folate Levels:** measures levels of B$_{12}$ and folate in the blood.

### 3. Physical Assessment of Anemia

**Signs and symptoms of anemia:** may or may not be present in all patients

- Fatigue
- Shortness of breath or dyspnea on exertion
- Headache
- Chest pain
- Paresthesias
- Inability to concentrate
- Feeling cold
- Lightheadedness
- Irritability

**Physical Exam Findings:** may or may not be present in all patients, commonly no physical abnormalities are found on examination. Cardiovascular signs are not usually present until hemoglobin falls below 7 gm/dL.

- Pallor
- Jaundice
- Hepatosplenomegaly
- Tachycardia
- Tachypnea
- Hypotension
- Glossitis
- Systolic murmur
- Impaired vibratory and position sense
- Spastic weakness

### 4. Differential Diagnosis of Anemia

Anemia is a sign of illness, not a disease itself. The challenge in diagnosis comes from the numerous and diverse etiologies of anemia. It is helpful to categorize anemias according to the size of the RBCs, as determined by the RBC indices and cell morphology. Microcytic anemias have small cells, macrocytic anemias have large cells and anemias with normal sized cells are normocytic. A significant elevation in the RDW indicates that the MCV is a less accurate assessment of RBC size, making this classification less useful.

Another important distinction in developing a differential diagnosis is the presence or absence of pancytopenia. The presence of pancytopenia suggests ineffective hematopoesis that affects all three cell lines. Pancytopenia results from distinctly different disorders than those that cause simple anemia. An examination of the bone marrow is required in the presence of pancytopenia.

Finally, anemias can be categorized by looking at the reticulocyte count to assess the bone marrow response to the anemic state. Increased reticulocyte counts are seen with accelerated RBC production, such as hemolysis and blood loss. Decreased reticuloctye counts indicate the marrow is not actively producing RBCs. This is demonstrated in iron deficiency and anemia of chronic disease.

**Section 8: Table 1**

**Common Cancer-Related Anemias and Their Treatment**

| Type | Classification | Causes | Characteristics | Treatment |
|---|---|---|---|---|
| Iron Deficiency Anemia | Microcytic, Hypochromic | • Inadequate intake of iron<br>• Inadequate absorption of iron, eg, malabsorption syndromes, s/p gastrectomy<br>• Excessive loss of iron through blood loss, GI bleeding, menorrhagia | • Low MCV<br>• Low MCHC<br>• Low to normal retic count<br>• Low ferritin<br>• Low iron<br>• Paresthesias, sore tongue, brittle nails, pica | • Oral iron supplements given between meals TID<br>• Response within 2 wks increased retic count, anemia corrected 6-8 weeks<br>• Transfusions rarely needed<br>• IV iron an option |
| Anemia of Chronic Disease (ACD) | Normocytic, normochromic | • Associated with infectious, inflammatory, malignant and connective tissue disorders of several weeks duration<br>• Etiology unknown, thought to be due to inadequate release of erythropoietin from the kidney or lack of iron release from its stored form<br>• May be found in combination with iron deficiency | • Mild anemia, Hbg >9 gm/dL<br>• Low or normal MCV<br>• Low serum iron and TIBC, normal or elevated ferritin<br>• No identifying symptoms, diagnosis of exclusion | • Identify and treat the underlying condition if possible<br>• Erythropoietin 10,000 U sq TIW or 40,000 U sq weekly until Hgb normal<br>• Darbepoietin is a newer formulation of erythropoietin with a longer half life, suggested initial dose 2.25 mcg/kg SQ once per week, some studies suggest it can be given every 2 weeks<br>• Start iron replacement orally with start of epo as pt. usually becomes iron deficient with correction of ACD |

(continued on next page)

## Common Cancer-Related Anemias and Their Treatment

| Type | Classification | Causes | Characteristics | Treatment |
|------|---------------|--------|-----------------|-----------|
| Vitamin $B_{12}$ Deficiency | Macrocytic, hyperchromic, megaloblastic | • Lack of intrinsic factor<br>• Intrinsic factor inhibition<br>• Gastric surgery<br>• Small intestine disorders<br>• Hyperthyroidism<br>• Pernicious anemia (intrinsic factor deficiency due to atrophy of gastric mucosa) | • Develops years after cessation of ingestion of $B_{12}$<br>• High MCV, high MCHC, increased ferritin, low $B_{12}$ level, normal folate level<br>• Megaloblastic features on peripheral smear<br>• Fatigue, weakness, paresthesias, glossitis<br>• Decreased vibratory sensation, loss of proprioception, ataxia, spastic weakness<br>• Can lead to permanent nerve damage if not corrected | • Weekly $B_{12}$ injections for initial repletion<br>• Monthly lifelong maintenance therapy |
| Folate Deficiency | Macrocytic, hyperchromic, megaloblastic | • Insufficient dietary intake<br>• Over-cooking of food<br>• Alcoholism<br>• Malabsorption<br>• Ingestion of folic acid antagonists | • Develops months after inadequate intake<br>• High MCV, high MCHC, increased ferritin, normal $B_{12}$ level, low folate level<br>• Megaloblastic features on peripheral smear<br>• Clinical findings similar to $B_{12}$ deficiency except for absence of neurological symptoms | • Folate 1 mg po daily<br>• Duration of treatment dependent upon the cause of the deficiency |
| Thalassemia | Mild anemia, microcytic, hypochromic | • Group of genetic disorders characterized by abnormal hemoglobin synthesis<br>• May co-exist with other anemias such as iron deficiency or ACD | • Primarily affects populations of Africa, Southeast Asia, and the Mediterranean<br>• Mild anemia, decreased MCV<br>• Increased or normal retic count<br>• Increased or normal ferritin<br>• May have microcytosis without decrease in hemoglobin<br>• Abnormal hemoglobin electrophoresis<br>• Target cells on blood smear<br>• No defining signs or symptoms | • No treatment may be necessary for thalassemia minor |

**177**

*(continued on next page)*

**Common Cancer-Related Anemias and Their Treatment**

| Type | Classification | Causes | Characteristics | Treatment |
|------|---------------|--------|-----------------|-----------|
| Acute Blood Loss | Normocytic, normochromic | • Rapid drop in hemoglobin with corresponding rise in RBC production as bone marrow attempts to replete the supply | • Rapidly falling hemoglobin<br>• Increased reticulocyte count<br>• Signs and symptoms usually evident, however occult bleeding can occur with retroperitoneal bleed after trauma | • Treat the cause of the bleed<br>• Replete blood supply with transfusions |
| Hypersplenism | Normocytic, normochromic | • Hyper-sequestration of blood in large spleen<br>• Premature destruction of red cells within the enlarged spleen<br>• Principle mechanism is hemodilution<br>• May be associated with sarcoidosis, leukemia, lymphoma | • Splenomegaly at three or more times normal size<br>• Reduction in one or more of the cellular elements<br>• Increased reticuloctye count | • Usually corrected by splenectomy |
| Hemolytic anemia | Normocytic, normochromic | • Premature destruction of RBCs<br>• Classified as extravascular or intravascular according to the primary site of RBC destruction<br>• May be a result of the tumor or can be a side effect of chemotherapy<br>• Many different types of hemolytic anemias | • Increased reticulocyte count<br>• Increased serum LDH and bilirubin<br>• Positive Coombs test<br>• Presence of schistocytes on peripheral smear | • Treatment directed at management of underlying process |

Casciato DA. Manual of Clinical Oncology. *5th ed. Philadelphia, Pa: Lippincott, Williams and Wilkins; 2004:642-645.*
Fischer DS, Knobf MT, Durivage HJ, Beaulieu NJ. The Cancer Chemotherapy Handbook. *6th ed. Philadelphia, Pa: Mosby; 2003.*
Gillespie T. Anemia in cancer. Cancer Nursing. *2003;26(2):119-128.*
Montoya VL, Wink D, Sole ML. Adult anemia: determine clinical significance. The Nurse Practitioner. *2002;27(3):38-53.*
Oncology Nursing Society. Chemotherapy and Biotherapy Guidelines and Recommendations for Practice. *Pittsburgh, Pa: Oncology Nursing Press; 2001:92-96.*
Rizzo JD, Lichtin AE, Woolf SH et al. Use of epoetin in patients with cancer: evidence-based clinical practice guidelines of the American Society of Clinical Oncology and the American Society of Hematology. *Journal of Clinical Oncology. 2002;20:4083.*
Sabbatini P, Cella D, Chanan-Khan A et al. Cancer and treatment-related anemia. Version 1.2004; 2004. National Comprehensive Cancer Network (NCCN) Clinical Practice Guidelines in Oncology. *Available at http://www.nccn.org/professionals/physician_gls/default.asp*

## 5. Cancer-Related Thrombocytopenia

Patients with cancer may have a low platelet count due to decreased numbers of platelets or altered platelet function. Underlying malignancy may alter the function of the platelets. Platelets may be destroyed by immune or nonimmune mechanisms. The most common cause of thrombocytopenia in the cancer patient is chemotherapy.

### Laboratory Assessment of Thrombocytopenia

A moderate risk of bleeding occurs when the platelet count falls below 50,000 cells per cubic millimeter. A major risk is associated with platelet counts below 20,000 and a critical risk is present with counts below 10,000.

### Signs and Symptoms of Thrombocytopenia
- petechiae
- common sites of hemorrhage:
    - gingiva
    - nose
    - bladder
    - GI tract
    - brain
- presence of signs and symptoms of anemia may be indicative of occult long-term bleeding

**Causes and Management of Cancer-Related Thrombocytopenia**

| Type | Classification and Causes | Signs & Symptoms | Management |
|---|---|---|---|
| Decreased platelet production | • Chemotherapy<br>• Tumor invasion of bone marrow<br>• Other drugs<br>• Viral infections | • Thrombocytopenia<br>• No coagulopathies<br>• Petechiae<br>• Hemorrhage | • Platelet transfusion, usually reserved for platelet count below 10,000 or patient's symptoms<br>• Preventive measures, see below<br>• Interleukin-11 (Oprelvekin/Neumega®) for the prevention of severe thrombocytopenia and the reduction of need for platelet transfusions in patients with non-myeloid malignancies who are at high risk of severe thromboctyopenia (<20,000) Dose is 50 mcg/kg SQ daily, given 6 to 24 hrs after chemo until count rises above 50,000, not more than 21 ds. |
| Splenic sequestration of platelets | Increased destruction of platelets by pooling in spleen | • Thrombocytopenia with normal megakaryocytes in bone marrow<br>• Enlarged spleen (3 to 4 times normal size)<br>• Decreased platelet life span<br>• Petechiae<br>• Hemorrhage | • Splenectomy<br>• Preventive measures, see below |
| Disseminated Intravascular Coagulation | Increased destruction of platelets by simultaneous bleeding and clotting | See Table 8-1 | See Table 8-1 |
| Idiopathic Thrombocytopenic Purpura (ITP) | Increased destruction of platelets, commonly seen in lymphoproliferative diseases, eg, CLL, lymphoma | • Thrombocytopenia with nondiagnostic bone marrow with normal or increased number of megakaryocytes<br>• Absence of DIC or drug-induced cause for thrombocytopenia<br>• Petechiae<br>• Hemorrhage | • Treat underlying cause if possible<br>• Preventive measures, see below:<br>  • Observation if asymptomatic with platelets above 50,000<br>  • Steroids<br>  • Single alkylating agents or vinca alkaloids helpful in some patients<br>  • High dose immunoglobulins<br>  • Splenectomy for those who fail above measures or have severe symptomatic thrombocytopenia |

(continued on next page)

## Causes and Management of Cancer-Related Thrombocytopenia

| Type | Classification and Causes | Signs & Symptoms | Management |
|---|---|---|---|
| Thrombotic Thrombocytopenic Purpura (TTP)/ Hemolytic Uremic Syndrome (HUS) | Increased platelet destruction, may be chemotherapy induced but rare; seen with mito-mycin C for adenocarci-noma; also associated with cisplatin and bleomycin; occurs 2-9 months after cessation of treatment, often precipitated by blood transfusion | • Severe thrombocytopenia<br>• Markedly elevated serum LDH<br>• Rapidly changing neurologic abnormalities<br>• Fever<br>• Renal dysfunction in HUS | • Plasma transfusions or intensive plasma-pheresis with or with-out antiplatelet drugs<br>• Immunopheresis in TTP/HUS<br>• Preventive measures, see below |

*Bacquiran DC.* Lippincott's Cancer Chemotherapy Handbook. *2nd ed. Philadelphia, Pa: Lippincott; 2001.*
*Casciato DA.* Manual of Clinical Oncology. *5th ed. Philadelphia, Pa: Lippincott, Williams & Wilkins; 2004.*
Drug Facts and Comparisons. *St. Louis, Mo: A Wolters-Kluwer Co; 2004.*
*Fischer DS, Knobf MT, Durivage HJ, Beaulieu NJ.* The Cancer Chemotherapy Handbook. *6th ed.*
*Philadelphia, Pa: Mosby; 2003.*

## Preventive Measures/Bleeding Precautions:

• Maintain safe environment to prevent trauma

• Avoid invasive procedures

• Maintain pressure for at least 5 minutes for IV injections and venipuncture

• Avoid straining at stools, use stool softeners, drink plenty of fluids

• Avoid aspirin and nonsteroidal anti-inflammatory drugs

• Soft toothbrush, electric razor

## 6. Cancer Related Neutropenia

White blood cells are the body's defense against infection. They neutralize and localize bacterial infections. Neutropenia is defined as an absolute neutrophil count of 1500 cells per cubic millimeter or less (see section 2 for calculation of ANC).

Neutropenia in the cancer patient is usually due to chemotherapy but may also be related to radiation therapy, other drugs or severe infection. Invasion of the bone marrow by tumor may also lead to neutropenia. Chemotherapy drugs that cause mild, moderate and severe neutropenia are listed in Table 4-1.

Infection can be life threatening in the cancer patient. A fever may be the first and only sign of infection. In the elderly patient, infection may manifest itself as a change in mental status, without fever. Neutropenic fevers usually warrant broad-spectrum antibiotics and should be treated as an emergency situation. Febrile neutropenia may delay or cause dose reduction in subsequent chemotherapy cycles.

**Risk Factors for Neutropenia**

- Age >65

- Serum albumin <3.5, elevated LDH

- Myelosuppressive chemotherapy regimen

- Previous radiation to marrow

- Bone marrow involvement

- Advanced cancer

- Extensive chemotherapy

- Pre-existing neutropenia

- History of febrile neutropenia

- Decreased immune function

- Open wounds

## Grades of Neutropenia

Grade I    1500 – 2000 cells/mm$^3$

Grade II   1000 – 1500 cells/mm$^3$

Grade III  500 – 1000 cells/mm$^3$

Grade IV  <500 cells/mm$^3$

## Laboratory Assessment

The patient with febrile neutropenia needs a complete fever workup. This includes CBC with differential, blood cultures and chest x-rays. In some institutions, urine cultures are done routinely as well. Sputum and stool cultures are usually added if the patient is symptomatic. Blood cultures should be taken from two sites (one peripheral and one central if the patient has a central venous access device) and should be taken prior to initiation of antipyretics or antibiotics.

Chemotherapy induced neutropenia usually reaches its nadir in 7 to 10 ds with recovery at 14 to 28 ds post chemotherapy.

## Signs and Symptoms of Infection

• Temperature greater than 100.4°F or 38°C

• Chills or rigors

• Inflammation, rash, swelling or tenderness of any site

• General malaise

• Tachypnea

• Headache

• Change in mental status in elderly patient

• Urinary frequency with or without pain

• Cough with or without sputum

## Management

Detailed management of febrile neutropenia is beyond the scope of this handbook. As previously mentioned, it should be treated as an emergency, with immediate medical attention, cultures and initiation of broad-spectrum antibiotics. Growth factors (G-CSF – granulocyte colony stimulating factor and GM-CSF – granulocyte macrophage colony stimulating factor) may be used to stimulate production of white blood cells during the period of neutropenia.

Growth factors have had a significant impact on the management of cancer-related neutropenia. The American Society of Clinical Oncology (ASCO) published guidelines in 1996, updated in 2000, on the use of these drugs. A summary of some of these recommendations follows.

1. Primary prophylactic CSF administration: should be reserved for patient's expected to experience levels of febrile neutropenia with an expected incidence of >40%; not recommended for previously untreated patients receiving most chemotherapy regimens.

2. Secondary prophylactic CSF administration: in the setting of many tumors exclusive of curable tumors (eg, germ cell tumors) dose reduction after an episode of severe neutropenia should be considered as a primary therapeutic option as no published regimens have demonstrated disease-free or overall survival benefits when dose was maintained or secondary prophylaxis was instituted.

3. Guidelines for CSF Therapy:
   *Afebrile patient:* not recommended for routine use in neutropenic patients who are afebrile.
   *Febrile patient:* should not be routinely used as adjunct therapy for treatment of uncomplicated febrile neutropenia; consider in the high risk patient (ANC <100/mcL), eg, uncontrolled primary disease, pneumonia, hypotension, multi-organ dysfunction, invasive fungal infection.

4. Guidelines for increasing chemotherapy dose intensity: no justification for the use of CSFs to increase chemo dose intensity or schedule or both outside of a clinical trial.

5. Guidelines for use of CSFs as adjuncts to progenitor cell transplantation: recommended to help mobilize peripheral blood progenitor cells (PBPCs) and after PBPC infusion; optimal dose of CSFs and chemo agents is subject of ongoing investigations but a higher dose (10 mcg/kg/d) in setting of mobilization may yield greater content of CD34+ progenitor cells.

6. CSFs should be avoided in patients receiving concomitant chemotherapy and radiation therapy.

7. Recommended doses:

G-CSF (filgrastim/Neupogen®) – 5 mcg/kg/d SQ or IV
GM-CSF (sargramostim/Leukine®) – 250 mcg/m2/d SQ or IV
Pegylated G-CSF (pegfilgrastim/Neulasta®) 6 mg SQ once
(day 2) for each 21- or 28-day chemotherapy cycle
Rounded dose to nearest vial size is an appropriate strategy
to maximize cost benefit.

Ozols H, Armitage JO, Bennett CL, et al. 2000 Update of recommendations for the use of hematopoetic colony stimulating factors: Evidence-based, clinical practice guidelines. American Society of Clinical Oncology web site. Submitted July, 2000.

Bacquiran DC. Lippincott's Cancer Chemotherapy Handbook. 2nd ed. Philadelphia, Pa: Lippincott; 2001.

Casciato DA. Manual of Clinical Oncology. 5th ed. Philadelphia, Pa: Lippincott, Williams and Wilkins; 2004.

Drug Facts and Comparisons 2004. St. Louis, Mo: A Wolters Kluwer Company. 2004.

Fischer DS, Knobf MT, Durivage HJ, Beaulieu NJ. The Cancer Chemotherapy Handbook. 6th ed. Philadelphia, Pa: Mosby; 2003.

Skeel RT. Handbook of Cancer Chemotherapy. 6th ed. Philadelphia, Pa: Lippincott, Williams and Wilkins; 2003.